The

LECTURES
ON FAITH

In Historical
Perspective

RELIGIOUS STUDIES CENTER PUBLICATIONS

BOOK OF MORMON SYMPOSIUM SERIES

The Book of Mormon: The
  Keystone Scripture
The Book of Mormon: First
  Nephi, the Doctrinal
  Foundation

The Book of Mormon: Second
  Nephi, the Doctrinal Structure

MONOGRAPH SERIES

Nibley on the Timely and the
  Timeless
Deity and Death
The Glory of God Is
  Intelligence
Reflections on Mormonism
Literature of Belief
The Words of Joseph Smith
Book of Mormon Authorship
Mormons and Muslims
The Temple in Antiquity
Isaiah and the Prophets
Scriptures for the Modern World

The Joseph Smith Translation:
  The Restoration of Plain and
  Precious Things
Apocryphal Writings and the
  Latter-day Saints
The Pearl of Great Price:
  Revelations From God
The Lectures on Faith in
  Historical Perspective

SPECIALIZED MONOGRAPH SERIES

Supporting Saints: Life Stories
  of Nineteenth-Century
  Mormons
The Call of Zion: The Story of
  the First Welsh Mormon
  Emigration
The Religion and Family
  Connection: Social Science
  Perspectives

Welsh Mormon Writings
  from 1844 to 1862: A
  Historical Bibliography
Peter and the Popes
John Lyon: The Life of a
  Pioneer Poet

OCCASIONAL PAPERS SERIES

Excavations at Seila, Egypt

The

LECTURES

ON FAITH

In Historical Perspective

Edited with a Preface by
Larry E. Dahl and Charles D. Tate, Jr.

VOLUME FIFTEEN
IN THE RELIGIOUS STUDIES CENTER MONOGRAPH SERIES

Religious Studies Center
Brigham Young University
Provo, Utah

Library of Congress Catalog Card Number: 89-63802

ISBN 0-88494-725-4

First Printing, 1990

Distributed by BOOKCRAFT, INC.
Salt Lake City, Utah

Printed in the United States of America

Contents

Preface

The Lectures on Faith were first given to the School of the Elders in the early part of the winter of 1834-35 in Kirtland, Ohio, when the elders who had been out on missions returned to their homes for the season. From 1835 to 1921 the Lectures were printed as the first part of the Doctrine and Covenants. Since 1921 they have been available for study mainly in a little booklet edition published by N. B. Lundwall about 1940, and in a Deseret Book Company version published in 1985.

As we studied the printed versions in connection with the symposium on the Lectures on Faith sponsored by the Religious Studies Center at Brigham Young University, we decided to prepare a newly edited version of the Lectures to correct several mistakes that had found their way into the printed versions. We also decided to try to make some of the long, complex sentences easier to read.

We present here a newly edited version of the Lectures on Faith. We have restricted our editing to making the language clearer and easier to read; we have not changed any of the doctrinal teachings.

We are pleased to be able to print a whole book containing the Lectures on Faith and discussions of those lectures. If our readers can gain as much from reading this book as we have from seeing it throughout the printing process, our efforts will be richly rewarded.

We wish to express gratitude to those who have helped us in this project. We are especially grateful for those who presented papers at the symposium, and to the staff of the Religious Studies Center Publications Office for their work in preparing the manuscripts for printing.

Larry E. Dahl and Charles D. Tate, Jr.

Authorship and History of the Lectures on Faith

Larry E. Dahl

J ust what are the Lectures on Faith? Who prepared them? Who delivered them—to whom, where, when, and why? What is the history of their publication? Why have they not been included in editions of the Doctrine and Covenants since 1921? What benefit might we derive from acquainting ourselves with the content of the Lectures on Faith? This paper addresses these questions. It will not provide definitive answers to them all, but it will summarize the literature about them and propose some answers. A bibliography of the sources examined in the process of preparing this paper appears in Appendix B to this volume. This bibliography will facilitate and, hopefully, encourage others to check the reasonableness of the conclusions drawn in this paper, and it will stimulate further searching for more sources and more answers—and even more questions.

What Are the Lectures on Faith?

Joseph Smith referred to the Lectures on Faith as "lectures on theology" (*History of the Church* 2:176; hereafter *HC*). There are seven of them. Lecture 1 explains what faith is; Lecture 2 describes how mankind comes to know about God; Lectures 3 and 4 make clear the necessary and unchanging attributes of God; Lecture 5 deals with the nature of God the Father, his Son Jesus Christ, and the Holy Ghost; Lecture 6 proclaims that the willingness to sacrifice all earthly things is prerequisite to gaining faith unto salvation; Lecture 7 treats the fruits of faith—perspective, power, and eventually perfection. In the original printing the lectures filled 74 pages. The lengths of the lectures differ, the longest being Lecture 2, and the shortest being Lecture 5. The format consists of numbered paragraphs in which principles are stated and scriptures quoted. Lectures 1 through 5 each sum up with a question and answer section, a kind of catechism pertaining to the principles stated in the lecture. These sections are often about as long as the lectures themselves. There are no questions and answers at the end of Lecture 6; rather, the following note appears: "This lecture is so plain and the facts set forth so self-evident that it is deemed unnecessary to form a catechism upon it. The student is, therefore, instructed to commit the whole to memory." Lecture 7 ends with a simple "Amen."

Who Wrote the Lectures on Faith?

It is a common understanding that Joseph Smith wrote the Lectures on Faith. Often we hear or read statements like "The Prophet Joseph Smith taught" as an introduction to a quotation from the Lectures. Those who have carefully studied the historical sources agree to the Prophet's close involvement with the Lectures, but acknowledge that others contributed heavily in their preparation, as the following representative quotations from Church leaders and others show:

> 1. The idea has been expressed that Sidney Rigdon wrote these lectures, but they were compiled by a number of the brethren and the Prophet himself had the final revision of them (Smith, *Church History* 137).

> 2. "Lectures on Faith" written by Sidney Rigdon and others . . . (Widtsoe 2).

2

3. Joseph Smith was not their sole author, but they were written by a committee over which he presided. . . . It is not known specifically which member, or members, of the committee put the *Lectures on Faith* in their written form. But there can be no doubt that the theological ideas which they contain came from Joseph Smith. All the major ideas within them can be found in his revelations and teachings before 1834 (Andrus 20 fn).

4. These statements that I now read were in part written by the Prophet and in whole approved by him and taught by him in the School of the Prophets (McConkie 4).

5. My analysis of the Lectures on faith [sic] leads me to three somewhat tentative conclusions: First, although Joseph Smith did not write the lectures as they appear in the 1835 version, his influence can be seen in images, examples, scriptural references, and phrasing. Second, Sidney Rigdon may well have prepared them for publication; however, the style throughout is not consistently his. Third, the lectures in their published version represent a compilation or collaboration rather than the work of a single person (Partridge 28).

It is instructive to review the evidence that links Joseph Smith and others to the writing of the Lectures. First, perhaps, it should be noted that a committee of four men—Joseph Smith, Oliver Cowdery, Sidney Rigdon, and Frederick G. Williams (all presiding officers in the Church)—was appointed 24 September 1834 "to arrange the items of the doctrine of Jesus Christ, for the government of the Church of Latter-day Saints. These items are to be taken from the Bible, Book of Mormon, and the revelations which have been given to the Church up to this date, or that shall be given until such arrangements are made" (*HC* 2:165). That committee reported to the priesthood councils of the Church nearly one year later, 17 August 1835, recommending the publication of a book they had prepared (*HC* 2:243-51). That book consisted of two parts. The first contained the Lectures on Faith; the second consisted of selected revelations and inspired declarations received since the beginning of this dispensation. The two parts together made up what were called the Doctrine and Covenants of the Church. The priesthood councils and other Church members assembled accepted the committee's recommendation. The result was the publication of the first edition of the Doctrine and Covenants, which came off the press about the middle of September 1835.[1]

The First Edition of the Doctrine and Covenants

A photographic reproduction of the title page of the 1835 edition of the Doctrine and Covenants is on the following page. The heading to the first part of the book (the Lectures) reads like this:

THEOLOGY.

LECTURE FIRST

ON THE DOCTRINE OF THE CHURCH OF THE

LATTER DAY SAINTS.

Of Faith.

SECTION I.

The first lecture follows this heading. Lecture 2 is introduced simply as:

LECTURE SECOND.

Of Faith.

SECTION II.

This same simple pattern introduces the rest of the lectures.

The title page of the second part of the book, containing the revelations, is photographically reproduced on page 6. The revelations follow in order labelled SECTION II, SECTION III, etc., through SECTION CII (or 102).

---

[1]Writing from Kirtland to the Saints in Missouri under the date of 16 September 1835, W. W. Phelps said, "We received some of the Commandments from Cleveland last week. I shall try and send 100 copies to the Saints in Zion this fall" (*Journal History* [16 Sep 1835]). An earlier compilation of revelations known as the Book of Commandments was being printed in 1833, when mobs destroyed the church press and all but a few copies of the book.

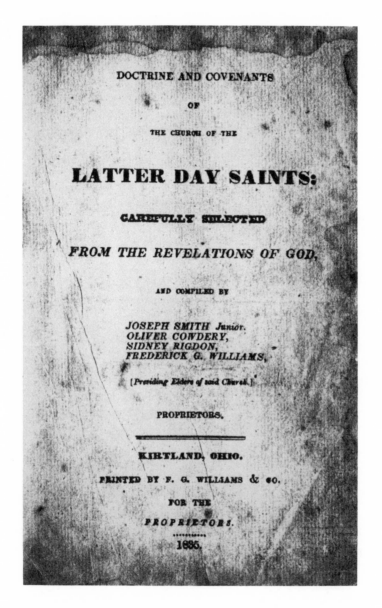

Title page — 1835 edition of the Doctrine and Covenants.
Courtesy of BYU Special Collections

PART SECOND.

COVENANTS AND COMMANDMENTS

OF THE LORD,

to his servants of the church of the

LATTER DAY SAINTS.

SECTION I.

1 Hearken, O ye people of my church, saith the voice of him who dwells on high, and whose eyes are upon all men; yea, verily I say, hearken ye people from afar, and ye that are upon the islands of the sea, listen together; for verily the voice of the Lord is unto all men, and there is none to escape, and there is no eye that shall not see, neither ear that shall not hear, neither heart that shall not be penetrated: and the rebellious shall be pierced with much sorrow, for their iniquities shall be spoken upon the house-tops, and their secret acts shall be revealed; and the voice of warning shall be unto all people, by the mouths of my disciples, whom I have chosen in these last days, and they shall go forth and none shall stay them, for I the Lord have commanded them.

2 Behold, this is mine authority, and the authority of my servants, and my preface unto the book of my commandments, which I have given them to publish unto you O inhabitants of the earth: wherefore fear and tremble, O ye people, for what I the Lord have decreed, in them shall be fulfilled. And verily, I say unto you, that they who go forth, bearing these tidings unto the inhabitants of the earth, to them is power given to seal both on earth and in heaven, the unbelieving and rebellious; yea, verily, to seal them up unto the day when the wrath of God shall be poured out upon the wicked without measure; unto the day when the Lord shall come to recompense unto every man according to his work, and measure to every man according to the measure which he has measured to his fellow man.

3 Wherefore the voice of the Lord is unto the ends of the earth, that all that will hear may hear: prepare ye, prepare ye

Title page — second part, 1835 Doctrine and Covenants.
Courtesy of BYU Special Collections

The preface to the first edition of the Doctrine and Covenants (1835) explains how the four committee members felt about the Lectures on Faith (see the preface on page 9). Although the preface is dated February 17, 1835, the book was not completed until August of that year.

A careful look at these divisions in the first edition of the Doctrine and Covenants shows that the Lectures on Faith were considered the "Doctrine," and the revelations were viewed as the "Covenants," or more precisely, "Covenants and Commandments." In the 1921 edition and all subsequent editions, the title *Doctrine and Covenants* was retained, though the Lectures were not published with the revelations. The title is appropriate, however, for the revelations themselves contain much doctrine.

Historical Evidence Concerning Authorship

The foregoing information demonstrates that preparing and printing the Lectures on Faith was an official, purposeful activity of the committee appointed to compile the first edition of the Doctrine and Covenants. Their preface says that the Lectures contain "the important doctrine of salvation," representing the belief of the committee members and what they perceived to be the beliefs of the Church as a body.

The question as to who actually wrote the Lectures then, may be of little consequence. However, we mortals are a curious lot, and sometimes pursue answers simply to have them, not because they are of great moment. Catering to that curiosity, we note now some historical evidence of Joseph Smith's participation in their preparation, and acknowledge two recent authorship studies which conclude that others, particularly Sidney Rigdon, were also involved.

At the end of October 1834, Joseph's history states, "It being the last of the month, and the Elders beginning to come in, it was necessary to make preparations for the school for the Elders, wherein they might be more perfectly instructed in the great things of God, during the coming winter. . . . No month ever

7

found me more busily engaged than November" (*HC* 2:169-70). It is possible, even probable, that some of the Prophet's busyness during that month pertained to the writing of the Lectures on Faith. Two months later, in January 1835, we find this entry— "During the month of January, I was engaged in the school of the Elders, and in preparing the lectures on theology for publication in the book of Doctrine and Covenants, which the committee appointed last September were now compiling" (*HC* 2:180). These two entries clearly establish Joseph Smith's close ties to preparing for the School of the Elders and to the content of the Lectures on Faith.

Authorship Studies

One of the authorship studies of the Lectures on Faith was done by Alan J. Phipps as a master's thesis in 1977. He compared the frequency of use of certain "function words" in the Lectures with the use of the same words in the writings of several persons who may have had a hand in writing the Lectures, ie, Joseph Smith, Oliver Cowdery, Sidney Rigdon, William W. Phelps, and Parley P. Pratt. He concludes:

> The study showed that Sidney Rigdon's use of function words corresponded very closely with that in Lectures One and Seven, and fairly well with Two, Three, Four, and Six. Joseph Smith's use of function words matched closely those in Lecture Five, with some evidence of his having co-authored or edited Two, Three, Four, and Six. . . . The data and tests appear, therefore, to assign the authorship of the Lectures on Faith mainly to Sidney Rigdon, with Lecture Five and perhaps some parts of the other lectures, except One and Seven, to Joseph Smith (66-67).

Using the same data as Phipps, but applying a somewhat different word-print analysis, Wayne A. Larsen and Alvin C. Rencher report: "Our conclusions largely support his results, with some differences . . ." (183-84). Both studies conclude that Sidney Rigdon was heavily involved, and that Joseph Smith was probably the author of Lecture 2. The differences suggest that Joseph Smith had less to do with Lectures 3, 4, and 6 than the Phipps study

PREFACE.

To the members of the church of the Latter Day Saints—

DEAR BRETHREN:

We deem it to be unnecessary to entertain you with a lengthy preface to the following volume, but merely to say, that it contains in short, the leading items of the religion which we have professed to believe.

There may be an aversion in the minds of some against receiving any thing purporting to be articles of religious faith, in consequence of there being so many now extant; but if men believe a system, and profess that it was given by inspiration, certainly, the more intelligibly they can present it, the better. It does not make a principle untrue to *print* it, neither does it make it true not to print it.

The church viewing this subject to be of importance, appointed, through their servants and delegates the High Council, your servants to select and compile this work. Several reasons might be adduced in favor of this move of the Council, but we only add a few words. They knew that the church was evil spoken of in many places—its faith and belief misrepresented, and the way of truth thus subverted. By some it was represented as disbelieving the bible, by others as being an enemy to all good order and uprightness, and by others as being injurious to the peace of all governments civil and political.

We have, therefore, endeavored to present, though in few words, *our* belief, and when we say this, humbly trust, the faith and principles of this society as a body.

We do not present this little volume with any other expectation than that we are to be called to answer to every principle advanced, in that day when the secrets of all hearts will be revealed, and the reward of every man's labor be given him.

With sentiments of esteem and sincere respect, we subscribe ourselves your brethren in the bonds of the gospel of our Lord Jesus Christ.

JOSEPH SMITH jr.
OLIVER COWDERY.
SIDNEY RIGDON.
F. G. WILLIAMS.

Kirtland, Ohio, February 17, 1835.

Preface—1835 Doctrine and Covenants.
Courtesy of BYU Special Collections

showed, and that William W. Phelps and/or Parley P. Pratt could have had at least some editorial influence on Lecture 5.[2] In fairness it should be recognized that Larsen's and Rencher's work with the Lectures on Faith was a peripheral, almost incidental glance, in a study of Book of Mormon authorship. If they were to focus primarily on the Lectures, perhaps they would adjust both the selection of data and perform additional tests and comparisons.

Conclusions About Authorship

What then can we conclude about authorship of the Lectures on Faith? It is clear that several of the brethren participated in writing them. It is also clear that Joseph Smith and perhaps others prepared them for publication after they were written. Undoubtedly, the Lectures were, in the words of President John Taylor, "published with the sanction and approval of the Prophet Joseph Smith" (Woodford 1:87). It would therefore seem appropriate to attribute the ideas, principles, and doctrines in the Lectures on Faith to the Prophet Joseph.

Who Delivered the Lectures—To Whom, When, Where, Why?

Trying to identify who delivered the Lectures on Faith is as difficult as trying to decide who wrote them. Contemporary historical records are scarce. Yet, official histories, books, and articles generally agree that Joseph Smith and Sidney Rigdon were the primary teachers, noting that others of the brethren may also have been involved (see Appendix B). Interestingly, however, there are seldom source citations for these conclusions, or the sources cited do not provide adequate historical data to clearly

---

[2]There is some historical evidence that W. W. Phelps could have had an editorial influence on the Lectures on Faith. The *History of the Church* (2:227) records that W. W. Phelps arrived in Kirtland from Missouri in May, 1835, lived in the Prophet Joseph's home, and "assisted the committee in compiling the Book of Doctrine and Covenants."

establish the point being made. It becomes at times a case of authors citing one another with no one having compelling documentary evidence.

Some information from two men who were at the scene in 1834 is available and of particular interest. Zebedee Coltrin, in an 1883 remembrance, differentiated between the 1833 School of the Prophets which was held in the Prophet's home above the Whitney store—and located in the valley—and the 1834 School for the Elders in which the Lectures on Faith were studied. He said, "It was in a larger school on the hill afterwards, where Sidney presided that the lectures on faith that appear in the Book of Doctrine and Covenants were given" (*Salt Lake* [11 Oct] 44). His reference to "the school on the hill" points to the printing office built on a lot near the temple site, on land of much higher elevation than the valley where the store was located. The printing office was a 30- by 38-foot two-story building completed in November 1834. The lower story of the printing office was used for the School for the Elders (*HC* 1:417-418; 2:169-170). Even though Brother Coltrin said that Sidney Rigdon "presided" at the school where the seven lectures were given, it is likely that it was Joseph Smith and not Sidney Rigdon who "presided" over the school in the sense of being in charge of it because Joseph Smith organized and attended the school, and was the President of the Church. Perhaps Zebedee Coltrin's "presided" meant "taught."

Heber C. Kimball tells us something of how the school was conducted and who the teachers were:

> In the winter of 1834-5 . . . I attended the Theological School established in Kirtland, in which the lectures on faith, contained in the book of Doctrine and Covenants, originated.
> A certain number were appointed to speak at each meeting. On one occasion I was called upon to speak on the principle of faith. Several brethren spoke before me and quoted every passage mentioned in the scriptures on the subject. I referred to an original circumstance which took place in my family. My daughter had broke a saucer; her mother promised her a whipping, when she returned from a visit on which she was just starting; she went out under an apple tree and prayed that her mother's heart might be softened, that when she returned she might not whip her; although

her mother was very punctual when she made a promise to her children to fulfil it, yet when she returned she had no disposition to chastise her child. Afterwards the child told her mother that she had prayed to God that she might not whip her.

Joseph wept like a child on hearing this simple narrative and its application (*Journal History* [22 Dec 1834]).

In addition to being instructed by their presiding officers, it appears that the elders taught one another in the school. The School for the Elders began sometime between 25 November and 1 December 1834. Under the date of 25 November the Prophet records, "I continued my labors daily, preparing for the school" (*HC* 2:170). On 1 December he says,

Our school for the Elders was now well attended, and with the lectures on theology, which were regularly delivered, absorbed for the time being everything else of a temporal nature. The classes, being mostly Elders gave the most studious attention to the all-important object of qualifying themselves as messengers of Jesus Christ, to be ready to do His will in carrying glad tidings to all that would open their eyes, ears and hearts (*HC* 2:175-76).

The Lectures on Faith phase of the School for the Elders evidently ended sometime before 22 December because on that date the Elders were joined by a number of sisters and also children—some one hundred thirty people total—and they all attended a grammar school with Sidney Rigdon and William E. McLellin as teachers (*HC* 2:200).[3] Heber C. Kimball explains: "On the 22nd of December a Grammar school was opened in Kirtland, under the superintendence of Sidney Rigdon and William E. McLellin teachers, —and nearly all the elders and myself, and many of the sisters commenced going to school" (Kimball 6:868). Evidently the grammar school was also held in the printing office where the elders had met to study the Lectures on Faith. The curriculum for this grammar school consisted of "penmanship, arithmetic, English grammar, and geography . . . and writing" (*HC* 2:200), and according to Heber C. Kimball,

---

[3] In reporting to the trustees of the "Kirtland School" in February 1835, W. E. McLellin indicated that because of overcrowding, they had dismissed the "small students," reducing the number to one hundred.

nearly all the elders were in attendance. In his February 1835 report to the school trustees, William E. McLellin made no mention of the Lectures on Faith or other missionary training in connection with the grammar school. Since the Prophet was busy in January preparing the Lectures for publication, we could assume that by then they had already been delivered. If the elders as a group did continue to study the Lectures on Faith after 22 December, the School for the Elders and the Kirtland Grammar School would necessarily have been two separate entities meeting at different times, but there is no specific mention of any such arrangement in the historical sources.

In answer then to the questions of who delivered the Lectures to whom, when, where, and why, I would say they were delivered by the presiding officers of the Church and some of the elders themselves to a School for the Elders, in the printing office in Kirtland, during November and December 1834, for the purpose of preparing the elders to be effective missionaries.

Publication History of the Lectures

The first publication of any of the Lectures on Faith was that of Lectures 5 and 6 in the May 1835 edition of the *Messenger and Advocate*, the Church monthly paper published in Kirtland. They were introduced with the following comments:

> The following are two short lectures which were delivered before a Theological class, in this place last winter. These lectures are being compiled and arranged with other documents of instruction and regulation for the church, titled "Doctrine and Covenants of the church of the Latter Day Saints," &c. It may be well, for the information of the churches abroad, to say, that this book will contain the important revelations on doctrine and church government now extant, and will, we trust, give them a perfect understanding of the doctrine believed by this society. Such a work has long been called for, and if we are prospered a few weeks, shall have this volume ready for distribution. A full detail of its contents will be given hereafter.

> In giving the following lectures we have thought best to insert the catechism, that the reader may fully understand the manner in which this science was taught. It was found, that by annexing a

catechism to the lectures as they were presented, the class made greater progress than otherwise; and in consequence of the additional scriptural proofs, it was preserved in compiling (Cowdery 122).

The next publication of any of the lectures was a broadside containing Lecture 1, probably published in June 1835.[4]

The first printing of all seven lectures was in September 1835, when they were printed as part of the first edition of the Doctrine and Covenants. Between 1835 and 1921 the Lectures were printed in almost all of the English language editions of the Doctrine and Covenants, and in many, but not all non-English editions.[5] The issue of why the Lectures have not been printed in editions of the Doctrine and Covenants since 1921 will be discussed later. But first, let us review instances when the Lectures on Faith were published by themselves.

Between 1840 and 1843, Parley P. Pratt printed all seven lectures in the *Millennial Star* in England.[6] Lecture 1, printed in September 1840, was introduced with the following comment: "We purpose to present our readers with a brief Course of Lectures on the first principles of Theology, or the Doctrine of the Church of Jesus Christ of Latter-day Saints; and commence our quotations from the Book of Doctrine and Covenants, p. 5" (Pratt, "Lecture on Theology" 129). Lecture 5 was printed in December 1842 with this note: "We have thought [it] proper to give this month in our Star the fifth lecture on Faith, extracted from the above work (Doctrine and Covenants). The four lectures preceding it were given in the first volume of the Star. Having often heard the desire expressed for the publication of the remaining lectures, it is our intention to give them forthwith. -Ed" (Pratt, "Lecture on Faith" 135). As promised, Lectures 6 and 7 were published in the next two issues of the *Millennial Star.*

---

[4]A comparison of the broadside and Lecture 1 as printed in the 1835 D&C by Wm. M. Powell is available in the Harold B. Lee Library, BYU—Mor/M208/Ala/#568.

[5]Evidently some English language pocket editions published in the early 1900s also did not contain the Lectures on Faith (see Lambert).

[6]See Appendix B under *Millennial Star* for editions containing the Lectures on Faith.

All the lectures were published in 1845-46 by Sidney Rigdon in Pittsburgh, Pennsylvania. He had left the Church after the death of Joseph Smith and started his own organization called the "Church of Christ." In Pittsburgh he published a paper also called *Messenger and Advocate*, in which he published the lectures serially each month from October 1845 through March 1846. Lectures 5 and 6 both appeared in the February 1846 issue. Rigdon did not include the catechisms at the end of each lecture except for Lecture 1. As he began publishing the Lectures, he explained:

> There will be found in this paper a lecture on faith copied from the Book of Doctrine and Covenants, which is the first of a course delivered before a theological class in Kirtland, O. in the winter of 1834 & 5. Faith being the first principle of action in all intelligent beings, and those lectures setting forth that principle in a clear and interesting manner, we thought perhaps we could not interest our readers more than by giving place to one of them at this time; we may copy others of them hereafter, if our space will admit (Rigdon 360-61).

Space did "admit," and all seven lectures were published as indicated above, without further editorial comment.

There are three other separate publications of the Lectures, all of them appearing in the 20th century, we need to mention. N. B. Lundwall of Salt Lake City published the Lectures on Faith along with a number of other items about 1940. We get the date from John W. Fitzgerald's master's thesis (346). Lundwall's is probably the most widely known publication of the Lectures in the Church. In 1952 the Reorganized Church of Jesus Christ of Latter Day Saints published the Lectures on Faith with an interesting preface written by their president, Israel A. Smith.[7] The Deseret Book Company of Salt Lake City also published a hardbound edition of the Lectures on Faith in 1985. This edition was the first to incorporate references to the book of Moses, much

---

[7]The title page reads "LECTURES ON FAITH delivered in Kirtland Temple in 1834 and 1835 by the Prophet Joseph Smith . . . with the Revelation on the Rebellion as an appendix published in 1952 by Herald House, Reorganized Church of Jesus Christ of Latter Day Saints, Independence, Missouri." See Appendix A for the full text of Israel A. Smith's preface. The

of which corresponds with the Joseph Smith Translation of Genesis.

As an endnote to the discussion of publication history, it is interesting to learn of the changes that have appeared in the titles through the years. In 1835, they were originally referred to as "Lecture First—Of Faith," "Lecture Second—Of Faith," etc. When Parley P. Pratt published them in England in the 1840s, he called them "Lecture 1—On Faith," "Lecture 2—On Faith," etc. All Liverpool editions of the Doctrine and Covenants thereafter used the "On Faith" label, while the American editions kept the "Of Faith" designation until 1876. For some reason Sidney Rigdon in 1845 in Pittsburgh also called them lectures "On Faith." The 1985 Deseret Book edition carries the title *Lectures on Faith*, but inside, the lectures are referred to simply as "Lecture First," "Lecture Second," "Lecture Third," etc., with no reference to "of" or "on." This 1990 edited version uses the common reference of *Lectures on Faith* and refers to each lecture by its number, such as Lecture 1, Lecture 2, etc.

Why No Lectures with the D&C Since 1921?

When a new edition of the Doctrine and Covenants was prepared in 1921, the Lectures on Faith were not included.[8] The answers proposed as to why the Lectures were not included are

---

RLDS published the Lectures on Faith in their editions of the Doctrine and Covenants from 1863 through 1896. Of their 1897 edition, Richard P. Howard writes: "The 1897 edition was somewhat of a departure from the previous format. The Lectures on Faith, printed in every edition through 1896, were removed. The background of this decision has not been established, but it seems reasonable to consider that the extensive quotations from the New Translation of the Bible taken from the unpublished manuscripts were unacceptable in the light of the work as published in 1867. Also, the materials in these pages (being simply outlines of the lectures given in a strictly local situation to a class of elders) had lost much of their relevance to the circumstances of the church over half a century later" (Howard 236).

[8]This was not the first time the question of omitting the Lectures had been raised. Orson Pratt proposed to President John Taylor in 1879 that they perhaps be published separately rather than in the Doctrine and Covenants. President Taylor's response was that "The Lectures on Faith were published with the sanction and approval of the Prophet Joseph Smith, and we do not feel that it is desirable to make any alteration in that regard, at any rate, not at present" (see Woodford 1:86-87).

varied. Many have pointed to the content of Lecture 5 concerning the Godhead, suggesting that it contains incomplete, if not erroneous doctrine—doctrine which was corrected or clarified in 1843 by Joseph Smith (D&C 130:22-23). The argument is that the Lectures were removed to avoid these inconsistencies. Some have claimed that the removal of the Lectures from the Doctrine and Covenants constitutes decanonization of material once affirmed by the Church as scripture. Those who take this view see the 1834 vote of the priesthood quorums and the general assembly to accept as true and to publish both the Lectures on Faith and the revelations of Joseph Smith in the first edition of the Doctrine and Covenants, as putting the Lectures on a par with the revelations, considering both to be canonized scripture (Van Wagoner, et al 72-77). Leaders of the Church, however, have consistently maintained that from the beginning a distinction was made between the Lectures on Faith and the revelations (see Penrose 16; *Modern Revelation* 34; Smith, *Essentials* 186). They also appeal to the occasion when the first edition of the Doctrine and Covenants was voted upon, citing the testimony of Elder John Smith, who represented the High Council in Kirtland. The minutes read as follows: Elder Smith "bore record that the *revelations* in said book were true, and that the *lectures* were judiciously arranged and compiled, and were profitable for doctrine. Whereupon, the High Council of Kirtland accepted and acknowledged them as the doctrine and covenants of their faith by a unanimous vote" (*HC* 2:244; emphasis added). Similarly, "Elder Levi Jackman, taking the lead for the High Council of the church in Missouri, bore testimony that the *revelations* in said book were true, and the said High Council of Missouri accepted and acknowledged them as the doctrine and covenants of their faith, by a unanimous vote" (*HC* 2:244; emphasis added). The minutes relative to the other quorums' acceptance of the work do not distinguish "revelations" from "lectures." They say only that these quorums gave testimony in favor of "*the book*" (*HC* 2:244; emphasis added).

It can be reasoned then that a distinction was made early between the seven lectures and the revelations, and that the vote to accept the lectures as "judiciously arranged . . . and profitable for doctrine" was not to equate them with the divine revelations. Such is the message in the "Explanatory Introduction" of the 1921 edition of the Doctrine and Covenants:

> Certain lessons, entitled "Lectures on Faith," which were bound in with the Doctrine and Covenants in some of its former issues, are not included in this edition. Those lessons were prepared for use in the School of the Elders, conducted in Kirtland, Ohio, during the winter of 1834-1835; but they were never presented to nor accepted by the Church as being otherwise than theological lectures or lessons (v).

Church leaders have acknowledged that the decision to omit the Lectures on Faith in the 1921 edition of the Doctrine and Covenants was based not only on the fact that they are not revelations, but it also had to do with some of the teachings about the Godhead in Lecture 5, as I mentioned earlier. Elders James E. Talmage, John A. Widtsoe, and Joseph Fielding Smith served as a committee to consider whether to continue to publish the Lectures on Faith with the revelations (Fitzgerald 345). Fitzgerald reports that he was told in a 22 July 1940 interview with Elder Joseph Fielding Smith:

> They are not complete as to their teachings regarding the Godhead. More complete instructions on this point of doctrine are given in section 130 of . . . The Doctrine and Covenants.
>
> It was thought by Elder James E. Talmage, chairman, and other members of the committee who were responsible for their omission that to avoid confusion and contention on this vital point of belief, it would be better not to have them bound in the same volume as the commandments or revelations which make up The Doctrine and Covenants (345).[9]

It is not the purpose of this paper to discuss the doctrinal issues raised by Lecture 5. Professor Millet's paper will address that subject. It is sufficient to note here that Lecture 5 was one of

---

[9] Elder Smith is also reported to have said in this same interview that the Lectures are explanations of the principle of faith "but are not doctrine." In this statement he may have been comparing certain items in the Lectures (perhaps Lecture 5) with doctrine as understood in 1940, and not making an "historically erroneous" statement as has been suggested by some.

the matters of concern influencing the decision not to publish the Lectures on Faith with the Doctrine and Covenants from 1921.

The Lectures on Faith were written and published in the Doctrine and Covenants by men called of God to lead the Church in 1834. The decision not to print them in the Doctrine and Covenants was made by men called of God to lead the Church in 1921. I submit that both actions were appropriate.

Summary and Conclusion

This paper has attempted to shed some light on the authorship and history of the Lectures on Faith by bringing together and briefly discussing information that is available in an array of histories, books, and articles. The motivation for preparing the paper and the bibliography in Appendix B has been to stimulate an interest in the Lectures—to encourage people to study them carefully.

I love the Lectures on Faith. For me they carry a special spirit. They are a rich source of doctrinal treasures couched in clear and powerful language. One can drink as deeply from them as he has a mind to. I commend them to you.

BIBLIOGRAPHY

Andrus, Hyrum. *Principles of Perfection*. Vol 2 of *Foundations of the Millennial Kingdom of Christ*. 3 vols. Salt Lake City: Bookcraft, 1968-73.

Cowdery, Oliver, ed. Untitled article. *The Latter-day Saints' Messenger and Advocate* (May 1835) 1:122-26.

Fitzgerald, John W. "A Study of the Doctrine and Covenants." Master's thesis. Provo, UT: Brigham Young Univ, 1940.

History of the Church. 7 vols. Salt Lake City: Deseret Book, 1978.

Howard, Richard P. *Restoration Scriptures.* Independence, MO: Herald House, 1969.

Journal History of the Church. Salt Lake City: The Church of Jesus Christ of Latter-day Saints, 1906- .

Kimball, Heber C. "Extracts from H. C. Kimball Journal." *Times and Seasons* (15 Apr 1845) 6:868.

Lambert, Asael Carlyle. *The Published Editions of the Book of Doctrine and Covenants of The Church of Jesus Christ of Latter-day Saints in All Languages 1833 to 1950.* N.p.: A. C. Lambert, 1950.

Larsen, Wayne A., and Alvin C. Rencher. "Who Wrote the Book of Mormon? An Analysis of Wordprints." *Book of Mormon Authorship.* Ed. Noel B. Reynolds and Charles D. Tate, Jr. Salt Lake City: Bookcraft, 1982. 157-88.

Lectures on Faith. Independence, MO: Herald House, 1953.

McConkie, Bruce R. "The Lord God of Joseph Smith." *Speeches of the Year, 1971-1972.* Provo, UT: Brigham Young Univ, 1972.

Modern Revelation: The History and Message of the Doctrine and Covenants. Young Men's Mutual Improvement Associations Manual #10, 1906-1907. Salt Lake City: General Board of YMMIA, 1906.

Partridge, Elinore H. "Characteristics of Joseph Smith's Style and Notes on the Authorship of the Lectures on Faith." Task Papers in LDS History series. Salt Lake City: The Church of Jesus Christ of Latter-day Saints, 1976 (Dec), no. 14, p 28.

Penrose, Charles W. *Conference Report* (3 Apr 1921) 9-17.

Phipps, Alan J. "The Lectures on Faith: An Authorship Study." Master's thesis. Provo, UT: Brigham Young Univ, 1977.

Pratt, Parley P., ed. "Lecture on Faith." *Millennial Star* (Dec 1842) 3:135-38.

———. "Lecture on Theology." *Millennial Star* (Sep 1840) 1:129-33.

Rigdon, Sidney, ed. "Faith." *Messenger and Advocate*. Pittsburgh, PA (15 Oct 1845) 1:360-61.

Salt Lake School of the Prophets Minute Book, 1883 . Ed. Merle H. Graffam. Palm Desert, CA: LDS Historical Department, ULC Press, 1981. In typescript copy, same publisher, same date.

Smith, Joseph Fielding. *Church History and Modern Revelation* . 2nd series. Salt Lake City: Council of the Twelve Apostles, 1947.

———. *Essentials in Church History*. Salt Lake City: Bookcraft, 1956.

Van Wagoner, Richard S., Steven C. Walker, and Allen D. Roberts. "The 'Lectures on Faith': A Case Study in Decanonization." *Dialogue* (Fall 1987) 20:71-77.

Widtsoe, John A. *The Message of the Doctrine and Covenants*. Salt Lake City: Bookcraft, 1969.

Woodford, Robert J. "The Historical Development of the Doctrine and Covenants." PhD dissertation. 3 vols. Provo, UT: Brigham Young Univ, 1974.

Larry E. Dahl is professor and chairman of Church History and Doctrine at Brigham Young University.

Introduction to the
1990 Edited Version

One of the major purposes in publishing this 1990 edited version of the Lectures on Faith is to maintain the integrity of the text of the 1835 edition and at the same time make the Lectures easier to read. To accomplish this we have used the 1835 edition as our base text. However, as we studied all the editions that have been published since 1835, we recognized that some of the changes made in the later editions have become so widely accepted and make such good sense that we need to retain them in this version. For example, the title to the early editions of the lectures was simply "Of Faith," but later editions changed it to "Lectures on Faith" (see "Authorship and History" above). We have also adopted the modern reference to the different lectures as "Lecture 1," "Lecture 2," in place of the 1835 "Lecture First," "Lecture Second," etc.

In our study of the 1835 Lectures, we found several places where the meaning is generally not clear or is difficult for the modern reader to understand. We have tried to make the text clearer and easier to read by doing several things: we have corrected misspelled words, misquotations, grammatical and clarity problems, and a few simple mistakes that were printed in the 1835 edition. For example, in one instance in the Question and Answer section to Lecture 2, Nahor is called Abraham's father. Nahor is the name of both Abraham's grandfather and one of his brothers, but his father was Terah. We changed "father" to "brother" since it is obvious from the context that the reference was to his brother. Also in Lecture 2, the names of Arphaxad and Methuselah are consistently misspelled. We have corrected those spellings.

We have made the text more readable and easier to understand by breaking several very long and complex sentences into shorter, easier-to-read units simply by punctuating those units with periods rather than colons or semi-colons. We have also made other difficult sentences clearer by rearranging the phrases and clauses to let the ideas flow more easily.

To show the reader precisely what we changed in the 1835 text, we have made a chart (Chart 1) showing all our specific word and phrase changes. When word changes or corrections are frequent and repetitive, we mention them in blanket statements at the beginning of the charts, and the reader can assume that each time the word appears in the 1990 edition, it has been changed from the 1835 edition.

The references to the Book of Mormon in the 1835 edition of the Lectures are to page numbers in the 1830 edition of that scripture[*] because the paragraphs or verses had not yet been numbered. We left the page number references as they were used in the 1835 edition of the Lectures and added references to the 1981 edition of the Book of Mormon in parentheses for our readers' convenience.

Additionally, we have made five blanket changes which we describe here but do not note in Chart 1. First, we have made all scriptural quotations conform to the language and spelling of the printed versions of the Joseph Smith Translation (JST), the King James Version, and the other scriptures.

The writers of the 1835 edition often indicated that they were "copying" a scriptural reference from the "New Translation," which came to be what we now call the Joseph Smith Translation (JST), but they were actually paraphrasing. They used the familiar pronouns *he*, *you*, and *your*, rather than the biblical

---

[*] The 1876 and 1891 editions of the Lectures on Faith cited different page numbers in the Book of Mormon references, indicating use of editions later than 1830.

thee, thou, thy, and *thine,* which are used in the JST, and they also left the biblical suffixes off the verbs. We have made all these references conform with the printed text. We have also added corresponding references to the book of Moses in the Pearl of Great Price, where applicable, following the 1985 Deseret Book edition, which was the first to do this.

Second, we have standardized internal scriptural citations by placing them in parentheses after the quotation or reference and using Arabic numerals to identify chapters and verses. The 1835 citations generally preceded the reference, and the chapter and verse notations were sometimes written out and other times listed in numerals.

Third, we have changed punctuation as we sensed it needed to be changed to facilitate the flow of the thought and to make this edition conform to modern punctuation rules.

Fourth, we have standardized the use of numbers within the text by changing all numbers above ten to numerals and writing out all numbers ten and below except in the lecture titles.

Fifth, we have added the heading "Questions and Answers" for Lectures 1, 2, 3, 4, and 5 to introduce what the original writers clearly thought were the second parts of those lectures. We numbered the questions to facilitate referencing. There were no question and answer sections for Lectures 6 or 7 in the 1835 edition.

We also deleted the subheadings SECTION I, SECTION II, etc., which appeared at the head of each lecture in the 1835 edition, and we have changed all references to these subheadings to refer to the lecture concerned instead. We did this because the section numbers were redundant with the numbers in the titles of the lectures and their use was discontinued after the 1876 edition.

We have also included a second comparative chart (Chart 2) showing the changes made in the 1876, 1891, and 1985 editions to facilitate further study.

Charles D. Tate, Jr., Editor

January 1990

Lectures on
Faith

A 1990 Edited Version

Preface

To the members of The Church of Jesus Christ of Latter-day Saints:*

We deem it to be unnecessary to entertain you with a lengthy preface to the following volume, but merely to say that it contains, in short, the leading items of the religion which we have professed to believe.

The first part of the book will be found to contain a series of lectures as delivered before a theological class in this place, and in consequence of their embracing the important doctrine of salvation, we have arranged them into the following work.

The second part** contains items or principles for the regulation of the church as taken from the revelations which have been given since its organization, as well as from former ones.

There may be an aversion in the minds of some against receiving anything purporting to be articles of religious faith, since there are so many now extant; but if men believe a system and profess that it was given by inspiration, certainly the more intelligibly they can present it, the better. It does not make a principle untrue to *print* it, neither does it make it true not to print it.

Viewing this subject to be of importance, the Church, through its servants and delegates, the High Council, appointed your servants to select and compile this work. Several reasons

---

*The 1835 edition says, "To the members of the church of the Latter Day Saints," one of the names it was known by at that time. The current name was revealed to the Prophet Joseph Smith on 26 April 1838 (see D&C 115:4). We have deleted the 1835 "Dear Brethren" reference to the School of the Elders.

**From 1835 to 1921, the Lectures on Faith were the "first part" or "Doctrine" of almost all of the editions of the Doctrine and Covenants. The "second part" referred to here is the "Covenants and Commandments " in the 1835 edition of the Doctrine and Covenants. Since 1921, only the "second part" has remained as the Doctrine and Covenants (see Dahl's "Authorship and History" herein).

might be adduced in favor of this move of the Council, but we add only a few words. They knew that the church was evil spoken of in many places—its faith and belief misrepresented, and the way of truth thus subverted. By some it was represented as disbelieving the Bible, by others as being an enemy to all good order and uprightness, and by others as being injurious to the peace of all governments, civil and political.

We have, therefore, endeavored to present our belief, though in few words, and when we say this, we humbly trust that it is the faith and principles of this society as a body.

We do not present this little volume with any other expectation than that we are to be called to answer to every principle advanced, in that day when the secrets of all hearts will be revealed and the reward of every man's labor be given him.

With sentiments of esteem and sincere respect, we subscribe ourselves your brethren in the bonds of the gospel of our Lord Jesus Christ.

> Joseph Smith, Jr.
> Oliver Cowdery
> Sidney Rigdon
> F. G. Williams

Kirtland, Ohio, February 17, 1835.

Lecture 1
ON FAITH

1. Faith, being the first principle in revealed religion and the foundation of all righteousness, necessarily claims the first place in a course of lectures designed to unfold to the understanding the doctrine of Jesus Christ.

2. In presenting the subject of faith, we shall observe the following order:

3. First, faith itself—what it is;

4. Secondly, the object on which it rests; and,

5. Thirdly, the effects which flow from it.

6. Agreeable to this order we have first to show what faith is.

7. The author of the epistle to the Hebrews gives the following definition of the word faith:

8. "Now faith is the substance [assurance]* of things hoped for, the evidence of things not seen" (11:1).

9. From this we learn that faith is the assurance which men have of the existence of things which they have not seen and that it is also the principle of action in all intelligent beings.

10. If men were duly to consider themselves and turn their thoughts and reflections to the operations of their own minds, they would readily discover that it is faith, and faith only, which is the moving cause of all action in them; that without it both mind

---

*Brackets in the 1835 edition. "Assurance" comes from the JST.

and body would be in a state of inactivity, and all their exertions would cease, both physical and mental.

11. Were each of you in this class to go back and reflect upon the history of your lives from the period of your first recollection, and ask yourselves what principle excited you to action, or what gave you energy and activity in all your lawful avocations, callings, and pursuits, what would be the answer? Would it not be that it was the assurance which you had of the existence of things which you had not seen as yet? Was it not the hope which you had, in consequence of your belief in the existence of unseen things, which stimulated you to action and exertion in order to obtain them? Are you not dependent on your faith, or belief, for the acquisition of all knowledge, wisdom, and intelligence? Would you exert yourselves to obtain wisdom and intelligence unless you did believe that you could obtain them? Would you have ever sown if you had not believed that you would reap? Would you have ever planted if you had not believed that you would gather? Would you have ever asked, unless you had believed that you would receive? Would you have ever sought unless you had believed that you would find? Or, would you have ever knocked, unless you had believed that it would be opened unto you? In a word, is there anything that you would have done, either physical or mental, if you had not previously believed? Are not all your exertions of every kind dependent on your faith? Or, may we not ask, what have you or what do you possess which you have not obtained by reason of your faith? Your food, your raiment, your lodgings—are they not all by reason of your faith? Reflect, and ask yourselves if these things are not so. Turn your thoughts to your own minds and see if faith is not the moving cause of all action in yourselves, and if it is the moving cause in you, is it not also the moving cause in all other intelligent beings?

12. And as faith is the moving cause of all action in temporal concerns, so it is in spiritual. For the Savior has said, and that truly, that "he that *believeth* and is baptized shall be saved" (Mark 16:16; emphasis in 1835).

13. As we receive by faith all temporal blessings, so we in like manner receive by faith all spiritual blessings. But faith is not only the principle of action, it is also the principle of power in all intelligent beings, whether in heaven or on earth. Thus says the author of the epistle to the Hebrews:

14. "Through faith we understand that the worlds were framed by the word of God, so that things which are seen were not made of things which do appear" (11:3).

15. By this we understand that the principle of power which existed in the bosom of God, by which he framed the worlds, was faith; and that it is by reason of this principle of power existing in the Deity that all created things exist; so that all things in heaven, on earth, or under the earth exist by reason of faith as it existed in him.

16. Had it not been for the principle of faith, the worlds would never have been framed, neither would man have been formed of the dust. It is the principle by which Jehovah works and through which he exercises power over all temporal as well as eternal things. Take this principle or attribute (for it is an attribute) from the Deity and he would cease to exist.

17. Who cannot see that if God framed the worlds by faith, it is by faith that he exercises power over them, and faith is the principle of power? And if it is the principle of power in the Deity, it must be so in man as well? This is the testimony of all the sacred writers and the lesson which they have been endeavoring to teach to man.

18. The Savior says the reason the disciples could not cast out the devil was their unbelief: "For verily I say unto you," said he, "If ye have faith as a grain of mustard seed, ye shall say unto this mountain, Remove hence to yonder place; and it shall remove; and nothing shall be impossible unto you" (Matt 17:19-20).

19. Moroni, while abridging and compiling the record of his fathers, gave us the following account of faith as the principle of power. He says on page 563 of the 1830 Book of Mormon that it was the faith of Alma and Amulek which caused the walls of

the prison to be rent (Ether 12:13), as recorded on the 264th page (Alma 14:27). It was the faith of Nephi and Lehi which caused a change to be wrought upon the hearts of the Lamanites when they were immersed with the Holy Spirit and with fire, as seen on the 421st page (Hel 5:43-45). And it was by faith that the mountain Zerin was removed when the brother of Jared spake in the name of the Lord. See also the 565th page (Ether 12:30).

20. In addition to this we are told in Hebrews that Gedeon, Barak, Samson, Jephthah, David, Samuel, and the prophets "through faith subdued kingdoms, wrought righteousness, obtained promises, stopped the mouths of lions, quenched the violence of fire, escaped the edge of the sword, out of weakness were made strong, waxed valiant in fight, turned to flight the armies of the aliens. Women received their dead raised to life again" (11:33-35), etc.

21. Also Joshua, in the sight of all Israel, bade the sun and moon to stand still, and it was done (Joshua 10:12-13).

22. We here understand that the sacred writers say that all these things were done by faith. It was by faith that the worlds were framed—God spake, chaos heard, and worlds came into order by reason of the faith there was in him. So with men also, they spake by faith in the name of God and the sun stood still, the moon obeyed, mountains removed, prisons fell, lions' mouths were closed, the human heart lost its enmity, fire its violence, armies their power, the sword its terror, and death its dominion; and all this by reason of the faith which was in them.

23. Had it not been for the faith which was in men, they might have spoken to the sun, the moon, the mountains, prisons, lions, the human heart, fire, armies, the sword, or to death in vain!

24. Faith, then, is the first great governing principle which has power, dominion, and authority over all things. By it they exist; by it they are upheld; by it they are changed; or by it they remain, agreeable to the will of God. Without it there is no power, and without power there could be no creation nor existence!

Questions and Answers for Lecture 1

1. *Question*—What is theology?

Answer—It is that revealed science which treats the being and attributes of God, his relations to us, the dispensations of his providence, his will with respect to our actions, and his purposes with respect to our end (*Buck's Theological Dictionary* 582).

2. Q—What is the first principle in this revealed science?

A—Faith (Lecture 1:1).

3. Q—Why is faith the first principle in this revealed science?

A—Because it is the foundation of all righteousness."Without faith it is impossible to please him [God]*" (Heb 11:6). "Little children, let no man deceive you: he that doeth righteousness is righteous, even as he [God]** is righteous" (1 John 3:7; Lecture 1:1).

4. Q—What arrangement should be followed in presenting the subject of faith?

A—First, it should be shown what faith is (Lecture 1:3); secondly, the object upon which it rests (Lecture 1:4); and thirdly, the effects which flow from it (Lecture 1:5).

5. Q—What is faith?

A—It is the "assurance of things hoped for, the evidence of things not seen" (JST Heb 11:1); that is, it is the assurance we have of the existence of unseen things. And being the assurance which we have of the existence of unseen things, it must be the principle of action in all intelligent beings. "Through faith we understand that the worlds were framed by the word of God" (Heb 11:3; Lecture 1:8-9).

6. Q—How do you prove that faith is the principle of action in all intelligent beings?

A—First, by duly considering the operations of your own mind; and secondly, by the direct declaration of scripture. "By faith Noah, being warned of God of things not seen as yet, moved

---

*Bracketed material in 1835 edition, but without brackets.

**Brackets in 1835 edition.

35

with fear, prepared an ark to the saving of his house; by the which he condemned the world, and became heir of the righteousness which is by faith. By faith Abraham, when he was called to go out into a place which he should after receive for an inheritance, obeyed; and he went out, not knowing whither he went. By faith he sojourned in the land of promise, as in a strange country, dwelling in tabernacles with Isaac and Jacob, the heirs with him of the same promise" (Heb 11:7-9). By faith Moses "forsook Egypt, not fearing the wrath of the king: for he endured, as seeing him who is invisible" (Heb 11:27; Lecture 1:10-11).

7. Q—Is not faith the principle of action in spiritual things as well as in temporal?

A—It is.

8. Q—How do you prove it?

A—"Without faith it is impossible to please him [God]*" (Heb 11:6). "He that believeth and is baptized shall be saved" (Mark 16:16). "Therefore it is of faith, that it might be by grace; to the end the promise might be sure to all the seed; not to that only which is of the law, but to that also which is of the faith of Abraham; who is the father of us all" (Rom 4:16; Lecture 1:12-13).

9. Q—Is faith anything else besides the principle of action?

A—It is.

10. Q—What is it?

A—It is the principle of power also (Lecture 1:13).

11. Q—How do you prove it?

A—First, it is the principle of power in the Deity as well as in man. "Through faith we understand that the worlds were framed by the word of God, so that things which are seen were not made of things which do appear" (Heb 11:3: Lecture 1:14-16).

Secondly, it is the principle of power in man also. Book of Mormon, page 264: Alma and Amulek are delivered from prison (Alma 14:27). Page 421: Nephi and Lehi, with the Lamanites, are immersed with the Spirit (Hel 5:43-45). Page 565: The mountain

---

*Bracketed material in 1835 edition, but without brackets.

Zerin, by the faith of the brother of Jared, is removed (Ether 12:30). "Then spake Joshua to the Lord in the day when the Lord delivered up the Amorites before the children of Israel, and he said in the sight of Israel, Sun, stand thou still upon Gibeon; and thou, Moon, in the valley of Ajalon. And the sun stood still, and the moon stayed, until the people had avenged themselves upon their enemies. Is not this written in the book of Jasher? So the sun stood still in the midst of heaven, and hasted not to go down about a whole day" (Joshua 10:12-13). "Then came the disciples to Jesus apart, and said, Why could not we cast him out? And Jesus said unto them, Because of your unbelief: for verily I say unto you, If ye have faith as a grain of mustard seed, ye shall say unto this mountain, Remove hence to yonder place; and it shall remove; and nothing shall be impossible unto you" (Matt 17:19-20). "And what shall I more say? for the time would fail me to tell of Gedeon, and of Barak, and of Samson, and of Jephthae; of David also, and Samuel, and of the prophets: Who through faith subdued kingdoms, wrought righteousness, obtained promises, stopped the mouths of lions, quenched the violence of fire, escaped the edge of the sword, out of weakness were made strong, waxed valiant in fight, turned to flight the armies of the aliens. Women received their dead raised to life again: and others were tortured, not accepting deliverance; that they might obtain a better resurrection" (Heb 11:32-35; Lecture 1:16-22).

12. Q—How would you define faith in its most unlimited sense?

A—It is the first great governing principle which has power, dominion, and authority over all things (Lecture 1:24).

13. Q—How do you convey to the understanding more clearly the idea that faith is the first great governing principle which has power, dominion, and authority over all things?

A—By it they exist, by it they are upheld, by it they are changed, and by it they remain, agreeable to the will of God. Without it there is no power, and without power there could be no creation nor existence! (Lecture 1:24).

Lecture 2
ON FAITH

1. Having shown in our previous lecture "faith itself—what it is," we shall proceed to show, secondly, the object on which it rests.

2. We here observe that God is the only supreme governor and independent being in whom all fulness and perfection dwell. He is omnipotent, omnipresent, and omniscient, without beginning of days or end of life. In him every good gift and every good principle dwell, and he is the Father of lights. In him the principle of faith dwells independently, and he is the object in whom the faith of all other rational and accountable beings centers for life and salvation.

3. In order to present this part of the subject in a clear and conspicuous point of light, it is necessary to go back and show the evidences which mankind have had to believe in the existence of a God and also to show the foundation on which these evidences are and have been based since the creation.

4. We do not mean those evidences which are manifested by the works of creation which we daily behold with our natural eyes. We are sensible that, after a revelation of Jesus Christ, the works of creation clearly exhibit his eternal power and Godhead throughout their vast forms and varieties. "For the invisible things of him from the creation of the world are clearly seen, being understood by the things that are made, even his eternal power and Godhead" (Rom 1:20). But we do mean those evidences by

which the first thoughts were suggested to the minds of men that there was a God who created all things.

5. We shall now proceed to examine the situation of man at his first creation. Moses, the historian, has given us the following account of him in Genesis. We copy from the New Translation:[*]

6. "And I, God, said unto mine Only Begotten, which was with me from the beginning, Let us make man in our image, after our likeness; and it was so.

7. "And I, God, said, Let them have dominion over the fishes of the sea, and over the fowl of the air, and over the cattle, and over all the earth, and over every creeping thing that creepeth upon the earth.

8. "And I, God, created man in mine own image, in the image of mine Only Begotten created I him; male and female created I them. And I, God, blessed them, and said unto them, Be fruitful, and multiply, and replenish the earth, and subdue it; and have dominion over the fish of the sea, and over the fowl of the air, and over every living thing that moveth upon the earth.

9. "And I, God, said unto man, Behold, I have given you every herb, bearing seed, which is upon the face of all the earth; and every tree in the which shall be the fruit of a tree, yielding seed; to you it shall be for meat" (JST Gen 1:27-31; see also Moses 2:26-29).

10. Again, in Genesis: "And I, the Lord God, took the man, and put him into the garden of Eden, to dress it, and to keep it. And I, the Lord God, commanded the man, saying, Of every tree of the garden thou mayest freely eat; But of the tree of the knowledge of good and evil, thou shalt not eat of it; Nevertheless, thou mayest choose for thyself, for it is given unto thee; but remember that I forbid it; For in the day thou eatest thereof thou shalt surely die. . . .

11. "And out of the ground, I the Lord God, formed every beast of the field, and every fowl of the air; and commanded that

---

[*]All references to the "New Translation" are to the Joseph Smith Translation.

they should come unto Adam, to see what he would call them. And . . . whatsoever Adam called every living creature, that should be the name thereof. And Adam gave names to all cattle, and to the fowl of the air, and to every beast of the field" (JST Gen 2:18-22, 25-27; see also Moses 3:15-17, 19-20).

12. From the foregoing we learn of man's situation at his first creation, the knowledge with which he was endowed, and the high and exalted station in which he was placed—lord, or governor, of all things on earth, and at the same time enjoying communion and intercourse with his Maker, without a veil to separate between. We shall next proceed to examine the account given of his fall and of his being driven out of the garden of Eden and from the presence of the Lord.

13. Moses proceeds: "And they [Adam and Eve]* heard the voice of the Lord God, as they were walking in the garden, in the cool of the day. And Adam and his wife went to hide themselves from the presence of the Lord God, amongst the trees of the garden. And I, the Lord God, called unto Adam, and said unto him, Where goest thou? And he said, I heard thy voice, in the garden, and I was afraid, because I beheld that I was naked, and I hid myself.

14. "And I, the Lord God, said unto Adam, Who told thee that thou wast naked? Hast thou eaten of the tree whereof I commanded thee that thou shouldst not eat, if so thou shouldst surely die? And the man said, The woman whom thou gavest me, and commanded that she should remain with me, she gave me of the fruit of the tree, and I did eat.

15. "And I, the Lord God, said unto the woman, What is this thing which thou hast done? And the woman said, The serpent beguiled me, and I did eat" (JST Gen 3:13-19; see also Moses 4:14-19).

16. And again, the Lord said unto the woman, "I will greatly multiply thy sorrow, and thy conception; in sorrow thou

---

*Brackets in the 1835 edition.

shalt bring forth children, and thy desire shall be to thy husband, and he shall rule over thee.

17. "And unto Adam, I, the Lord God, said, Because thou hast hearkened unto the voice of thy wife, and hast eaten of the fruit of the tree, of which I commanded thee, saying, Thou shalt not eat of it, cursed shall be the ground for thy sake; in sorrow shalt thou eat of it all the days of thy life; thorns also and thistles shall it bring forth to thee; and thou shalt eat the herb of the field; by the sweat of thy face shalt thou eat bread, until thou shalt return unto the ground, for thou shalt surely die; for out of it wast thou taken, for dust thou wast, and unto dust shalt thou return" (JST Gen 3:22-25; see also Moses 4:22-25). This was immediately followed by the fulfilment of what we previously said: Man was driven or sent out of Eden.

18. Two important items are shown from the former quotations: First, after man was created, he was not left without intelligence or understanding to wander in darkness and spend an existence in ignorance and doubt on the great and important point which effected his happiness as to the real fact by whom he was created, or unto whom he was amenable for his conduct. God conversed with him face to face: in his presence he was permitted to stand, and from his own mouth he was permitted to receive instruction. He heard his voice, walked before him, and gazed upon his glory, while intelligence burst upon his understanding and enabled him to give names to the vast assemblage of his Maker's works.

19. Secondly, we have seen that though man did transgress, his transgression did not deprive him of the previous knowledge with which he had been endowed relative to the existence and glory of his Creator; for no sooner did he hear his voice than he sought to hide himself from his presence.

20. Having shown, then, in the first instance, that God began to converse with man immediately after he "breathed into his nostrils the breath of life," and that he did not cease to manifest himself to him, even after his fall, we shall next proceed to show, that even though man was cast out from the garden of Eden, he

did not lose his knowledge of the existence of God, neither did God cease to manifest his will unto him.

21. We next proceed to present the account of the direct revelation which man received after he was cast out of Eden, and further copy from the New Translation:

22. After Adam had been driven out of the garden, he "began to till the earth, and to have dominion over all the beasts of the field, and to eat his bread by the sweat of his brow, as I, the Lord had commanded him. . . . And Adam called upon the name of the Lord, and Eve also, his wife; and they heard the voice of the Lord, from the way towards the garden of Eden, speaking unto them, and they saw him not; for they were shut out from his presence. And he gave unto them commandments, that they should worship the Lord their God; and should offer the firstlings of their flocks for an offering unto the Lord. And Adam was obedient unto the commandments of the Lord.

23. "And after many days, an angel of the Lord appeared unto Adam, saying, Why dost thou offer sacrifices unto the Lord. And Adam said unto him, I know not, save the Lord commanded me.

24. "And then the angel spake, saying, This thing is a similitude of the sacrifice of the Only Begotten of the Father, which is full of grace and truth; wherefore, thou shalt do all that thou doest, in the name of the Son. And thou shalt repent, and call upon God, in the name of the Son for evermore. And in that day, the Holy Ghost fell upon Adam, which beareth record of the Father and the Son" (JST Gen 4:1, 4-9; see also Moses 5:1, 4-9).

25. This last quotation shows this important fact: even though our first parents were driven out of the garden of Eden and were separated from the presence of God by a veil, they still retained a knowledge of his existence, and that sufficiently to move them to call upon him. And further, no sooner was the plan of redemption revealed to man and he began to call upon God, than the Holy Spirit was given, bearing record of the Father and Son.

26. Moses also gives us an account of the transgression of Cain, of the righteousness of Abel, and of the revelations of God to them. He says, "In process of time . . . Cain brought of the fruit of the ground an offering unto the Lord. And Abel, he also brought, of the firstlings of his flock, and of the fat thereof; and the Lord had respect unto Abel, and to his offering, but unto Cain, and to his offering, he had not respect. Now Satan knew this, and it pleased him. And Cain was very wroth, and his countenance fell. And the Lord said unto Cain, Why art thou wroth? Why is thy countenance fallen? If thou doest well thou shalt be accepted, and if thou doest not well, sin lieth at the door; and Satan desireth to have thee, and except thou shalt hearken unto my command-ments, I will deliver thee up, and it shall be unto thee according to his desire. . . .

27. "And Cain went into the field, and Cain talked with Abel his brother; and it came to pass, that while they were in the field, Cain rose up against Abel his brother, and slew him. And Cain gloried in that which he had done, saying, I am free; surely the flocks of my brother falleth into my hands.

28. "And the Lord said unto Cain, Where is Abel, thy brother? And he said, I know not, am I my brother's keeper? And the Lord said, What hast thou done? The voice of thy brother's blood cries unto me from the ground. And now, thou shalt be cursed from the earth, which hath opened her mouth to receive thy brother's blood from thy hand. When thou tillest the ground, it shall not henceforth yield unto thee her strength; a fugitive and a vagabond shalt thou be in the earth.

29. "And Cain said unto the Lord, Satan tempted me, because of my brother's flock; and I was wroth also, for his offering thou didst accept, and not mine. My punishment is greater than I can bear. Behold, thou hast driven me out this day from the face of the Lord, and from thy face shall I be hid; and I shall be a fugitive and a vagabond in the earth; and it shall come to pass, that he that findeth me shall slay me, because of mine iniquities, for these things are not hid from the Lord. And I, the Lord, said unto him, Whosoever slayeth thee, vengeance shall be

taken on him seven-fold; and I, the Lord, set a mark upon Cain, lest any finding him should kill him" (JST Gen 5:6-9, 17-25; see also Moses 5:19-23, 32-40).

30. The object of the foregoing quotation is to show to this class that the way by which mankind were first made acquainted with the existence of a God was by a manifestation of God to man. Also after man's transgression God continued to manifest himself to him and to his posterity. And notwithstanding they were separated from his immediate presence so that they could not see his face, they continued to hear his voice.

31. Adam, thus being made acquainted with God, communicated the knowledge which he had unto his posterity. And it was through this means that the thought was first suggested to their minds that there was a God, which laid the foundation for the exercise of their faith, through which they could obtain a knowledge of his character and also of his glory.

32. Not only was there a manifestation made unto Adam of the existence of a God, but Moses informs us, as before quoted, that God also condescended to talk with Cain after his great transgression in slaying his brother. And Cain knew that it was the Lord who was talking with him, so when he was driven out from the presence of his brethren, he carried with him the knowledge of the existence of a God. And through this means, doubtless, his posterity became acquainted with the fact that such a being existed.

33. From this we can see that the whole human family in the early age of their existence and in all their different branches had this knowledge disseminated among them; so that the existence of God became an object of faith in the early age of the world. And the evidence which these men had of the existence of a God was the testimony of their fathers, in the first instance.

34. The reason we have been thus particular on this part of our subject is that this class may see by what means it was that God became an object of faith among men after the Fall, and also may see what it was that stirred up the faith of multitudes to feel after him, to search after a knowledge of his character, perfections,

and attributes, until they became extensively acquainted with him. Not only were they to commune with him and behold his glory, but they were also to be partakers of his power and stand in his presence.

35. Let this class mark particularly that the testimony which these men had of the existence of a God was the testimony of man. For previous to the time that any of Adam's posterity had obtained a manifestation of God to themselves, Adam, their common father, had testified unto them of the existence of God and of his eternal power and Godhead.

36. For instance, Abel, before he received the assurance from heaven that his offerings were acceptable unto God, had received the important information from his father that such a being who had created and who did uphold all things did exist. Neither can there be any doubt existing in the mind of any person but that Adam was the first who did communicate the knowledge of the existence of a God to his posterity. The whole faith of the world from that time down to the present is in a certain degree dependent on the knowledge first communicated to them by their common progenitor; and it has been handed down to the day and generation in which we live, as we shall show from the face of the sacred records.

37. First, Adam was 130 years old when Seth was born (Gen 5:3). And the days of Adam, after he had begotten Seth, were 800 years, making him 930 years old when he died (5:4-5). Seth was 105 when Enos was born (5:6); Enos was 90 when Cainan was born (5:9); Cainan was 70 when Mahalaleel was born (5:12); Mahalaleel was 65 when Jared was born (5:15); Jared was 162 when Enoch was born (5:18); Enoch was 65 when Methuselah was born (5:21); Methuselah was 187 when Lamech was born (5:25); Lamech was 182 when Noah was born (5:28).

38. From this account it appears that Lamech, the eighth* from Adam, and the father of Noah, was 56 years old when Adam

---

*The 1835 text says "9th," but the sequence above shows that Lamech is the eighth generation from Adam.

died; Methuselah, 243; Enoch, 308; Jared, 470; Mahalaleel, 535; Cainan, 605; Enos, 695; and Seth, 800.

39. So Lamech the father of Noah, Methuselah, Enoch, Jared, Mahalaleel, Cainan, Enos, Seth, and Adam, were all living at the same time, and, beyond all controversy, were all preachers of righteousness.

40. Moses further informs us that Seth lived 807 years after he begat Enos, making him 912 years old at his death (Gen 5:7-8). And Enos lived 815 years after he begat Cainan, making him 905 years old when he died (5:10-11). And Cainan lived 840 years after he begat Mahalaleel, making him 910 years old at his death (5:13-14). And Mahalaleel lived 830 years after he begat Jared, making him 895 years old when he died (5:16-17). And Jared lived 800 years after he begat Enoch, making him 962 years old at his death (5:19-20). And Enoch walked with God 300 years after he begat Methuselah, making him 365 years old when he was translated (5:22-23).* And Methuselah lived 782 years after he begat Lamech, making him 969 years old when he died (5:26-27). Lamech lived 595 years after he begat Noah, making him 777 years old when he died (5:30-31).

41. Agreeable to this account, Adam died in the 930th year of the world; Enoch was translated in the 987th; Seth died in the 1042nd; Enos in the 1140th; Cainan in the 1235th; Mahalaleel in the 1290th; Jared in the 1422nd; Lamech in the 1651st; and Methuselah in the 1656th, it being the same year in which the flood came.

42. So Noah was 84 years old when Enos died, 179** when Cainan died, 234 when Mahalaleel died, 366 when Jared died, 595 when Lamech died, and 600 when Methuselah died.

---

*Doctrine and Covenants 107:49 reads: "And he [Enoch] saw the Lord, and he walked with him, and was before his face continually; and he walked with God three hundred and sixty-five years, making him four hundred and thirty years old when he was translated."

**The 1835 edition here says Noah was 176 when Cainan died, but the mathematics show him to have been 179, and the 1835 edition corrects itself in the Question and Answer section of this lecture, answer to Question 62.

43. We can see from this that Enos, Cainan, Mahalaleel, Jared, Methuselah, Lamech, and Noah, all lived on the earth at the same time, and that Enos, Cainan, Mahalaleel, Jared, Methuselah, and Lamech, were all acquainted with both Adam and Noah.

44. From the foregoing, it is easy to see not only how the knowledge of God came into the world but also upon what principle it was preserved. From the time it was first communicated, it was retained in the minds of righteous men who taught not only their own posterity but also the world. So there was no need of a new revelation to man after Adam's creation to Noah to give them the first idea or notion of the existence of a God, and not only of a God, but the true and living God.

45. Having traced the chronology of the world from Adam to Noah, we will now trace it from Noah to Abraham. Noah was 502 years old when Shem was born; 98 years afterwards the flood came, being the 600th year of Noah's age (Gen 7:11). And Moses informs us that Noah lived 350 years after the flood, making him 950 years old when he died (Gen 9:28-29).

46. Shem was 100 years old when Arphaxad was born (Gen 11:10). Arphaxad was 35 when Salah was born (11:12); Salah was 30 when Eber was born (11:14); Eber was 34 when Peleg was born, in whose days the earth was divided (11:16); Peleg was 30 when Reu was born (11:18); Reu was 32 when Serug was born (11:20); Serug was 30 when Nahor was born (11:22); Nahor was 29 when Terah was born (11:24); Terah was 70 when Haran and Abraham were born (11:26).

47. There is some difficulty in the account given by Moses of Abraham's birth. Some have supposed that Abraham was not born until Terah was 130 years old. This conclusion is drawn from a variety of scriptures, but it is not our purpose at present to quote them. Neither is it a matter of any consequence to us whether Abraham was born when Terah was 70 years old or 130. But so there may be no doubt about the present chronology, we will date the birth of Abraham at the later period, that is, when

Terah was 130 years old. It appears from this account that the time from the flood to the birth of Abraham was 352 years.

48. Moses informs us that Shem lived 500 years after he begat Arphaxad (Gen 11:11); this added to 100 years, which was his age when Arphaxad was born, makes him 600 years old when he died. Arphaxad lived 403 years after he begat Salah (11:13); this added to 35 years, which was his age when Salah was born, makes him 438 years old when he died. Salah lived 403 years after he begat Eber (11:15); this added to 30 years, which was his age when Eber was born, makes him 433 years old when he died. Eber lived 430 years after he begat Peleg (11:17); this added to 34 years, which was his age when Peleg was born, makes him 464 years old when he died. Peleg lived 209 years after he begat Reu (11:19); this added to 30 years, which was his age when Reu was born, makes him 239 years old when he died. Reu lived 207 years after he begat Serug (11:21); this added to 32 years, which was his age when Serug was born, makes him 239 years old when he died. Serug lived 200 years after he begat Nahor (11:23); this added to 30 years, which was his age when Nahor was born, makes him 230 years old when he died. Nahor lived 119 years after he begat Terah (11:25); this added to 29 years, which was his age when Terah was born, makes him 148 years old when he died. Terah was 130 years old when Abraham was born, and is supposed to have lived 75 years after his birth, making him 205 years old when he died.

49. Agreeable to this last account, Peleg died in the 1996th year of the world, Nahor in the 1997th, and Noah in the 2006th. So that Peleg, in whose days the earth was divided, and Nahor, the grandfather of Abraham, both died before Noah: the former being 239 years old, and the latter 148. And who cannot but see that they must have had a long and intimate acquaintance with Noah?

50. Reu died in the 2026th year of the world, Serug in the 2049th, Terah in the 2083rd, Arphaxad in the 2096th, Salah in the 2126th, Shem in the 2158th, Abraham in the 2183rd, and Eber in

the 2187th, which was four years after Abraham's death. And Eber was the fourth from Noah.

51. Nahor, Abraham's brother, was 58 years old when Noah died, Terah 128, Serug 187, Reu 219, Eber 283, Salah 313, Arphaxad 348,* and Shem 448.

52. It appears from this account that Nahor, brother of Abraham, Terah, Nahor, Serug, Reu, Peleg, Eber, Salah, Arphaxad, Shem, and Noah, all lived on the earth at the same time. Abraham was 18 years old when Reu died, 41 when Serug and his brother Nahor died, 75 when Terah died, 88 when Arphaxad died, 118 when Salah died, 150 when Shem died, and that Eber lived four years after Abraham's death. Shem, Arphaxad, Salah, Eber, Reu, Serug, Terah, and Nahor, brother of Abraham, and Abraham, lived at the same time. Nahor, brother of Abraham, Terah, Serug, Reu, Eber, Salah, Arphaxad, and Shem, were all acquainted with both Noah and Abraham.

53. We have now traced the chronology of the world from Adam to Abraham agreeable to the account given in our present Bible, and have clearly determined beyond the power of controversy that there was no difficulty in preserving the knowledge of God in the world from the creation of Adam, and the manifestation made to his immediate descendants, as set forth in the former part of this lecture. So the students in this class need not have any doubt in their minds on this subject, for they can easily see that it is impossible for it to be otherwise, but that the knowledge of the existence of a God must have continued from father to son, as a matter of tradition at least. For we cannot suppose that a knowledge of this important fact could have existed in the mind of any of the before-mentioned individuals without their having made it known to their posterity.

54. We have now shown how it was by reason of the manifestation which God first made to our father Adam, when he stood in his presence and conversed with him face to face at the

*The 1835 edition here puts Arphaxad's age at 344 when Noah died, but he was actually 348, and the 1835 edition corrects itself in the answer to Question 122 in the Question and Answer section of this lecture.

time of his creation, that the first thought ever existed in the mind of any individual that there was such a being as a God who had created and did uphold all things.

55. Let us here observe that after any members of the human family are made acquainted with the important fact that there is a God who has created and does uphold all things, the extent of their knowledge respecting his character and glory will depend upon their diligence and faithfulness in seeking after him, until, like Enoch, the brother of Jared, and Moses, they shall obtain faith in God and power with him to behold him face to face.

56. We have now clearly set forth how it is, and how it was, that God became an object of faith for rational beings, and also, upon what foundation the testimony was based which excited the inquiry and diligent search of the ancient Saints to seek after and obtain a knowledge of the glory of God. We have also seen that it was human testimony, and human testimony only, that excited this inquiry in their minds in the first instance. It was the credence they gave to the testimony of their fathers, it having aroused their minds to inquire after the knowledge of God. That inquiry frequently terminated, indeed always terminated when rightly pursued, in the most glorious discoveries and eternal certainty.

Questions and Answers for Lecture 2

1. *Question*—Is there a being who has faith in himself, independently?

Answer—There is.

2. Q—Who is it?

A—It is God.

3. Q—How do you prove that God has faith in himself independently?

A—Because he is omnipotent, omnipresent, and omniscient, without beginning of days or end of life, and in him all fulness dwells. "Which is his body, the fulness of him that filleth all in all" (Eph 1:23). "For it pleased the Father that in him should all fulness dwell" (Col 1:19; see also Lecture 2:2).

4. Q—Is he the object in whom the faith of all other rational and accountable beings centers for life and salvation?

A—He is.

5. Q—How do you prove it?

A—"Look unto me, and be ye saved, all the ends of the earth: for I am God, and there is none else" (Isa 45:22). "For who hath known the mind of the Lord? or who hath been his counsellor? or who hath first given to him, and it shall be recompensed unto him again? For of him, and through him, and to him, are all things: to whom be glory for ever. Amen" (Rom 11:34-36). "O Zion, that bringest good tidings, [or, O thou that tellest good tidings to Zion,]* get thee up into the high mountain; O Jerusalem, that bringest good tidings, [or, O thou that tellest good tidings to Jerusalem,]* lift up thy voice with strength; lift it up, be not afraid; say unto the cities of Judah, Behold your God! Behold, the Lord God will come with strong hand, [or, against the strong,]* and his arm shall rule for him: behold, his reward is with him, and his work before him [or, recompense for his work].* He shall feed his flock like a shepherd: he shall gather the lambs with his arm, and carry them in his bosom, and shall gently lead those that are with young. Who hath measured the waters in the hollow of his hand, and meted out heaven with the span, and comprehended the dust of the earth in a measure, and weighed the mountains in scales, and the hills in a balance? Who hath directed the Spirit of the Lord, or being his counsellor hath taught him? With whom took he counsel, and who instructed him, and taught him in the path of judgment, and taught him knowledge, and shewed to him the way of understanding? Behold, the nations are as a drop of a bucket, and are counted as the small dust of the balance: behold, he taketh up the isles as a very little thing. And Lebanon is not sufficient to burn, nor the beasts thereof sufficient for a burnt

---

*Brackets in the 1835 edition.

offering. All nations before him are as nothing; and they are counted to him less than nothing, and vanity" (Isa 40:9-17). "He [the Lord]* hath made the earth by his power, he hath established the world by his wisdom, and hath stretched out the heaven by his understanding. When he uttereth his voice, there is a multitude of waters in the heavens; and he causeth the vapours to ascend from the ends of the earth: he maketh lightnings with rain, and bringeth forth the wind out of his treasures" (Jer 51:15-16). "But to us there is but one God, the Father, of whom are all things, and we in him; and one Lord Jesus Christ, by whom are all things, and we by him" (1 Cor 8:6; see Lecture 2:2).

6. Q—How did men first come to the knowledge of the existence of a God so as to exercise faith in him?

A—In order to answer this question, it will be necessary to go back and examine man at his creation, the circumstances in which he was placed, and the knowledge which he had of God (Lecture 2:3-11).

First, when man was created, he stood in the presence of God (Gen 1:27-31). From this we learn that man at his creation stood in the presence of his God and had a most perfect knowledge of his existence.

Secondly, God conversed with him after his transgression (Gen 3:8-21; Lecture 2:13-17). From this we learn that even though man did transgress, he was not deprived of the previous knowledge which he had of the existence of God (Lecture 2:19).

Thirdly, God conversed with man after he cast him out of the garden (Lecture 2:22-25).

Fourthly, God also conversed with Cain after he had slain Abel (Gen 4:9-15; Lecture 2:26-29).

7. Q—What is the object of the foregoing quotations?

A—It is that it may be clearly seen how it was that the first thoughts of the existence of God were suggested to the minds of men and how extensively this knowledge was spread among the immediate descendants of Adam (Lecture 2:30-33).

---

*Brackets in 1835 edition.

8. Q—What testimony did the immediate descendants of Adam have in proof of the existence of a God?

A—The testimony of their father. And after they were made acquainted with God's existence by the testimony of their father, they were dependent upon the exercise of their own faith for a knowledge of his character, perfections, and attributes (Lecture 2:23-26).

9. Q—Did any other of the human family, besides Adam, have a knowledge of the existence of God, in the first instance, by any other means than human testimony?

A—They did not. For previous to the time that they could have power to obtain a manifestation for themselves, that all-important fact had been communicated to them by their common father. And so, the knowledge of his existence was communicated from father to child as extensively as it was known. For it was by this means that men had a knowledge of his existence in the first instance (Lecture 2:35-36).

10. Q—How do you know that the knowledge of the existence of God was communicated in this manner throughout the different ages of the world?

A—By the chronology obtained through the revelations of God.

11. Q—How would you divide that chronology in order to convey it to the understanding clearly?

A—Into two parts: First, by embracing that period of the world from Adam to Noah, and secondly, from Noah to Abraham. The knowledge of the existence of God has been so general from that period that it is a matter of no dispute in what manner the idea of his existence has been retained in the world.

12. Q—How many noted righteous men lived from Adam to Noah?

A—Nine, which includes Abel, who was slain by his brother.

13. Q—What are their names?

A—Abel, Seth, Enos, Cainan, Mahalaleel, Jared, Enoch, Methuselah, and Lamech.

14. Q—How old was Adam when Seth was born?
A—130 years (Gen 5:3).

15. Q—How many years did Adam live after Seth was born?
A—800 years (5:4).

16. Q—How old was Adam when he died?
A—930 years (5:5).

17. Q—How old was Seth when Enos was born?
A—105 years (5:6).

18. Q—How old was Enos when Cainan was born?
A—90 years (5:9).

19. Q—How old was Cainan when Mahalaleel was born?
A—70 years (5:12).

20. Q—How old was Mahalaleel when Jared was born?
A—65 years (5:15).

21. Q—How old was Jared when Enoch was born?
A—162 years (5:18).

22. Q—How old was Enoch when Methuselah was born?
A—65 years (5:21).

23. Q—How old was Methuselah when Lamech was born?
A—187 years (5:25).

24. Q—How old was Lamech when Noah was born?
A—182 years (5:28). For this chronology, see Lecture 2:37.

25. Q—How many years, according to this account, was it from Adam to Noah?
A—1056 years.

26. Q—How old was Lamech when Adam died?
A—Lamech, the ninth from Adam (including Abel) and father of Noah, was 56 years old when Adam died.

27. Q—How old was Methuselah?
A—243 years.

28. Q—How old was Enoch?
A—308 years.

29. Q—How old was Jared?
A—470 years.

30. Q—How old was Mahalaleel?

A—535 years.

31. Q—How old was Cainan?

A—605 years.

32. Q—How old was Enos?

A—695 years.

33. Q—How old was Seth?

A—800 years. For this item of the account, see Lecture 2:38.

34. Q—How many of these noted men were contemporary with Adam?

A—Nine.

35. Q—What are their names?

A—Abel, Seth, Enos, Cainan, Mahalaleel, Jared, Enoch, Methuselah and Lamech (Lecture 2:39).

36. Q—How long did Seth live after Enos was born?

A—807 years (Gen 5:7).

37. Q—What was Seth's age when he died?

A—912 years (5:8).

38. Q—How long did Enos live after Cainan was born?

A—815 years (5:10).

39. Q—What was Enos's age when he died?

A—905 years (5:11).

40. Q—How long did Cainan live after Mahalaleel was born?

A—840 years (5:13).

41. Q—What was Cainan's age when he died?

A—910 years (5:14).

42. Q—How long did Mahalaleel live after Jared was born?

A—830 years (5:16).

43. Q—What was Mahalaleel's age when he died?

A—895 years (5:17).

44. Q—How long did Jared live after Enoch was born?

A—800 years (5:19).

45. Q—What was Jared's age when he died?

A—962 years (5:20).

46. Q—How long did Enoch walk with God after Methuselah was born?

A—300 years (Gen 5:22).

47. Q—What was Enoch's age when he was translated?
A—365 years (5:23).*

48. Q—How long did Methuselah live after Lamech was born?
A—782 years (5:26).

49. Q—What was Methuselah's age when he died?
A—969 years (5:27).

50. Q—How long did Lamech live after Noah was born?
A—595 years (5:30).

51. Q—What was Lamech's age when he died?
A—777 years (5:31). For the account of the last item see Lecture 2:40.

52. Q—In what year of the world did Adam die?
A—In the 930th.

53. Q—In what year was Enoch translated?
A—In the 987th.

54. Q—In what year did Seth die?
A—In the 1042nd.

55. Q—In what year did Enos die?
A—In the 1140th.

56. Q—In what year did Cainan die?
A—In the 1235th.

57. Q—In what year did Mahalaleel die?
A—In the 1290th.

58. Q—In what year did Jared die?
A—In the 1422nd.

59. Q—In what year did Lamech die?
A—In the 1651st.

60. Q—In what year did Methuselah die?
A—In the 1656th. For this account see Lecture 2:41.

61. Q—How old was Noah when Enos died?
A—84 years.

62. Q—How old when Cainan died?

---

*Doctrine and Covenants 107:49 reads: "And he [Enoch] saw the Lord, and he walked with him, and was before his face continually; and he walked with God three hundred and sixty-five years, making him four hundred and thirty years old when he was translated."

A—179 years.

63. Q—How old when Mahalaleel died?

A—234 years.

64. Q—How old when Jared died?

A—366 years.

65. Q—How old when Lamech died?

A—595 years.

66. Q—How old when Methuselah died?

A—600 years. See Lecture 2:42, for the last item.

67. Q—How many of those men lived in the days of Noah?

A—Six.

68. Q—What are their names?

A—*Enos, Cainan, Mahalaleel, Jared, Methuselah, and Lamech (Lecture 2:43).

69. Q—How many of those men were contemporary with Adam and Noah both?

A—Six.

70. Q—What are their names?

A—Enos, Cainan, Mahalaleel, Jared, Methuselah, and Lamech (Lecture 2:43).

71. Q—According to the foregoing account, how was the knowledge of the existence of God first suggested to the minds of men?

A—By the manifestation made to our father Adam when he was in the presence of God, both before and while he was in Eden (Lecture 2:44).

72. Q—How was the knowledge of the existence of God disseminated among the inhabitants of the world?

A—By tradition from father to son (Lecture 2:44).

73. Q—How old was Noah when Shem was born?

A—502 years (Gen 5:32; 11:10).**

---

*The 1835 edition has Seth listed here, but he died some fourteen years before Noah was born.

**Gen 5:32 says Noah was 500 years old when Shem was born, but a genealogy workup based on Gen 11:10 shows he must have been 502 years as stated in the 1835 edition.

74. Q—What was the term of years from the birth of Shem to the flood?

A—98 years.

75. Q—What was the term of years that Noah lived after the flood?

A—350 years (Gen 9:28).

76. Q—What was Noah's age when he died?

A—950 years (9:29; Lecture 2:45).

77. Q—What was Shem's age when Arphaxad was born?

A—100 years (Gen 11:10).

78. Q—What was Arphaxad's age when Salah was born?

A—35 years (11:12).

79. Q—What was Salah's age when Eber was born?

A—30 years (11:14).

80. Q—What was Eber's age when Peleg was born?

A—34 years (11:16).

81. Q—What was Peleg's age when Reu was born?

A—30 years (11:18).

82. Q—What was Reu's age when Serug was born?

A—32 years (11:20).

83. Q—What was Serug's age when Nahor was born?

A—30 years (11:22).

84. Q—What was Nahor's age when Terah was born?

A—29 years (11:24).

85. Q—What was Terah's age when Nahor, the brother* of Abraham, was born?

A—70 years (11:26).

86. Q—What was Terah's age when Abraham was born?

A—Some suppose 130 years and others 70 (12:4; 11:26; Lecture 2:46).

87. Q—What was the number of years from the flood to the birth of Abraham?

---

*All previous editions have said "father," but Nahor is either the grandfather or brother of Abraham. The context indicates his brother.

A—Supposing Abraham to have been born when Terah was 130 years old, it was 352 years; but if he was born when Terah was 70 years old, it was 292 years (Lecture 2:47).

88. Q—How long did Shem live after Arphaxad was born?

A—500 years (Gen 11:11).

89. Q—What was Shem's age when he died?

A—600 years.

90. Q—What number of years did Arphaxad live after Salah was born?

A—403 years (11:13).

91. Q—What was Arphaxad's age when he died?

A—438 years.

92. Q—What number of years did Salah live after Eber was born?

A—403 years (11:15).

93. Q—What was Salah's age when he died?

A—433 years.

94. Q—What number of years did Eber live after Peleg was born?

A—430 years (11:17).

95. Q—What was Eber's age when he died?

A—464 years.

96. Q—What number of years did Peleg live after Reu was born?

A—209 years (11:19).

97. Q—What was Peleg's age when he died?

A—239 years.

98. Q—What number of years did Reu live after Serug was born?

A—207 years (11:21).

99. Q—What was Reu's age when he died?

A—239 years.

100.Q—What number of years did Serug live after Nahor was born?

A—200 years (11:23).

101.Q—What was Serug's age when he died?

A—230 years.

102. Q—What number of years did Nahor live after Terah was born?

A—119 years (Gen 11:25).

103. Q—What was Nahor's age when he died?

A—148 years.

104. Q—What number of years did Terah live after Abraham was born?

A—Supposing Terah to have been 130 years old when Abraham was born, he lived 75 years; but if Abraham was born when Terah was 70 years old, he lived 135.

105. Q—What was Terah's age when he died?

A—205 years (11:32). For this account, from the birth of Arphaxad to the death of Terah see Lecture 2:48.

106. Q—In what year of the world did Peleg die?

A—Agreeable to the foregoing chronology, he died in the 1996th year of the world.

107. Q—In what year of the world did Nahor die?

A—In the 1997th.

108. Q—In what year of the world did Noah die?

A—In the 2006th.

109. Q—In what year of the world did Reu die?

A—In the 2026th.

110. Q—In what year of the world did Serug die?

A—In the 2049th.

111. Q—In what year of the world did Terah die?

A—In the 2083rd.

112. Q—In what year of the world did Arphaxad die?

A—In the 2096th.

113. Q—In what year of the world did Salah die?

A—In the 2126th.

114. Q—In what year of the world did Abraham die?

A—In the 2183rd.

115. Q—In what year of the world did Eber die?

A—In the 2187th.

For this account of the year of the world in which those men died see Lecture 2:49-50.

116. Q—How old was Nahor, Abraham's brother, when Noah died?

A—58 years.

117. Q—How old was Terah?

A—128 years.

118. Q—How old was Serug?

A—187 years.

119. Q—How old was Reu?

A—219 years.

120. Q—How old was Eber?

A—283 years.

121. Q—How old was Salah?

A—313 years.

122. Q—How old was Arphaxad?

A—348 years.

123. Q—How old was Shem?

A—448 years. For the last account see Lecture 2:51.

124. Q—How old was Abraham when Reu died?

A—18 years, if he was born when Terah was 130 years old.

125. Q—What was his age when Serug and Nahor, Abraham's brother, died?

A—41 years.

126. Q—What was his age when Terah died?

A—75 years.

127. Q—What was his age when Arphaxad died?

A—88 years.

128. Q—What was his age when Salah died?

A—118 years.

129. Q—What was his age when Shem died?

A—150 years. For this see Lecture 2:52.

130. Q—How many noted characters lived from Noah to Abraham?

A—Ten.

131. Q—What are their names?

A—Shem, Arphaxad, Salah, Eber, Peleg, Reu, Serug, Nahor, Terah, and Nahor, Abraham's brother (Lecture 2:52).

132. Q—How many of these were contemporary with Noah?

A—The whole.

133. Q—How many with Abraham?

A—Eight.

134. Q—What are their names?

A—Nahor, Abraham's brother, Terah, Serug, Reu, Eber, Salah, Arphaxad, and Shem (Lecture 2:52).

135. Q—How many were contemporary with both Noah and Abraham?

A—Eight.

136. Q—What are their names?

A—Shem, Arphaxad, Salah, Eber, Reu, Serug, Terah, and Nahor, Abraham's brother (Lecture 2:52).

137. Q—Did any of these men die before Noah?

A—They did.

138. Q—Who were they?

A—Peleg, in whose days the earth was divided, and Nahor, Abraham's grandfather (Lecture 2:49).

139. Q—Did any one of them live longer than Abraham?

A—There was one (Lecture 2:50).

140. Q—Who was he?

A—Eber, the fourth from Noah (Lecture 2:50).

141. Q—In whose days was the earth divided?

A—In the days of Peleg.

142. Q—Where have we the account given that the earth was divided in the days of Peleg?

A—Genesis 10:25.

143. Q—Can you repeat the sentence?

A—"Unto Eber were born two sons: the name of one was Peleg; for in his days was the earth divided."

144. Q—What testimony did men have, in the first instance, that there is a God?

A—Human testimony, and human testimony only (Lecture 2:56).

145.Q—What excited the ancient Saints to seek diligently after a knowledge of the glory of God, his perfections, and attributes?

A—The credence they gave to the testimony of their fathers (Lecture 2:56).

146.Q—How do men obtain a knowledge of the glory of God, his perfections, and attributes?

A—By devoting themselves to his service, through prayer and supplication incessantly, strengthening their faith in him, until, like Enoch, the brother of Jared, and Moses, they obtain a manifestation of God to themselves (Lecture 2:55).

147.Q—Is the knowledge of the existence of God a matter of mere tradition founded upon human testimony alone until persons receive a manifestation of God to themselves?

A—It is.

148.Q—How do you prove it?

A—From the whole of the first part of Lecture 2.

Lecture 3

ON FAITH

1. In the second lecture we showed how the knowledge of the existence of God came into the world and by what means the first thoughts were suggested to the minds of men that such a being did actually exist. We also showed that it was by reason of the knowledge of his existence that there was a foundation laid for the exercise of faith in him as the only being in whom faith could center for life and salvation. For faith could not center in a being of whose existence we had no idea, because the idea of his existence, in the first instance, is essential to the exercise of faith in him. "How then shall they call on him in whom they have not believed? and how shall they believe in him of whom they have not heard? and how shall they hear without a preacher?" (or one sent to tell them?) (Rom 10:14). So, then, faith comes by hearing the word of God.

2. Let us here observe that three things are necessary for any rational and intelligent being to exercise faith in God unto life and salvation.

3. First, the idea that he actually exists;

4. Secondly, a *correct* idea of his character, perfections, and attributes;

5. Thirdly, an actual knowledge that the course of life which one is pursuing is according to His will. For without an acquaintance with these three important facts, the faith of every rational being must be imperfect and unproductive. But with this

understanding, it can become perfect and fruitful, abounding in righteousness unto the praise and glory of God the Father and the Lord Jesus Christ.

6. Having previously shown the way that both the idea and the fact of his existence came into the world, we shall proceed to examine his character, perfections, and attributes, so this class may see not only the just grounds which they have to exercise faith in him for life and salvation, but the reasons that all the world, also, may have to exercise faith in him, the Father of all living, as far as the idea of his existence extends.

7. As we are indebted for the idea of his existence to a revelation which God made of himself to his creatures, in the first instance, so in like manner we are indebted to the revelations which he has given to us for a correct understanding of his character, perfections, and attributes. Because without the revelations which he has given to us, no man by searching could find out God (see Job 11:7-9). "But as it is written, Eye hath not seen, nor ear heard, neither have entered into the heart of man, the things which God hath prepared for them that love him. But God hath revealed them unto us by his Spirit: for the Spirit searcheth all things, yea, the deep things of God. For what man knoweth the things of a man, save the spirit of man which is in him? even so the things of God knoweth no man, but the Spirit of God" (1 Cor 2:9-11).

8. Having said so much, we proceed to examine the character which the revelations give of God.

9. Moses gives us the following account in Exodus: "And the Lord passed by before him, and proclaimed, The Lord, the Lord God, merciful and gracious, longsuffering, and abundant in goodness and truth" (Ex 34:6). "The Lord executeth righteousness and judgment for all that are oppressed. He made known his ways unto Moses, his acts unto the children of Israel. The Lord is merciful and gracious, slow to anger, and plenteous in mercy" (Ps 103:6-8). "But the mercy of the Lord is from everlasting to everlasting upon them that fear him, and his righteousness unto children's children; to such as keep his covenant, and to those that

remember his commandments to do them" (Ps 103:17-18). "Before the mountains were brought forth, or ever thou hadst formed the earth and the world, even from everlasting to everlasting, thou art God" (Ps 90:2). "And, Thou, Lord, in the beginning hast laid the foundation of the earth; and the heavens are the works of thine hands: They shall perish; but thou remainest; and they all shall wax old as doth a garment; and as a vesture shalt thou fold them up, and they shall be changed: but thou art the same, and thy years shall not fail" (Heb 1:10-12). "Every good gift and every perfect gift is from above, and cometh down from the Father of lights, with whom is no variableness, neither shadow of turning" (James 1:17). "For I am the Lord, I change not; therefore ye sons of Jacob are not consumed" (Mal 3:6).

10. "For God doth not walk in crooked paths; neither doth he turn to the right hand nor the left; neither doth he vary from that which he hath said: therefore his paths are strait and his course is one eternal round" (Book of Commandments 2:1; D&C 3:2). "Listen to the voice of the Lord your God, even Alpha and Omega, the beginning and the end, whose course is one eternal round, the same today as yesterday and forever" (Book of Commandments 37:1; D&C 35:1).

11. "God is not a man, that he should lie; neither the son of man, that he should repent" (Num 23:19). "He that loveth not knoweth not God; for God is love" (1 John 4:8). "Then Peter opened his mouth, and said, Of a truth I perceive that God is no respecter of persons: But in every nation he that feareth him, and worketh righteousness, is accepted with him" (Acts 10:34-35).

12. From the foregoing testimonies, we learn the following things respecting the character of God:

13. First, he was God before the world was created, and the same God he was after it was created.

14. Secondly, he is merciful and gracious, slow to anger, abundant in goodness, and he was so from everlasting, and will be to everlasting.

15. Thirdly, he does not change, neither does he vary; but he is the same from everlasting to everlasting, being the same yesterday, today, and forever; and his course is one eternal round, without variation.

16. Fourthly, he is a God of truth and cannot lie.

17. Fifthly, he is no respecter of persons; but in every nation he that fears God and works righteousness is accepted of him.

18. Sixthly, he is love.

19. An acquaintance with these attributes in the divine character is essential so the faith of any rational being can center in him for life and salvation. For if, in the first instance, he did not believe him to be God, that is, the creator and upholder of all things, he could not *center* his faith in him for life and salvation, for fear there should be a greater one than he who would thwart all his plans, and he, like the gods of the heathen, would be unable to fulfil his promises. But seeing he is God over all, from everlasting to everlasting, the creator and upholder of all things, no such fear can exist in the minds of those who put their trust in him, so that in this respect their faith can be unwavering.

20. But secondly, unless God was merciful and gracious, slow to anger, long-suffering and full of goodness, such is the weakness of human nature and so great the frailties and imperfections of men that unless they believed that these excellencies existed in the divine character, they could not have the faith necessary to salvation. For doubt would take the place of faith, and those who know their weakness and liability to sin would be in constant doubt of salvation if it were not for the idea which they have of the excellency of the character of God, that he is slow to anger, long-suffering, and of a forgiving disposition, and does forgive iniquity, transgression, and sin. Having an idea of these facts does away with doubt and makes faith exceedingly strong.

21. But in order to have faith in him, it is equally as necessary that men should have the idea that he is a God who does not change as it is to have the idea that he is gracious and long-suffering. For without the idea of unchangeableness in the

character of the Deity, doubt would take the place of faith. But with the idea that he does not change, faith lays hold upon the excellencies in his character with unshaken confidence, believing he is the same yesterday, today, and forever, and that his course is one eternal round.

22. And again, the idea that he is a God of truth and cannot lie is equally as necessary to the exercise of faith in him as is the idea of his unchangeableness. For without the idea that he is a God of truth and cannot lie, men could not have the confidence in his word necessary to exercise faith in him. But having the idea that he is not a man who can lie gives power to the minds of men to exercise faith in him.

23. But it is also necessary that men should have an idea that God is no respecter of persons, for with the idea of all the other excellencies in his character, and this one wanting, men could not exercise faith in him. Because if he were a respecter of persons, they could not tell what their privileges were, nor how far they were authorized to exercise faith in him, or whether they were authorized to do it at all. All must be confusion. But no sooner are the minds of men made acquainted with the truth on this point, that he is no respecter of persons, than they see that they have authority by faith to lay hold on eternal life, the richest boon of heaven, because God is no respecter of persons, and every man in every nation has an equal privilege.

24. And lastly, but not less important to the exercise of faith in God, is the idea that he is love. For without this one characteristic to influence all the other excellencies in his character, they could not have such powerful dominion over the minds of men. But when the idea is planted in the mind that he is love, who cannot see the just ground that men of every nation, kindred, and tongue have to exercise faith in God so as to obtain eternal life?

25. From the above description of the character of the Deity which is given him in the revelations to men, there is a sure foundation for the exercise of faith in him among every people, nation, and kindred, from age to age, and from generation to generation.

26. Let us here observe that the foregoing is the character which is given of God in his revelations to the Former-day Saints, and it is also the character which is given of him in his revelations to the Latter-day Saints. So the Saints of former days and those of latter days are both alike in this respect: the Latter-day Saints have as good grounds to exercise faith in God as the Former-day Saints had, because the same character is given of him to both.

Questions and Answers for Lecture 3

1. *Question*—What was shown in the second lecture?

Answer—It was shown how the knowledge of the existence of God came into the world (Lecture 3:1).

2. Q—What is the effect of the idea of his existence among men?

A—It lays the foundation for the exercise of faith in him (Lecture 3:1).

3. Q—Is the idea of his existence, in the first instance, necessary in order for the exercise of faith in him?

A—It is (Lecture 3:1).

4. Q—How do you prove it?

A—By Romans 10:14 (Lecture 3:1).

5. Q—How many things are necessary for us to understand, respecting the Deity and our relation to him, so we may exercise faith in him for life and salvation?

A—Three (Lecture 3:2).

6. Q—What are they?

A—First, that God does actually exist; secondly, correct ideas of his character, his perfections and attributes; and thirdly, that the course which we pursue is according to his mind and will (Lecture 3:3-5).

7. Q—Would the idea of any one or two of the above-mentioned things enable a person to exercise faith in God?

A—It would not. For without the idea of them all, faith would be imperfect and unproductive (Lecture 3:5).

8. Q—Would an idea of these three things lay a sure foundation for the exercise of faith in God, so as to obtain life and salvation?

A—It would. For by the idea of these three things, faith could become perfect and fruitful, abounding in righteousness unto the praise and glory of God (Lecture 3:5).

9. Q—How are we to be made acquainted with the before-mentioned things respecting the Deity and ourselves?

A—By revelation (Lecture 3:6).

10. Q—Could these things be found out by any other means than by revelation?

A—They could not.

11. Q—How do you prove it?

A—By the scriptures (Job 11:7-9; 1 Cor 2:9-11; see Lecture 3:7).

12. Q—What things do we learn in the revelations of God respecting his character?

A—We learn the six following things: First, he was God before the world was created, and the same God that he was after it was created. Secondly, he is merciful and gracious, slow to anger, abundant in goodness, and he was so from everlasting, and will be so to everlasting. Thirdly, he does not change, neither does he vary, and his course is one eternal round. Fourthly, he is a God of truth, and cannot lie. Fifthly, he is no respecter of persons. And sixthly, he is love (Lecture 3:12-18).

13. Q—Where do you find the revelations which give us this idea of the character of the Deity?

A—In the Bible and the Book of Commandments [the Doctrine and Covenants], and they are quoted in the third lecture (Lecture 3:9-11).

14. Q—What effect would it have on any rational being not to have an idea that the Lord was God, the creator and upholder of all things?

A—It would prevent him from exercising faith in him unto life and salvation.

15. Q—Why would it prevent him from exercising faith in God?

A—Because he would be as the heathen, not knowing but that there might be a being greater and more powerful than he, and thereby he would be prevented from fulfilling his promises (Lecture 3:19).

16. Q—Does this idea prevent this doubt?

A—It does. For persons having this idea are enabled thereby to exercise faith without this doubt (Lecture 3:19).

17. Q—Is it not also necessary to have the idea that God is merciful and gracious, long-suffering and full of goodness?

A—It is (Lecture 3:20).

18. Q—Why is it necessary?

A—Because of the weakness and imperfections of human nature and the great frailties of man. For such is the weakness of man, and such his frailties, that he is liable to sin continually. And if God were not long-suffering, full of compassion, gracious and merciful, and of a forgiving disposition, man would be cut off from before him; consequently, he would be in continual doubt and could not exercise faith. For where doubt is, there faith has no power. But by man's believing that God is full of compassion and forgiveness, long-suffering and slow to anger, he can exercise faith in him and overcome doubt, so as to be exceedingly strong (Lecture 3:20).

19. Q—Is it not equally as necessary that man should have an idea that God does not change, neither does he vary, in order to exercise faith in him unto life and salvation?

A—It is. Because without this, he would not know how soon God's mercy might change into cruelty, his long-suffering into rashness, his love into hatred. In consequence of this doubt, man would be incapable of exercising faith in him. But having the idea that he is unchangeable, man can have faith in him continually, believing that what he was yesterday he is today, and will be forever (Lecture 3:21).

20. Q—Is it not necessary, also, for men to have an idea that God is a being of truth before they can have perfect faith in him?

A—It is. For unless men have this idea, they cannot place confidence in his word. And not being able to place confidence in his word, they could not have faith in him. But believing that he is a God of truth and that his word cannot fail, they can rest their faith in him without doubt (Lecture 3:22).

21. Q—Could man exercise faith in God so as to obtain eternal life unless he believed that God was no respecter of persons?

A—He could not. Because without this idea, he could not certainly know that it was his privilege so to do, and in consequence of this doubt his faith could not be sufficiently strong to save him (Lecture 3:23).

22. Q—Would it be possible for a man to exercise faith in God, so as to be saved, unless he had an idea that God was love?

A—It would not. Man could not love God unless he had an idea that God was love; and if he did not love God, he could not have faith in him (Lecture 3:24).

23. Q—What is the description which the sacred writers give of the character of the Deity calculated to do?

A—It is calculated to lay a foundation for the exercise of faith in him, as far as the knowledge extends among all people, tongues, languages, kindreds, and nations, and that from age to age, and from generation to generation (Lecture 3:25).

24. Q—Is the character which God has given of himself uniform?

A—It is. In all his revelations, whether to the Former-day Saints, or to the Latter-day Saints, God's character is uniform so that they all have the authority to exercise faith in him and to expect, by the exercise of their faith, to enjoy the same blessings (Lecture 3:26).

Lecture 4

ON FAITH

1. We showed in the third lecture that it is necessary to have correct ideas of the character of God to exercise faith in him unto life and salvation, and that without correct ideas of his character, the minds of men could not have sufficient power with God to exercise the faith necessary to enjoy eternal life. But having correct ideas of his character lays a foundation, as far as his character is concerned, for the exercise of faith so as to enjoy the fulness of the blessing of the gospel of Jesus Christ, even that of eternal glory. We shall now proceed to show the connection between having correct ideas of the attributes of God and exercising faith in him unto eternal life.

2. Let us here observe that the real design which the God of heaven had in view in making the human family acquainted with his attributes was that they might be enabled to exercise faith in him through the idea of the existence of his attributes, and through exercising faith in him, might obtain eternal life. For without the idea of the existence of the attributes which belong to God, the minds of men could not have power to exercise faith in him so as to lay hold upon eternal life. The God of heaven, understanding most perfectly the constitution of human nature and the weakness of men, knew what was necessary to be revealed and what ideas needed to be planted in their minds to enable them to exercise faith in him unto eternal life.

3. Having said so much, we shall proceed to examine the attributes of God as set forth in his revelations to the human family and to show how necessary having correct ideas of his attributes is to enable men to exercise faith in him. For without these ideas being planted in the minds of men, it would be out of the power of any person or persons to exercise faith in God so as to obtain eternal life. Consequently, the divine communications made to men, in the first instance, were designed to establish in their minds the ideas necessary to enable them to exercise faith in God, and through this means to be partakers of his glory.

4. We have the following account of his attributes in the revelations which he has given to the human family:

5. First, knowledge. "Known unto God are all his works from the beginning of the world" (Acts 15:18). "Remember the former things of old: for I am God, and there is none else; I am God, and there is none like me, *declaring the end from the beginning*, and from ancient times the things that are not yet done, saying, My counsel shall stand, and I will do all my pleasure" (Isa 46:9-10; emphasis in 1835).

6. Secondly, faith or power. "Through faith we understand that the worlds were framed by the word of God" (Heb 11:3). "In the beginning God created the heaven and the earth" (Gen 1:1). "The Lord of hosts hath sworn, saying, Surely as I have thought, so shall it come to pass; and as I have purposed, so shall it stand. . . . For the Lord of hosts hath purposed, and who shall disannul it? and his hand is stretched out, and who shall turn it back?" (Isa 14:24, 27).

7. Thirdly, justice. "Justice and judgment are the habitation of thy throne" (Ps 89:14). "Tell ye, and bring them near; yea, let them take counsel together: who hath declared this from ancient time? . . . have not I the Lord? and there is no God else beside me; a just God and a Saviour" (Isa 45:21). "The just Lord is in the midst thereof" (Zeph 3:5). "Rejoice greatly, O daughter of Zion; shout, O daughter of Jerusalem: behold, thy King cometh unto thee: he is just, and having salvation" (Zech 9:9).

8. Fourthly, judgment. "Justice and judgment are the habitation of thy throne" (Ps 89:14). "He is the Rock, his work is perfect: for all his ways are judgment: a God of truth and without iniquity, just and right is he" (Deut 32:4). "But the Lord shall endure for ever: he hath prepared his throne for judgment" (Ps 9:7). "The Lord is known by the judgment which he executeth" (Ps 9:16).

9. Fifthly, mercy. "Mercy and truth shall go before thy face" (Ps 89:14). "And the Lord passed by before him, and proclaimed, The Lord, the Lord God, merciful and gracious" (Ex 34:6). "But thou art a God ready to pardon, gracious and merciful" (Neh 9:17).

10. And sixthly, truth. "Mercy and truth shall go before thy face" (Ps 89:14). "Longsuffering, and abundant in goodness and truth" (Ex 34:6). "He is the Rock, his work is perfect: for all his ways are judgment: a God of truth and without iniquity, just and right is he" (Deut 32:4). "Into thine hand I commit my spirit: thou hast redeemed me, O Lord God of truth" (Ps 31:5).

11. A little reflection shows that the idea of the existence of these attributes in the Deity is necessary to enable any rational being to exercise faith in him. For without the idea of the existence of these attributes in the Deity, men could not exercise faith in him for life and salvation, seeing that without the knowledge of all things God would not be able to save any portion of his creatures. For it is the knowledge which he has of all things from the beginning to the end that enables him to give that understanding to his creatures by which they are made partakers of eternal life. And if it were not for the idea existing in the minds of men that God has all knowledge, it would be impossible for them to exercise faith in him.

12. And it is not less necessary that men should have the idea of the existence of the attribute power in the Deity. For unless God had power over all things, and was able by his power to control all things and thereby deliver his creatures who put their trust in him from the power of all beings that might seek their destruction, whether in heaven, on earth, or in hell, men could

not be saved. But with the idea of the existence of this attribute planted in the mind, men who put their trust in God feel as though they have nothing to fear, believing that he has power to save all who come to him to the very uttermost.

13. It is also necessary that men should have the idea of the existence of the attribute justice in God in order to exercise faith in him unto life and salvation. For without the idea of the existence of the attribute justice in the Deity, men could not have confidence sufficient to place themselves under his guidance and direction. For they would be filled with fear and doubt lest the Judge of all the earth would not do right, and thus fear or doubt existing in the mind would preclude the possibility of the exercise of faith in him for life and salvation. But when the idea of the existence of the attribute justice in the Deity is fairly planted in the mind, it leaves no room for doubt to get into the heart; and the mind is enabled to cast itself upon the Almighty without fear, and without doubt, and with the most unshaken confidence, believing that the Judge of all the earth will do right.

14. It is also of equal importance that men should have the idea of the existence of the attribute judgment in God, so they may exercise faith in him for life and salvation. For without the idea of the existence of this attribute in the Deity, it would be impossible for men to exercise faith in him for life and salvation, seeing that it is through the exercise of this attribute that the faithful in Christ Jesus are delivered out of the hands of those who seek their destruction. For if God were not to come out in swift judgment against the workers of iniquity and the powers of darkness, his saints could not be saved; for it is by judgment that the Lord delivers his saints out of the hands of all their enemies and those who reject the gospel of our Lord Jesus Christ. But no sooner is the idea of the existence of this attribute planted in the minds of men than it gives power to their minds for the exercise of faith and confidence in God. They are thus enabled by faith to lay hold on the promises which are set before them and to wade through all the tribulations and afflictions to which they are subjected by reason of the persecution from those who know not

God and obey not the gospel of our Lord Jesus Christ. They believe that in due time the Lord will come out in swift judgment against their enemies, who shall be cut off from before him, and that in his own due time he will bear them off conquerors, and more than conquerors, in all things.

15. And again, it is equally important that men should have the idea of the existence of the attribute mercy in the Deity in order to exercise faith in him for life and salvation. For without the idea of the existence of this attribute in the Deity, the spirits of the Saints would faint in the midst of the tribulations, afflictions, and persecutions which they have to endure for righteousness' sake. But when the idea of the existence of this attribute is once established in the mind, it gives life and energy to the spirits of the Saints, who believe then that the mercy of God will be poured out upon them in the midst of their afflictions, and that he will be compassionate to them in their sufferings, and that the mercy of God will lay hold of them and secure them in the arms of his love, so that they will receive a full reward for all their sufferings.

16. And lastly, but not less important to the exercise of faith in God, is the idea of the existence of the attribute truth in him. For without the idea of the existence of this attribute, the mind of man could have nothing upon which it could rest with certainty: all would be confusion and doubt. But with the idea of the existence of this attribute in the Deity in the mind, all the teachings, instructions, promises, and blessings become realities. And the mind is enabled to lay hold of them with certainty and confidence, believing that these things and all that the Lord has said shall be fulfilled in their time, and that all the cursings, denunciations, and judgments pronounced upon the heads of the unrighteous will also be executed in the due time of the Lord. By reason of the truth and veracity of him, the mind beholds its deliverance and salvation as being certain.

17. Let the mind once reflect sincerely and candidly upon the ideas of the existence of the before-mentioned attributes in the Deity, and it will see that there is a sure foundation laid for

the exercise of faith in him for life and salvation as far as his attributes are concerned. For inasmuch as God possesses the attribute knowledge, he can make all things known to his saints that are necessary for their salvation. And as he possesses the attribute power, he is able thereby to deliver them from the power of all enemies. Seeing, also, that justice is an attribute of the Deity, he will deal with them upon the principles of righteousness and equity, and will grant them a just reward for all their afflictions and sufferings for the truth's sake. And as judgment is an attribute of the Deity, also, his saints can have the most unshaken confidence that, in due time, they will obtain a perfect deliverance out of the hands of all their enemies and a complete victory over all those who have sought their hurt and destruction. And as mercy is also an attribute of the Deity, his saints can have confidence that it will be exercised towards them, and through the exercise of that attribute towards them comfort and consolation will be administered unto them abundantly, amid all their afflictions and tribulations. Lastly, realizing that truth is an attribute of the Deity, the mind is led to rejoice amid all its trials and temptations in hope of that glory which is to be brought at the revelation of Jesus Christ. It will do this in view of that crown which is to be placed upon the heads of the Saints in the day when the Lord shall distribute rewards unto them, and in prospect of that eternal weight of glory which the Lord has promised to bestow upon them when he shall bring them in the midst of his throne to dwell in his presence eternally.

18. In view, then, of the existence of these attributes, the faith of the Saints can become exceedingly strong, abounding in righteousness unto the praise and glory of God. And it can exert its mighty influence in searching after wisdom and understanding, until it has obtained a knowledge of all things that pertain to life and salvation.

19. Such, then, is the foundation which is laid for the exercise of faith in him for life and salvation through the revelation of the attributes of God. And seeing that these attributes of the Deity are unchangeable—being the same yesterday, today,

and forever—gives to the minds of the Latter-day Saints the same power and authority to exercise faith in God which the Former-day Saints had. All the Saints, in this respect, have been, are, and will be alike until the end of time; for God never changes. Therefore, his attributes and character remain forever the same. And as it is through the revelation of these attributes that a foundation is laid for the exercise of faith in God unto life and salvation, the foundation for the exercise of faith, therefore, was, is, and ever will be, the same. Consequently all men have had and will have an equal privilege.

Questions and Answers for Lecture 4

1. *Question*—What was shown in the third lecture?

Answer—It was shown that having correct ideas of the character of God is necessary to exercise faith in him unto life and salvation, and that without correct ideas of his character, men could not have power to exercise faith in him unto life and salvation. But having correct ideas of his character, as far as it is concerned in the exercise of faith in him, lays a sure foundation for the exercise of it (Lecture 4:1).

2. Q—What object did the God of heaven have in revealing his attributes to men?

A—That through an acquaintance with his attributes they might be enabled to exercise faith in him so as to obtain eternal life (Lecture 4:2).

3. Q—Could men exercise faith in God so as to be enabled to lay hold of eternal life, without an acquaintance with his attributes?

A—They could not (Lecture 4:2-3).

4. Q—What account is given of the attributes of God in his revelations?

A—First, knowledge; secondly, faith or power; thirdly, justice; fourthly, judgment; fifthly, mercy; and sixthly, truth (Lecture 4:4-10).

5. Q—Where are the revelations to be found which give this relation of the attributes of God?

A—In the Old and New Testaments, and they are quoted in Lecture 4:5-10.*

6. Q—Is the idea of the existence of these attributes in the Deity necessary to enable any rational being to exercise faith in him unto life and salvation?

A—It is.

7. Q—How do you prove it?

A—By Lecture 4:11-16.*

8. Q—Does the idea of the existence of these attributes in the Deity enable a rational being to exercise faith in him unto life and salvation, as far as his attributes are concerned?

A—It does.

9. Q—How do you prove it?

A—By Lecture 4:17-18.*

10. Q—Do the Latter-day Saints have as much authority given them through the revelation of the attributes of God to exercise faith in him as the Former-day Saints had?

A—They have.

11. Q—How do you prove it?

A—By Lecture 4:19.*

---

*Note: Let the student turn and commit these paragraphs to memory [1835 footnote].

Lecture 5

ON FAITH

1. In our former lectures we treated the being, character, perfections, and attributes of God. What we mean by perfections is the perfections which belong to all the attributes of his nature. We shall, in this lecture, speak of the Godhead: we mean the Father, Son, and Holy Spirit.

2. There are two personages who constitute the great, matchless, governing, and supreme power over all things, by whom all things were created and made, whether visible or invisible, whether in heaven, on earth, in the earth, under the earth, or throughout the immensity of space. They are the Father and the Son: the Father being a personage of spirit, glory, and power, possessing all perfection and fulness. The Son, who was in the bosom of the Father, is a personage of tabernacle, made or fashioned like unto man, being in the form and likeness of man, or rather man was formed after his likeness and in his image. He is also the express image and likeness of the personage of the Father, possessing all the fulness of the Father, or the same fulness with the Father; being begotten of him, and ordained from before the foundation of the world to be a propitiation for the sins of all those who should believe on his name. He is called the Son because of the flesh. And he descended in suffering below that which man can suffer; or, in other words, he suffered greater sufferings and was exposed to more powerful contradictions than any man can be. But notwithstanding all this, he kept the law of

God and remained without sin, showing thereby that it is in the power of man to keep the law and remain also without sin. And also that by him a righteous judgment might come upon all flesh, that all who walk not in the law of God may justly be condemned by the law and have no excuse for their sins. He, being the Only Begotten of the Father, full of grace and truth, and having overcome, received a fulness of the glory of the Father, possessing the same mind with the Father, which mind is the Holy Spirit that bears record of the Father and the Son. These three are one; or, in other words, these three constitute the great, matchless, governing, and supreme power over all things, by whom all things were created and made. And these three constitute the Godhead and are one. The Father and the Son possess the same mind, the same wisdom, glory, power, and fulness—filling all in all. The Son, being filled with the fulness of the mind, glory, and power, or in other words, the spirit, glory, and power, of the Father, possesses all knowledge and glory and the same kingdom, and sits at the right hand of power in the express image and likeness of the Father. He is a mediator for man, being filled with the fulness of the mind of the Father, or, in other words, the Spirit of the Father, which Spirit is shed forth upon all who believe on his name and keep his commandments. And all those who keep his commandments shall grow from grace to grace and become heirs of the heavenly kingdom, and joint-heirs with Jesus Christ. They will possess the same mind, being transformed into the same image or likeness, even the express image of him who fills all in all, being filled with the fulness of his glory and becoming one in him, even as the Father, Son, and Holy Spirit are one.

3. From the foregoing account of the Godhead, which is given in his revelations, the Saints have a sure foundation laid for the exercise of faith unto life and salvation through the atonement and mediation of Jesus Christ. By his blood they have a forgiveness of sins and also a sure reward laid up for them in heaven, even that of partaking of the fulness of the Father and the Son through the Spirit. As the Son partakes of the fulness of the Father through the Spirit, so the Saints are, by the same Spirit, to be

84

partakers of the same fulness, to enjoy the same glory. For as the Father and the Son are one, so, in like manner, the Saints are to be one in them, through the love of the Father, the mediation of Jesus Christ, and the gift of the Holy Spirit. They are to be heirs of God and joint-heirs with Jesus Christ.

Questions and Answers for Lecture 5

1. *Question*—What subjects do the foregoing lectures treat?
Answer—The being, perfections, and attributes of the Deity (Lecture 5:1).

2. Q—What are we to understand by the perfections of the Deity?
A—The perfections which belong to his attributes.

3. Q—How many personages are there in the Godhead?
A—Two: the Father and Son (Lecture 5:1).

4. Q—How do you prove that there are two personages in the Godhead?
A—By the scriptures. "And I, God, said unto mine Only Begotten, which was with me from the beginning, Let us make man in our image, after our likeness; and it was so" (JST Gen 1:27; see also Moses 2:26; Lecture 2:6). "And I, the Lord God, said unto mine Only Begotten, Behold, the man is become as one of us, to know good and evil" (JST Gen 3:28; see also Moses 4:28). "And now, O Father, glorify thou me with thine own self with the glory which I had with thee before the world was" (John 17:5; see also Lecture 5:2).

5. Q—What is the Father?
A—He is a personage of glory and of power (Lecture 5:2).

6. Q—How do you prove that the Father is a personage of glory and of power?
A—First, of glory. "The sun shall be no more thy light by day; neither for brightness shall the moon give light unto thee: but the Lord shall be unto thee an everlasting light, and thy God thy glory" (Isa 60:19). "Thine, O Lord, is the greatness, and the

power, and the glory" (1 Chr 29:11). "The voice of the Lord is upon the waters: the God of glory thundereth" (Ps 29:3). "Help us, O God of our salvation, for the glory of thy name" (Ps 79:9). "And changed the glory of the uncorruptible God into an image made like to corruptible man" (Rom 1:23).

Secondly, of power. "Thine, O Lord, is the greatness, and the power, and the glory" (1 Chr 29:11). "Ah Lord God! behold, thou hast made the heaven and the earth by thy great power and stretched out arm, and there is nothing too hard for thee" (Jer 32:17). "And because he loved thy fathers, therefore he chose their seed after them, and brought thee out in his sight with his mighty power" (Deut 4:37). "God is my strength and power" (2 Sam 22:33). "He stretcheth out the north over the empty place, and hangeth the earth upon nothing. He bindeth up the waters in his thick clouds; and the cloud is not rent under them. He holdeth back the face of his throne, and spreadeth his cloud upon it. He hath compassed the waters with bounds, until the day and night come to an end. The pillars of heaven tremble and are astonished at his reproof. He divideth the sea with his power, and by his understanding he smiteth through the proud. By his spirit he hath garnished the heavens; his hand hath formed the crooked serpent. Lo, these are parts of his ways: but how little a portion is heard of him? but the thunder of his power who can understand?" (Job 26:7-14).

7. Q—What is the Son?

A—First, he is a personage of tabernacle (Lecture 5:2).

8. Q—How do you prove it?

A—"Jesus saith unto him, Have I been so long time with you, and yet hast thou not known me, Philip? he that hath seen me hath seen the Father; and how sayest thou then, Shew us the Father? Believest thou not that I am in the Father, and the Father in me? the words that I speak unto you I speak not of myself: but the Father that dwelleth in me, he doeth the works. Believe me that I am in the Father, and the Father in me" (John 14:9-11).

Secondly, and being a personage of tabernacle, the Son was made or fashioned like unto man, or being in the form and likeness of man (Lecture 5:2). "Let this mind be in you, which was also in Christ Jesus: who, being in the form of God, thought it not robbery to be equal with God: but made himself of no reputation, and took upon him the form of a servant, and was made in the likeness of men: and being found in fashion as a man, he humbled himself, and became obedient unto death, even the death of the cross" (Philip 2:5-8). "Forasmuch then as the children are partakers of flesh and blood, he also himself likewise took part of the same. . . . For verily he took not on him the nature of angels; but he took on him the seed of Abraham" (Heb 2:14, 16).

Thirdly, he is also in the likeness of the personage of the Father (Lecture 5:2). "God, who at sundry times and in divers manners spake in time past unto the fathers by the prophets, hath in these last days spoken unto us by his Son, whom he hath appointed heir of all things, by whom also he made the worlds; who being the brightness of his glory, and the express image of his person" (Heb 1:1-3). Again, "Let this mind be in you, which was also in Christ Jesus: who, being in the form of God, thought it not robbery to be equal with God" (Philip 2:5-6).

9. Q—Was it by the Father and the Son that all things were created and made?

A—It was. "Who is the image of the invisible God, the firstborn of every creature: for by him were all things created, that are in heaven, and that are in earth, visible and invisible, whether they be thrones, or dominions, or principalities, or powers: all things were created by him, and for him: and he is before all things, and by him all things consist" (Col 1:15-17). "In the beginning God created the heaven and the earth" (Gen 1:1). "[God]* hath in these last days spoken unto us by his Son, whom he hath appointed heir of all things, by whom also he made the worlds" (Heb 1:2).

10. Q—Does the Son possess the fulness of the Father?

---

*Brackets in the 1835 edition.

A—He does. "For it pleased the Father that in him should all fulness dwell. . . . For in him dwelleth all the fulness of the Godhead bodily" (Col 1:19; 2:9). "Which is his [Christ's]* body, the fulness of him that filleth all in all" (Eph 1:23).

11. Q—Why was he called the Son?

A—Because of the flesh. "That holy thing which shall be born of thee, shall be called the Son of God" (Luke 1:35). "And Jesus when he was baptized, went up straightway out of the water; and John saw, and lo, the heavens were opened unto him, and he [John]* saw the Spirit of God descending like a dove and lighting upon Jesus. And lo, he heard a voice from heaven, saying, This is my beloved Son, in whom I am well pleased" (JST Matt 3:45-46; see also KJV Matt 3:16-17).

12. Q—Was he ordained of the Father from before the foundation of the world to be a propitiation for the sins of all those who should believe on his name?

A—He was. "Forasmuch as ye know that ye were not redeemed with corruptible things, as silver and gold, from your vain conversation received by tradition from your fathers; but with the precious blood of Christ, as of a lamb without blemish and without spot: who verily was foreordained before the foundation of the world, but was manifest in these last times for you" (1 Peter 1:18-20). "And all that dwell upon the earth shall worship him [the beast],* whose names are not written in the book of life of the Lamb slain from the foundation of the world" (Rev 13:8). "But we speak the wisdom of God in a mystery, even the hidden wisdom, which God ordained before the world unto our glory" (1 Cor 2:7).

13. Q—Do the Father and the Son possess the same mind?

A—They do. "I [Christ]* can of mine own self do nothing: as I hear, I judge: and my judgment is just; because I seek not mine own will, but the will of the Father which hath sent me" (John 5:30). "For I [Christ]* came down from heaven, not to do

---

*Brackets in the 1835 edition.

mine own will, but the will of him that sent me" (John 6:38). "I [Christ]* and my Father are one" (John 10:30).

14. Q—What is this mind?

A—The Holy Spirit. "But when the Comforter is come, whom I will send unto you from the Father, even the Spirit of truth, which proceedeth from the Father, he shall testify of me [Christ]'" (John 15:26). "And because ye are sons, God hath sent forth the Spirit of his Son into your hearts" (Gal 4:6).

15. Q—Do the Father, Son, and Holy Spirit constitute the Godhead?

A—They do (Lecture 5:2). Let the student commit this paragraph to memory.

16. Q—Do the believers in Christ Jesus, through the gift of the Spirit, become one with the Father and the Son, as the Father and the Son are one?

A—They do. "Neither pray I for these [the apostles]** alone, but for them also which shall believe on me through their word; that they all may be one; as thou, Father, art in me, and I in thee, that they also may be one in us: that the world may believe that thou hast sent me" (John 17:20-21).

17. Q—Does the foregoing account of the Godhead lay a sure foundation for the exercise of faith in him unto life and salvation?

A—It does.

18. Q—How do you prove it?

A—By Lecture 5:3. Let the student commit this also.

---

*Brackets in the 1835 edition.

**Bracketed material in 1835 edition, but without the brackets.

Lecture 6
ON FAITH

1. Having treated the ideas of the character, perfections, and attributes of God in the preceding lectures, we next proceed to treat the knowledge which persons must have that the course of life which they pursue is according to the will of God, so they may be enabled to exercise faith in him unto life and salvation.

2. This knowledge supplies an important place in revealed religion; for it was by reason of it that the ancients were enabled to endure "as seeing him who is invisible" (Heb 11:27). It is essential for any person to have an actual knowledge that the course of life which he is pursuing is according to the will of God to enable him to have that confidence in God without which no person can obtain eternal life. It was this that enabled the ancient Saints to endure all their afflictions and persecutions and to take joyfully the spoiling of their goods, knowing (not believing merely) that they had a more enduring substance (Heb 10:34).

3. Having the assurance that they were pursuing a course which was agreeable to the will of God, they were enabled to take not only the spoiling of their goods and the wasting of their substance joyfully, but also to suffer death in its most horrid forms, knowing (not merely believing) that when this "earthly house of this tabernacle [was]* dissolved, we have a building of

---
*Bracketed material in 1835 edition, but without brackets.

God, an house not made with hands, eternal in the heavens" (2 Cor 5:1).

4. Such was and always will be the situation of the Saints of God. Unless they have an actual knowledge that the course they are pursuing is according to the will of God, they will grow weary in their minds and faint. For such has been and always will be the opposition in the hearts of unbelievers and those who know not God against the pure and unadulterated religion of heaven (the only thing which ensures eternal life). They will persecute to the uttermost all who worship God according to his revelations, receive the truth in the love of it, and submit themselves to be guided and directed by his will. And they will drive them to such extremities that nothing short of an actual knowledge of their being the favorites of heaven and of their having embraced that order of things which God has established for the redemption of man will enable them to exercise that confidence in him necessary for them to overcome the world and obtain that crown of glory which is laid up for them that fear God.

5. For a man to lay down his all—his character and reputation, his honor and applause, his good name among men, his houses, his lands, his brothers and sisters, his wife and children, and even his own life also, counting all things but filth and dross for the excellency of the knowledge of Jesus Christ—requires more than mere belief or supposition that he is doing the will of God. It requires actual knowledge, realizing that when these sufferings are ended, he will enter into eternal rest and be a partaker of the glory of God.

6. For unless a person does know that he is walking according to the will of God, it would be offering an insult to the dignity of the Creator were he to say that he would be a partaker of his glory when he should be done with the things of this life. But when he has this knowledge and most assuredly knows that he is doing the will of God, his confidence can be equally strong that he will be a partaker of the glory of God.

7. Let us here observe that a religion that does not require the sacrifice of all things never has power sufficient to produce

the faith necessary unto life and salvation. For from the first existence of man, the faith necessary unto the enjoyment of life and salvation never could be obtained without the sacrifice of all earthly things. It is through this sacrifice, and this only, that God has ordained that men should enjoy eternal life. And it is through the medium of the sacrifice of all earthly things that men do actually know that they are doing the things that are well pleasing in the sight of God. When a man has offered in sacrifice all that he has for the truth's sake, not even withholding his life, and believing before God that he has been called to make this sacrifice because he seeks to do His will, he does know, most assuredly, that God does and will accept his sacrifice and offering and that he has not sought nor will he seek His face in vain. Under these circumstances, then, he can obtain the faith necessary for him to lay hold on eternal life.

8. It is in vain for persons to fancy to themselves that they are heirs with those, or can be heirs with them, who have offered their all in sacrifice, and by this means obtained faith in God and favor with him so as to obtain eternal life, unless they in like manner offer unto him the same sacrifice and through that offering obtain the knowledge that they are accepted of him.

9. It was in offering sacrifices that Abel, the first martyr, obtained knowledge that he was accepted of God. And from the days of righteous Abel to the present time, the knowledge that men have that they are accepted in the sight of God is obtained by offering sacrifice. And in the last days before the Lord comes, he is to gather together his saints who have made a covenant with him by sacrifice. "Our God shall come, and shall not keep silence: a fire shall devour before him, and it shall be very tempestuous round about him. He shall call to the heavens from above, and to the earth, that he may judge his people. Gather my saints together unto me; those that have made a covenant with me by sacrifice" (Ps 50:3-5).

10. Those, then, who make the sacrifice will have the testimony that their course is pleasing in the sight of God. And those who have this testimony will have faith to lay hold on

eternal life and will be enabled, through faith, to endure unto the end and receive the crown that is laid up for them that love the appearing of our Lord Jesus Christ. But those who do not make the sacrifice cannot enjoy this faith, because men are dependent upon this sacrifice in order to obtain this faith. Therefore, they cannot lay hold upon eternal life, because the revelations of God do not guarantee unto them the authority so to do; and without this guarantee faith could not exist.

11. All the Saints of whom we have account in all the revelations of God which are extant obtained the knowledge which they had of their acceptance in his sight through the sacrifice which they offered unto him. And through the knowledge thus obtained, their faith became sufficiently strong to lay hold upon the promise of eternal life and to endure "as seeing him who is invisible" (Heb 11:27). They were enabled through faith to combat the powers of darkness, contend against the wiles of the adversary, overcome the world, and obtain the end of their faith, even the salvation of their souls.

12. But those who have not made this sacrifice to God do not know that the course which they pursue is well pleasing in his sight. For whatever may be their belief or their opinion, it is a matter of doubt and uncertainty in their mind; and where doubt and uncertainty are, there faith is not, nor can it be. For doubt and faith do not exist in the same person at the same time. So persons whose minds are under doubts and fears cannot have unshaken confidence, and where unshaken confidence is not, there faith is weak. And where faith is weak, the persons will not be able to contend against all the opposition, tribulations, and afflictions which they will have to encounter in order to be heirs of God and joint-heirs with Christ Jesus. But they will grow weary in their minds, and the adversary will have power over them and destroy them.*

---

*Note: This lecture is so plain and the facts set forth so self-evident that it is deemed unnecessary to form a catechism upon it. The student is, therefore, instructed to commit the whole to memory [1835 footnote].

Lecture 7
ON FAITH

1. In the preceding lectures, we treated what faith was and the object on which it rested. Agreeable to our plan, we now proceed to speak of its effects.

2. As we have seen in our former lectures that faith is the principle of action and of power in all intelligent beings both in heaven and on earth, it will not be expected that we will attempt to unfold all its effects in a lecture of this description. Neither is it necessary to our purpose so to do, for it would embrace all things in heaven and on earth and encompass all the creations of God with all their endless varieties. For no world has yet been framed that was not framed by faith, neither has there been an intelligent being on any of God's creations who did not get there by reason of faith as it existed in himself or in some other being. Nor has there been a change or a revolution in any of the creations of God but it has been effected by faith. Neither will there be a change or a revolution in any of the vast creations of the Almighty unless it is effected in the same way, for it is by faith that the Deity works.

3. Let us here offer some explanation in relation to faith that our meaning may be clearly comprehended. We ask, then, what are we to understand by a man's working by faith? We answer: we understand that when a man works by faith he works by mental exertion instead of physical force. It is by words, instead of by exerting his physical powers, with which every being works when he works by faith. God said, "Let there be

light: and there was light" (Gen 1:3). Joshua spake and the great lights which God had created stood still (Joshua 10:12-13). Elijah commanded and the heavens were stayed for the space of three years and six months, so that it did not rain; he again commanded and the heavens gave forth rain (1 Kings 17:1; 18:1, 41-45). All this was done by faith. And the Savior says: "If ye have faith as a grain of mustard seed, ye shall say unto this mountain, Remove . . . and it shall remove" (Matt 17:20); or "say unto this sycamine tree, Be thou plucked up . . . and . . . planted in the sea; and it should obey you" (Luke 17:6). Faith, then, works by words; and with these its mightiest works have been and will be performed.

4. It surely will not be required of us to prove that this is the principle upon which all eternity has acted and will act, for every reflecting mind must know that it is by reason of this power that all the hosts of heaven perform their works of wonder, majesty, and glory. Angels move from place to place by virtue of this power. It is by reason of it that they are enabled to descend from heaven to earth. And were it not for the power of faith, they never could be ministering spirits to them who should be heirs of salvation, neither could they act as heavenly messengers. For they would be destitute of the power necessary to enable them to do the will of God.

5. It is only necessary for us to say that the whole visible creation as it now exists is the effect of faith. It was faith by which it was framed, and it is by the power of faith that it continues in its organized form and by which the planets move round their orbits and sparkle forth their glory. So, then, faith is truly the first principle in the science of theology, and, when understood, it leads the mind back to the beginning and carries it forward to the end, or, in other words, from eternity to eternity.

6. As faith, then, is the principle by which the heavenly hosts perform their works and by which they enjoy all their felicity, we might expect to find it set forth in a revelation from God as the principle upon which his creatures here below must act to obtain the felicities enjoyed by the Saints in the eternal

world. And when God would undertake to raise up men for the enjoyment of himself, he would teach them the necessity of living by faith, and the impossibility of their enjoying the blessedness of eternity without it, seeing that all the blessings of eternity are the effects of faith.

7. Therefore, it is said, and appropriately too, that "without faith it is impossible to please him [God]*"(Heb 11:6). If it should be asked why it is impossible to please God without faith, the answer would be that without faith it is impossible for men to be saved. As God desires the salvation of men, he must, of course, desire that they should have faith; and he could not be pleased unless they had it, or else he could be pleased with their destruction.

8. From this we learn that the many exhortations to have faith in him which have been given by inspired men to those who had received the word of the Lord were not mere common-place matters, but were for the best of all reasons. And that reason is that without it there is no salvation, neither in this world nor in that which is to come. When men begin to live by faith, they begin to draw near to God; and when their faith is perfected, they are like him. And because he is saved, they are saved also; for they will be in the same situation he is in, because they have come to him. And "when he shall appear, we shall be like him; for we shall see him as he is" (1 John 3:2).

9. As all the visible creation is an effect of faith, so is salvation also. (We mean salvation in its most extensive latitude of interpretation, whether it is temporal or spiritual.) In order to have this subject clearly set before the mind, let us ask, what situation must a person be in in order to be saved? or, what is the difference between a saved man and one who is not saved? We answer from what we have before seen of the heavenly worlds that they must be persons who can work by faith and who are able, by faith, to be ministering spirits to them who shall be heirs of salvation. They must have faith to enable them to act in the

---

*Bracketed material in the 1835 edition, but without brackets.

presence of the Lord; otherwise, they cannot be saved. And what constitutes the real difference between a saved person and one not saved is the difference in the degree of their faith. One's faith has become perfect enough to lay hold upon eternal life, and the other's has not. But to be a little more particular, let us ask, where shall we find a prototype into whose likeness we may be assimilated, so we may be made partakers of life and salvation? or, where shall we find a saved being? For if we can find a saved being, we may ascertain without much difficulty what all others must be in order to be saved—they must be like that individual or they cannot be saved. We think that it will not be a matter of dispute that two beings who are unlike each other cannot both be saved; for whatever constitutes the salvation of one will constitute the salvation of every creature which will be saved. And if we find one saved being in all existence, we may see what all others must be or else not be saved. We ask, then, where is the prototype? or, where is the saved being? We conclude as to the answer of this question that there will be no dispute among those who believe the Bible that it is Christ. All will agree that he is the prototype or standard of salvation, or in other words, that he is a saved being. And if we should continue our interrogation and ask how it is that he is saved, the answer would be that he is a just and holy being. If he were anything different from what he is, he would not be saved; for his salvation depends on his being precisely what he is and nothing else. For if it were possible for him to change in the least degree, surely Christ would fail of salvation and lose all his dominion, power, authority and glory, which constitute salvation. For salvation consists in the glory, authority, majesty, power and dominion which Jehovah possesses and in nothing else; and no being can possess it but himself or one like him. Thus says John: "Beloved, now are we the sons of God, and it doth not yet appear what we shall be: but we know that, when he shall appear, we shall be like him; for we shall see him as he is. And every man that hath this hope in him purifieth himself, even as he is pure" (1 John 3:2-3). Why purify themselves as he is pure? Because if they do not, they cannot be like him.

10. The Lord said unto Moses, "Speak unto all the congregation of the children of Israel, and say unto them, Ye shall be holy: for I the Lord your God am holy" (Lev 19:2). And Peter says, "But as he which hath called you is holy, so be ye holy in all manner of conversation; because it is written, Be ye holy; for I am holy" (1 Peter 1:15-16). And the Savior says, "Be ye therefore perfect, even as your Father which is in heaven is perfect" (Matt 5:48). If any should ask, why all these sayings? the answer is to be found from what is before quoted from John's epistle, that when he (the Lord) shall appear, the Saints will be like him; and if they are not holy, as he is holy, and perfect, as he is perfect, they cannot be like him. For no beings can enjoy his glory without possessing his perfections and holiness, no more than they could reign in his kingdom without his power.

11. This clearly sets forth the propriety of the Savior's saying: "Verily, verily, I say unto you, He that believeth on me, the works that I do shall he do also; and greater works than these shall he do; because I go unto my Father" (John 14:12). This taken in connection with some of the sayings in the Savior's prayer recorded in John 17 gives great clearness to his expressions. He says, "Neither pray I for these alone, but for them also which shall believe on me through their word; that they all may be one; as thou, Father, art in me, and I in thee, that they also may be one in us: that the world may believe that thou hast sent me. And the glory which thou gavest me I have given them; that they may be one, even as we are one: I in them, and thou in me, that they may be made perfect in one; and that the world may know that thou hast sent me, and hast loved them, as thou hast loved me. Father, I will that they also, whom thou hast given me, be with me where I am; that they may behold my glory, which thou hast given me: for thou lovedst me before the foundation of the world" (John 17:20-24).

12. All these sayings put together give as clear an account of the state of the glorified Saints as language could give—the works that Jesus had done they were to do, and greater works than those which he had done among them should they do, and that

99

because he went to the Father. He does not say that they should do these works in time; but they should do greater works, because he went to the Father. He says, "Father, I will that they also, whom thou hast given me, be with me where I am; that they may behold my glory" (John 17:24). These sayings taken together make it very plain that the greater works which those who believed on his name were to do were to be done in eternity, where he was going and where they should behold his glory. He had said in another part of his prayer that he desired of his Father that those who believed on him should be one in him, as he and the Father were one in each other. "Neither pray I for these [the apostles]* alone, but for them also which shall believe on me through their word; that they all may be one"; that is, they who believe on him through the apostles' words, as well as the apostles themselves, "that they all may be one; as thou, Father, art in me, and I in thee, that they also may be one in us" (John 17:20-21).

13. What language can be plainer than this? The Savior surely intended to be understood by his disciples, and he spake that they might understand him. For he declares to his Father, in language not to be easily mistaken, that he wanted his disciples, even all of them, to be as himself and the Father are, for as he and the Father were one so they might be one with them (John 17:21). And what is said in the 22nd verse is calculated to establish this belief more firmly, if it needs anything to establish it. He says: "And the glory which thou gavest me I have given them; that they may be one, even as we are one" (v 22). This is as much as to say that unless they have the glory which the Father had given him, they could not be one with them. For he says he had given them the glory that the Father had given him that they might be one, or, in other words, to make them one.

14. This fills up the measure of information on this subject and shows most clearly that the Savior wished his disciples to understand that they were to be partakers with him in all things, not even his glory excepted.

_____

*Bracketed material in the 1835 edition, but without brackets.

100

15. It is scarcely necessary here to observe what we have previously noticed: that the Father and the Son have the glory they have because they are just and holy beings; and if they were lacking in one attribute or perfection which they have, they could never enjoy the glory which they have, for it requires them to be precisely what they are in order to enjoy it. And if the Savior gives this glory to any others, he must do it in the very way set forth in his prayer to his Father: by making them one with him as he and the Father are one. In so doing he would give them the glory which the Father has given him; and when his disciples are made one with the Father and Son, as the Father and the Son are one, who cannot see the propriety of the Savior's saying, "The works that I do shall [they]* do also; and greater works than these shall [they]* do; because I go unto my Father" (John 14:12).

16. These teachings of the Savior most clearly show unto us the nature of salvation and what he proposed unto the human family when he proposed to save them: he proposed to make them like unto himself, and he was like the Father, the great prototype of all saved beings. For any portion of the human family to be assimilated into their likeness is to be saved, and to be unlike them is to be destroyed. On this hinge turns the door of salvation.

17. Who cannot see, then, that salvation is the effect of faith? For as we have previously observed, all the heavenly beings work by this principle; and it is because they are able so to do that they are saved, for nothing but this could save them. And this is the lesson which the God of heaven has been endeavoring to teach to the world by the mouth of all his holy prophets. Hence we are told that "without faith it is impossible to please him [God]**" (Heb 11:6), and that salvation "is of faith, that it might be by grace; to the end the promise might be sure to all the seed" (Rom 4:16). And "Israel, which followed after the law of righteousness, hath not attained to the law of righteousness. Wherefore? Because they sought it not by faith, but as it were by

---

*Bracketed material in the 1835 edition, but without brackets. John 14:12 uses "he."

**Bracketed material in the 1835 edition, but without brackets.

the works of the law. For they stumbled at that stumblingstone" (Rom 9:31-32). And Jesus said unto the man who brought his son to him to get the devil who tormented him cast out: "If thou canst believe, all things are possible to him that believeth" (Mark 9:23). These references with a multitude of other scriptures which might be quoted plainly set forth the light in which the Savior, as well as the Former-day Saints, viewed the plan of salvation. It was a system of faith—it begins with faith, it continues by faith, and every blessing which is obtained in relation to it is the effect of faith, whether it pertains to this life or that which is to come. All the revelations of God bear witness to this. If there were children of promise, they were the effects of faith, not even the Savior of the world excepted. "Blessed is she that believed," said Elizabeth to Mary, when she went to visit her, "for there shall be a performance of those things which were told her from the Lord" (Luke 1:45). Nor was the birth of John the Baptist any the less a matter of faith. For in order that his father Zacharias might believe, he was struck dumb. And through the whole history of the scheme of life and salvation, it is a matter of faith. Every man received according to his faith: according as his faith was, so were his blessings and privileges. And nothing was withheld from him when his faith was sufficient to receive it. He could stop the mouths of lions, quench the violence of fire, escape the edge of the sword, wax valiant in fight, and put to flight the armies of the aliens; women could, by their faith, receive their dead children to life again (see Heb 11:33-35). In a word, there was nothing impossible for them who had faith. All things were in subjection to the Former-day Saints, according as their faith was. By their faith they could obtain heavenly visions and the ministering of angels. They could have knowledge of the spirits of just men made perfect, of the general assembly and church of the Firstborn whose names are written in heaven, of God, the Judge of all, and of Jesus, the Mediator of the new covenant. And they could become familiar with the third heavens, see and hear things which were not only unutterable but were unlawful to utter. Peter, in view of the power of faith, says to the Former-day Saints: "Grace and peace be multiplied unto you through the knowledge of God, and of Jesus our Lord, according as his divine power hath given unto us all things that pertain unto life and godliness, through the knowledge of him that hath called us to glory and virtue" (2 Peter 1:2-3). In the first epistle, he says: "Blessed be the God and Father of our Lord Jesus Christ, which according to his abundant mercy hath begotten us again unto a lively hope by the resurrection of Jesus Christ from the dead, to an inheritance incorruptible and undefiled, and that fadeth not away, reserved in heaven for you, who are kept by the power of God through faith unto salvation ready to be revealed in the last time" (1 Peter 1:3-5).

18.* These sayings put together show the Apostle's views most clearly, so as to admit of no mistake in the mind of any individual. He says that all things that pertain to life and godliness were given unto them through the knowledge of God and our Savior Jesus Christ. And if the question is asked, how were they to obtain the knowledge of God? (For there is a great difference between believing in God and knowing him—knowledge implies more than faith. And notice that all things that pertain to life and godliness were given through the knowledge of God.) The answer is that through faith they were to obtain this knowledge; and, having power by faith to obtain the knowledge of God, they could with it obtain all other things which pertain to life and godliness.

19. By these sayings of the Apostle Peter, we learn that it was by obtaining a knowledge of God that men got the knowledge of all things which pertain to life and godliness, and this knowledge was the effect of faith. So all things which pertain to life and godliness are the effects of faith.

20. From this we may extend as far as any circumstances may require, whether on earth or in heaven, and we will find it the testimony of all inspired men or heavenly messengers that all things that pertain to life and godliness are the effects of faith and

---

*Paragraphs 18, 19, and 20 in this edition were misnumbered 16, 17, and 18 in the 1835 edition.

nothing else. All learning, wisdom, and prudence fail, and every-thing else as a means of salvation but faith. This is the reason that the fishermen of Galilee could teach the world, because they sought by faith and by faith obtained. And this is the reason that Paul counted all things but filth and dross—what he formerly called his gain he called his loss. Yea, he counted "all things but loss for the excellency of the knowledge of Christ Jesus my Lord," because he had to suffer "the loss of all things" to obtain the faith by which he could enjoy the knowledge of Christ Jesus the Lord (Philip 3:7-8). This is the reason that the Former-day Saints knew more and understood more of heaven and of heavenly things than all others beside, because this information is the effect of faith—to be obtained by no other means. And this is the reason that men, as soon as they lose their faith, run into strifes, conten-tions, darkness, and difficulties. For the knowledge which tends to life disappears with faith, but returns when faith returns. For when faith comes, it brings its train of attendants with it—apostles, prophets, evangelists, pastors, teachers, gifts, wisdom, knowledge, miracles, healings, tongues, interpretation of tongues, etc. All these appear when faith appears on the earth and disappear when it disappears from the earth. For these are the effects of faith and always have attended and always will attend it. For where faith is, there will the knowledge of God be, also, with all things which pertain thereto: revelations, visions, and dreams, as well as every other necessary thing, so the possessors of faith may be perfected and obtain salvation. For God must change; otherwise, faith will prevail with him. And he who possesses it will obtain all neces-sary knowledge and wisdom through it until he shall know God and the Lord Jesus Christ, whom he has sent, whom to know is eternal life. Amen.

Charles D. Tate, Jr. is professor of English and Ancient Scripture at Brigham Young University.

Comparative Charts

Introduction to the
Comparative Charts

The following charts show the textual changes in the Lectures on Faith since they were first published in 1835. Chart 1 shows changes between the 1835 edition and this 1990 edited version. Chart 2 lists the progressive changes between the 1835 edition and three other major editions that followed it (1876, 1891, 1985). The **P** column gives paragraph numbers and the year columns show changes in the respective editions.

In compiling these charts, we found that some changes among the editions were so recurrent and consistent that it was not in the interest of space to list them with each occurrence. Such changes include: spelling of names and titles such as *Arphaxad* and *Methuselah* (spelled *Arphaxed* and *Methuseleh* or *Methusaleh* in the 1835 edition), *Savior* (spelled *Saviour* in 1876 and 1985), *Former-day* and *Latter-day* (both originally spelled as two words with no hyphen); and spelling modernization such as *agreeable* (from *agreeably* in 1835), *center* (spelled *centre* in 1876), *fulness* (spelled *fullness* in 1891 and 1985), and *long-suffering* (which was two words in 1835 but hyphenated thereafter). Some of these spelling changes do not apply to Bible quotations. Differences in punctuation, capitalization, and referencing format are not recorded here, unless other significant textual changes accompany them.

The headings to the Lectures have been altered over the years, but those alterations are not listed in these charts. Please see Dahl's "Authorship and History" (above) for a discussion of the various headings to the Lectures on Faith.

Paragraphs in the Question and Answer sections of past editions were not numbered; this edition assigns a number to each question, and assumes the same numbering for past editions regardless of their format.

These comparative charts were prepared by Rebecca Ann Harrison and Scott W. Gardner, editorial assistants in the Religious Studies Center Publications office at Brigham Young University.

Comparative Chart 1:
1835 and 1990 Editions
of the Lectures on Faith

The 1990 edition has corrected and standardized all scripture references in the Lectures on Faith to current editions of the scriptures and the Joseph Smith Translation. In keeping with the 1985 edition, we have added references to the book of Moses, where appropriate, to facilitate referencing. However, none of these corrections or additions are reflected in this chart. For any changes of this kind, refer to Chart 2 (beginning on page 135), which shows the correcting of scripture references over the years.

In the genealogies of Lecture 2, the word *years* was sometimes left off when ages were given in the 1835 edition. To save space, this chart does not list the occasions where the 1990 edition has added the word to provide uniformity.

P	1835	1990

Preface

P	1835	1990
1	To the members of the church of the Latter Day Saints-- DEAR BRETHREN:	To the members of The Church of Jesus Christ of Latter-day Saints:
2-4	No changes	------
5	any thing	anything
	in consequence of there being so many	since there are so many
6	The church viewing this subject to be of importance, appointed, through their servants and delegates the High Council, your servants to select and compile this work.	Viewing this subject to be of importance, the Church, through its servants and delegates, the High Council, appointed your servants to select and compile this work.
	we only add a few words	we add only a few words
7	to present, though in few words, *our* belief, and when we say this, humbly trust, the faith	to present our belief, though in few words, and when we say this, we humbly trust that it is the faith

109

P	1835	1990
8-10	No changes	------

Lecture 1

1	lectures which are designed	lectures designed
2-8	No changes	------
9	have not seen; and the principle	have not seen and that it is also the principle
10	No changes	------
11	Were this class to go back and reflect upon the history of their lives, from the period of their first recollection, and ask themselves, what principle excited them to action, or what gave them energy and activity, in all their lawful avocations	Were each of you in this class to go back and reflect upon the history of your lives from the period of your first recollection, and ask yourselves what principle excited you to action, or what gave you energy and activity in all your lawful avocations
	assurance which we had	assurance which you had
	which we had not	which you had not
	dependant	dependent
	you would have found	you would find
	it would have been opened	it would be opened
	any thing	anything
	dependant	dependent
	thoughts on your own	thoughts to your own
	and if the moving cause in you, is it not in all	and if it is the moving cause in you, is it not also the moving cause in all
12	No changes	------
13	temporal blessings that we do receive,	temporal blessings,

P	1835	1990
	spiritual blessings that we do receive.	spiritual blessings.
	but of power, also	it is also the principle of power
14	No changes	------
15	by which the worlds were framed,	by which he framed the worlds,
16	No changes	------
17	faith, that it is by	faith, it is by
	and that faith is the principle	and faith is the principle
	And that if the principle of power, it must be so in men as well as in the Deity	And if it is the principle of power in the Deity, it must be so in man as well
18	The Savior says, Matthew 17:19,20, in explaining the reason why the disciples could not cast out the devil, that it was because of their unbelief.	The Savior says the reason the disciples could not cast out the devil was their unbelief:
19	has given us	gave us
	He says, page 563, that	He says on page 563 of the 1830 Book of Mormon that
	wrent	rent
	that it was the faith	It was the faith
	and that it was by faith	And it was by faith
	also 565th	also the 565th
20-21	No changes	------
22	So with man also--he spake	So with men also--they spake
23	which was in man	which was in men
24	No changes	------

P	1835	1990

Lecture 1 Questions and Answers

P	1835	1990
1	treats of the being	treats the being
	page 582	582
2-3	No changes	------
4	First, Should be	First, it should be
5	unseen things, must be	unseen things, it must be
6	of my own mind	of your own mind
7-8	No changes	------
9	faith any thing else beside	faith anything else besides
10	No changes	------
11	Do. page 421.	Page 421:
	Do. page 565.	Page 565:
12	No changes	------
13	or by it	and by it
	and without it	Without it

Lecture 2

P	1835	1990
1	No changes	------
2	all fulness and perfection dwells	all fulness and perfection dwell
	who is	He is
	and that in him every good gift, and every good principle dwells;	In him every good gift and every good principle dwell,
	and that he is	and he is

P	1835	1990
3	mankind have had, and the foundation on which these evidences are, or were based, since the creation, to believe in the existence of a God.	mankind have had to believe in the existence of a God and also to show the foundation on which these evidences are and have been based since the creation.
4	the works of creation, throughout their vast forms and varieties, clearly exhibit his eternal power and Godhead.	the works of creation clearly exhibit his eternal power and Godhead throughout their vast forms and varieties.
	But we mean	But we do mean
5-11	No changes	------
12	we learn man's	we learn of man's
	vail	veil
13-18	No changes	------
19	was endowed	had been endowed
20	show, that, though he was cast out from the garden of Eden, his knowledge of the existence of God was not lost,	show, that even though man was cast out from the garden of Eden, he did not lose his knowledge of the existence of God,
21-24	No changes	------
25	quotation, or summary, shows this	quotation shows this
	that though	even though
	were even separated	were separated
	vail	veil
	And further, that no sooner	And further, no sooner
26	Cain, and the righteousness	Cain, of the righteousness
27-29	No changes	------
30	quotations is	quotation is
	existence of a God: that it was by	existence of a God was by

P	1835	1990
	and that God continued, after man's transgression to manifest himself to him and his posterity:	Also after man's transgression God continued to manifest himself to him and to his posterity.
	presence that they	presence so that they
31	No changes	------
32	God condescended	God also condescended
	and that Cain knew that it was the Lord that was talking with him: so that when	And Cain knew that it was the Lord who was talking with him, so when
33	existence, in all evidences which	existence and in all evidence which
34	reason why we	reason we
	Fall; and what it was	Fall, and also may see what it was
	and not only commune with him	Not only were they to commune with him
	but be partakers	but they were also to be partakers
35	No changes	------
36	information of his father, that such a being did exist, who had created, and who did uphold all things. Neither can there be a doubt existing on the mind of any person, that	information from his father that such a being who had created and who did uphold all things did exist. Neither can there be any doubt existing in the mind of any person but that
	and that the whole faith	The whole faith
37	No changes	------
38	Lamech, the 9th from Adam	Lamech, the eighth from Adam
39	So that Lamech	So Lamech
40	Seth lived, after he begat Enos, 807 years;	Seth lived 807 years after he begat Enos,
	Enos lived, after he begat Cainan, 815 years:	Enos lived 815 years after he begat Cainan,

114

P	1835	1990
	Cainan lived, after he begat Mahalaleel, 840 years:	Cainan lived 840 years after he begat Mahalaleel,
	Mahalaleel lived, after he begat Jared, 830 years:	Mahalaleel lived 830 years after he begat Jared,
	Jared lived, after he begat Enoch, 800 years:	Jared lived 800 years after he begat Enoch,
	with God, after he begat Methuseleh 300 years:	with God 300 years after he begat Methuselah,
	Methuseleh lived, after he begat Lamech, 782 years:	Methuselah lived 782 years after he begat Lamech,
	Lamech lived, after he begat Noah, 595 years:	Lamech lived 595 years after he begat Noah,
41	No changes	------
42	So that Noah	So Noah
43	No changes	------
44	it is easily to be seen	it is easy to see
	world, but upon	world but also upon
	that from the time	From the time
	but the world; so that there	but also the world. So there
	but of the true	but the true
45	afterward	afterwards
	Noah lived after the flood, 350 years:	Noah lived 350 years after the flood,
46	No changes	------
47	of scriptures, which are not to our purpose at present to quote	of scriptures, but it is not our purpose at present to quote them
	But in order that there may no doubt exist upon any mind, in relation to the object lying immediately before us, in presenting the present chronology	But so there may be no doubt about the present chronology

P	1835	1990
	latest period	later period
	that from the flood	that the time from the flood
48	Shem lived, after he begat Arphaxed, 500	Shem lived 500 years after he begat Arphaxad
	Arphaxed lived, after he begat Salah, 403 years	Arphaxad lived 403 years after he begat Salah
	Salah lived, after he begat Eber, 403 years	Salah lived 403 years after he begat Eber
	Eber lived, after he begat Peleg, 430 years	Eber lived 430 years after he begat Peleg
	years old.	years old when he died.
	Peleg lived, after he begat Reu, 209 years	Peleg lived 209 years after he begat Reu
	Reu lived, after he begat Serug, 207 years	Reu lived 207 years after he begat Serug
	Serug lived, after he begat Nahor, 200 years	Serug lived 200 years after he begat Nahor
	Nahor lived, after he begat Terah, 119 years	Nahor lived 119 years after he begat Terah
49	grand-father	grandfather
50	Selah	Salah
51	No changes	------
52	And that Abraham	Abraham
	And that Shem	Shem
	Nahor, the brother	Nahor, brother
	And that Nahor	Nahor
53	world, agreeably to the account given in our present bible, from Adam to Abraham,	world from Adam to Abraham agreeable to the account given in our present Bible,
	so that the students, in this class need not have any dubiety resting on their minds	So the students in this class need not have any doubt in their minds

P	1835	1990
	before mentioned	before-mentioned
54	We have now shown how it was that the first thought ever existed in the mind of any individual, that there was such a being as a God, who had created and did uphold all things: that it was by reason of the manifestation which he first made to our father Adam, when he stood in his presence, and conversed with him face to face, at the time of his creation.	We have now shown how it was by reason of the manifestation which God first made to our father Adam, when he stood in his presence and conversed with him face to face at the time of his creation, that the first thought ever existed in the mind of any individual that there was such a being as a God who had created and did uphold all things.
55	any portion of	any members of
56	enquiry	inquiry
	and we have seen	We have also seen
	enquiry, in the first instance in their minds	inquiry in their minds in the first instance
	this testimony having aroused	it having aroused
	enquire	inquire
	the enquiry	That inquiry
	persued	pursued

Lecture 2 Questions and Answers

1-5	No changes	------
6	had most perfect	had a most perfect
	that, though man	that even though man
7	quotation	quotations
	thoughts were suggested to the minds of man, of the existence of God, and	thoughts of the existence of God were suggested to the minds of men and

P	1835	1990
8	What testimony had the immediate descendants of Adam, in proof	What testimony did the immediate descendants of Adam have in proof
	with his existence	with God's existence
	dependant	dependent
9	Had any others of the human family, beside Adam, a knowledge	Did any other of the human family, besides Adam, have a knowledge
	They had not	They did not
	the all-important	that all-important
	and so, from father to child, the knowledge was communicated as extensively, as the knowledge of his existence was known; for it was by this means, in the first instance, that men had a knowledge of his existence	And so, the knowledge of his existence was communicated from father to child as extensively as it was known. For it was by this means that men had a knowledge of his existence in the first instance
10	thro'	through
11	Frst	First
	from which period the knowledge of the existence of God has been so general, that	The knowledge of the existence of God has been so general from that period that
12-27	No changes	------
28	Three hundred nnd eight years.	308 years.
29-33	No changes	------
34	cotemporary	contemporary
35-46	No changes	------
47	translatedd	translated
48-49	No changes	------
50	Five hundred and n e y five years	595 years
51-67	No changes	------

P	1835	1990
68	Seth, Enos, Cainan	Enos, Cainan
69	cotemporary	contemporary
70-84	No changes	------
85	father	brother
86-123	No changes	------
124	he were born	he was born
125-131	No changes	------
132	cotemporary	contemporary
133	No changes	------
134	Selah	Salah
135	cotemporary	contemporary
136-137	No changes	------
138	grand-father	grandfather
139	No changes	------
140	Who was it	Who was he
141-143	No changes	------
144	What testimony have men	What testimony did men have
145-146	No changes	------
147	until a person receives	until persons receive
148	the first lecture of the second section	the first part of Lecture 2

Lecture 3

1	it was shown how it was that the knowledge	we showed how the knowledge
	and that it was by reason	We also showed that is was by reason

P	1835	1990
2	in order that any rational and intelligent being may exercise	for any rational and intelligent being to exercise
3-4	No changes	------
5	which he is pursuing	which one is pursuing
6	Having previously been made acquainted with the way the idea of his existence came into the world, as well as the fact of his existence,	Having previously shown the way that both the idea and the fact of his existence came into the world,
	in order that this class	so this class
	for the exercise of	to exercise
	also, as far as the idea of his existence extends, may have to exercise faith in him the Father of all living.	also, may have to exercise faith in him, the Father of all living, as far as the idea of his existence extends.
7	As we have been indebted to a revelation which God made of himself to his creatures in the first instance, for the idea of his existence, so in	As we are indebted for the idea of his existence to a revelation which God made of himself to his creatures, in the first instance, so in
8	have given	give
9-12	No changes	------
13	First, That he was	First, he was
	God that he was	God he was
14	Secondly, That he is	Secondly, he is
	and that he was	and he was
15	Thirdly, That he changes not, neither is there variableness with him;	Thirdly, he does not change, neither does he vary;
	but that he	but he
	to-day	today
	and that his	and his
16	Fourthly, That he is	Fourthly, he is

P	1835	1990
17	Fifthly, That he is	Fifthly, he is
18	Sixthly, That he is	Sixthly, he is
19	is essentially necessary, in order that the faith	is essential so the faith
	if he did not, in the first instance, believe	if, in the first instance, he did not believe
	greater than	greater one than
	without wavering	unwavering
20	Unless he was	unless God was
	the faith necessary to salvation could not exist;	they could not have the faith necessary to salvation.
	An idea of these facts does away doubt	Having an idea of these facts does away with doubt
21	But it is equally as necessary that men should have the idea that he is a God who changes not, in order to have faith in him, as	But in order to have faith in him, it is equally as necessary that men should have the idea that he is a God who does not change as
	unchangibleness	unchangeableness
	he changes not	he does not change
	to-day	today
22	as the idea	as is the idea
	that he was a God of truth and could not lie, the confidence necessary to be placed in his word in order to the exercise of faith in him, could not exist.	that he is a God of truth and cannot lie, men could not have the confidence in his word necessary to exercise faith in him.
	he is not man that he can lie, it gives	he is not a man who can lie gives
23	that he is	that God is
	but all must be	All must be
	and that every man	and every man

121

P	1835	1990
24	for with all the other excellencies in his character, without this one to influence them, they could not	For without this one characteristic to influence all the other excellencies in his character, they could not
25	No changes	------
26	so that the saints	So the Saints
	having as good grounds	have as good grounds

Lecture 3 Questions and Answers

P	1835	1990
1-4	No changes	------
5	in order that we	so we
6	No changes	------
7	above mentioned	above-mentioned
8	No changes	------
9	before mentioned	before-mentioned
	Deity, and respecting ourselves	Deity and ourselves
10-11	No changes	------
12	First, that he was	First, he was
	Secondly, that he is	Secondly, he is
	goodness, and that he was	goodness, and he was
	Thirdly, that he changes not, neither is there variableness with him, and that his course	Thirdly, he does not change, neither does he vary, and his course
	Fourthly, that he is	Fourthly, he is
	Fifthly, that he is	Fifthly, he is
	and Sixthly, that he is	And sixthly, he is
13	and book of commandments	and the Book of Commandments
14	No changes	------

P	1835	1990
15	but there might be	but that there might be
	thereby he be	thereby he would be
16-17	No changes	------
18	long suffering, and full	long-suffering, full
	him in consequence of which, he	him; consequently, he
19	God changes not, neither is there variableness with him,	God does not change, neither does he vary,
	the mercy of God	God's mercy
	and in consequence of which doubt	In consequence of this doubt
	to day	today
20	their faith can rest in him	they can rest their faith in him
21	No changes	------
22	He could not; because man	It would not. Man
23	No changes	------
24	saints, so that	Saints, God's character is uniform so that

Lecture 4

1	Having shown in the third lecture, that correct ideas of the character of God are necessary in order to the exercise of faith	We showed in the third lecture that it is necessary to have correct ideas of the character of God to exercise faith
	power with God to the exercise of faith necessary to the enjoyment of eternal life, and that correct ideas of his character lay	power with God to exercise the faith necessary to enjoy eternal life. But having correct ideas of his character lays
	the connection there is between correct	the connection between having correct

123

P	1835	1990
	and the exercise of faith	and exercising faith
2	that they through the ideas of the existence of his attributes, might be enabled to exercise faith in him, and through the exercise of faith	that they might be enabled to exercise faith in him through the idea of the existence of his attributes, and through exercising faith
	faith on him	faith in him
	weakness of man	weakness of men
	must be	needed to be
	in their minds in order that they might be enabled	in their minds to enable them
3	how necessary correct ideas of his attributes are to enable	how necessary having correct ideas of his attributes is to enable
	So that the divine	Consequently, the divine
	made to man	made to men
4	We have, in the revelations which he has given to the human family, the following account of his attributes.	We have the following account of his attributes in the revelations which he has given to the human family:
5-10	No changes	------
11	By a little reflection it will be seen, that	A little reflection shows that
	for it is by reason of the knowledge	For it is the knowledge
	had all knowledge	has all knowledge
12	men feel as though they had nothing to fear, who put their trust in God,	men who put their trust in God feel as though they have nothing to fear,
13	It is also necessary, in order to the exercise in faith in God, unto life and salvation, that men should have the idea of the existence of the attribute justice, in him.	It is also necessary that men should have the idea of the existence of the attribute justice in God in order to exercise faith in him unto life and salvation.
	sufficiently	sufficient

124

P	1835	1990
	with most unshaken	with the most unshaken
14	in order that they	so they
	power to the mind	power to their minds
	and they are enabled	They are thus enabled
	and wade	and to wade
	believing, that	They believe that
	enemies, and they shall be	enemies, who shall be
15	saints: believing that	Saints, who believe then that
	will compassionate them	will be compassionate to them
16	Lord: and by reason	Lord. By reason
17	before mentioned	before-mentioned
	and it will be seen, that as far as his attributes are concerned, there is a sure foundation laid for the exercise of faith in him for life and salvation.	and it will see that there is a sure foundation laid for the exercise of faith in him for life and salvation as far as his attributes are concerned.
	in as much	inasmuch
	saints necessary	saints that are necessary
	and seeing also	Seeing, also
	and a just reward will be granted unto them for	and will grant them a just reward for
	that they will, in due time, obtain	that, in due time, they will obtain
	exercised toward	exercised towards
	attribute toward	attribute towards
	And lastly	Lastly
	and in view of that crown	It will do this in view of that crown
	into the midst	in the midst
18	and can exert	And it can exert

P	1835	1990
19	laid, through the revelation of the attributes of God, for the exercise of faith in him for life and salvation; and seeing that these are attributes of the Deity, they are unchangeable	laid for the exercise of faith in him for life and salvation through the revelation of the attributes of God. And seeing that these attributes of the Deity are unchangeable
	to day	today
	which gives to the minds	gives to the minds
	so that all the saints	All the Saints
	these that a foundation	these attributes that a foundation
	the foundation, therefore, for the exercise of faith, was, is and ever will be the same. So that all men	the foundation for the exercise of faith, therefore, was, is, and ever will be, the same. Consequently all men

Lecture 4 Questions and Answers

1	that correct ideas of the character of God are necessary in order to exercise	that having correct ideas of the character of God is necessary to exercise
	but that correct ideas of his character, as far as his character is concerned	But having correct ideas of his character, as far as it is concerned
	lay a sure foundation	lays a sure foundation
2	What object had the God of heaven in	What object did the God of heaven have in
3	God without an acquaintance with his attributes, so as to be enabled to lay hold of eternal life	God so as to be enabled to lay hold of eternal life, without an acquaintance with his attributes
4-5	No changes	------
6	those attributes	these attributes
	necessary in order to enable	necessary to enable
7	No changes	------

P	1835	1990
8	Deity, as far as his attributes are concerned, enable a rational being to exercise faith in him unto life and salvation	Deity enable a rational being to exercise faith in him unto life and salvation, as far as his attributes are concerned
9	No changes	------
10	Have the Latter Day Saints as much authoity	Do the Latter-day Saints have as much authority
11	No changes	------

Lecture 5

1	we treated of the being	we treated the being
2	were created and made, that are created and made, whether	were created and made, whether
	earth, or in the earth	earth, in the earth
	Father, a personage	Father, is a personage
	man, or being in the form	man, being in the form
	Fathe	Father
	and was ordained	and ordained
	and is called	He is called
	and descended	And he descended
	words, suffered	words, he suffered
	flesh, and that all who	flesh, that all who
	And he being	He, being
	and these three are one	These three are one
	were created and made that were created and made: and	were created and made. And
	Son possessing the same mind	Son possess the same mind
	possessing all knowledge	possesses all knowledge

P	1835	1990
	kingdom: sitting at the right hand	kingdom, and sits at the right hand
	Father--a Mediator	Father. He is a mediator
	grow up from grace to grace	grow from grace to grace
	joint heirs	joint-heirs
	Christ; possessing the same mind	Christ. They will possess the same mind
	and become one	and becoming one
3	by whose blood	By his blood
	joint heirs	joint-heirs

Lecture 5 Questions and Answers

1	Of what do	What subjects do
	Of the being	The being
2	No changes	------
3	Father and the Son	Father and Son
4-5	No changes	------
6	[No equivalent]	First, of glory.
7	No changes	------
8	tabernacle, was made	tabernacle, the Son was made
9	created and made, that were created and made?	created and made?
10	Does he possess	Does the Son possess
11-15	No changes	------
16	Does the believer in Christ	Do the believers in Christ
17-18	No changes	------

P	1835	1990

Lecture 6

1	Having treated, in the preceding lectures, of the ideas of the character, perfections and attributes of God, we	Having treated the ideas of the character, perfections, and attributes of God in the preceding lectures, we
	treat of the knowledge	treat the knowledge
	personsmust	persons must
	in order that they may	so they may
2	An actual knowledge to any person that the course of life which he pursues is according to the will of God, is essentially necessary to enable	It is essential for any person to have an actual knowledge that the course of life which he is pursuing is according to the will of God to enable
3	No changes	------
4	that unless they	Unless they
	course that they are pursuing	course they are pursuing
	and those that know not God	and those who know not God
	that they will persecute, to the uttermost, all that worship God	They will persecute to the uttermost all who worship God
	and drive	And they will drive
5	but actual knowledge	It requires actual knowledge
6	No changes	------
7	it was through the sacrifice	It is through this sacrifice
	sacrifice & offering, & that he was not nor will not seek	sacrifice and offering and that he has not sought nor will he seek
8-10	No changes	------
11	and were enabled	They were enabled
12	doubt and uncertainty is	doubt and uncertainty are
	So that persons whose minds	So persons whose minds
	joint heirs	joint-heirs

P	1835	1990
	and they will grow weary	But they will grow weary

Lecture 7

1	we treated of what faith was, and of the object on	we treated what faith was and the object on
2	faith was the principle	faith is the principle
	that we will, in a lecture of this description attempt to unfold all its effects;	that we will attempt to unfold all its effects in a lecture of this description.
	revolution unless it is effected in the same way, in any of the vast creations of the Almighty;	revolution in any of the vast creations of the Almighty unless it is effected in the same way,
3	instead of exerting	instead of by exerting
4	eternty	eternity
5	undrstood, leads	understood, it leads
6	act, in order, to obtain	act to obtain
	and that when God	And when God
	impossibility there was of their	impossibility of their
7	Why is it impossible to please God without faith? the answer would be, because, without	why it is impossible to please God without faith, the answer would be that without
	and as God desires	As God desires
	they had, or else	they had it, or else
8	exhortations which have been given by inspired men to those who had received the word of the Lord, to have faith in him, were	exhortations to have faith in him which have been given by inspired men to those who had received the word of the Lord were
	and that was, because, without it there was no salvation	And that reason is that without it there is no salvation
	when faith is perfected	when their faith is perfected

130

P	1835	1990
9	heavenly worlds, they	heavenly worlds that they
	And they must have faith	They must have faith
	assimulated, in order that we	assimilated, so we
	or in other words, where	or, where
	existance	existence
	question there	question that there
	agree in this that	agree that
	interogation	interrogation
	answer would be, because he is	answer would be, that he is
	and if he were any thing	If he were anything
	so sure he would fail	surely Christ would fail
	constitutes	constitute
	purify himself	purify themselves
10	being can enjoy	beings can enjoy
11	No changes	------
12	that Jesus done	that Jesus had done
	which he done	which he had done
	taken in connection, make	taken together make
	those that believed	those who believed
13	and he so spake that	and he spake that
	the Father: for	the Father are, for
	to more firmly establish this belief, if it needs any thing	to establish this belief more firmly, if it needs anything
	As much as to say	This is as much as to say
14	No changes	------

P	1835	1990
15	That the glory which the Father and the Son have, is because they are just and holy beings; and that if	that the Father and the Son have the glory they have because they are just and holy beings; and if
	have, the glory which they have, never could be enjoyed by them; for	have, they could never enjoy the glory which they have, for
	Father and the Son	Father and Son
16	them--That he proposed	them: he proposed
	And for any portion	For any portion
	assimulated	assimilated
	and on this hinge	On this hinge
17	the God of heaven, by the mouth of all his holy prophets, has been endeavoring to teach to the world.	the God of heaven has been endeavoring to teach to the world by the mouth of all his holy prophets.
	And that Israel	And "Israel
	These with	These references with
	That it was a system	It was a system
	and continues by faith	it continues by faith
	To this, all the revelations of God bear witness	All the revelations of God bear witness to this
	baptist the less	Baptist any the less
	receive the dead	receive their dead
	nothing impossible with them	nothing impossible for them
	visions, the ministering of angels, have	visions and the ministering of angels. They could have
	first born	firstborn
	all, of Jesus	all, and of Jesus
	and become	And they could become

P	1835	1990
18{16}*	mistake on the mind	mistake in the mind
	answer is given, through faith	answer is that through faith
19{17}*	the Apostle	the Apostle Peter
	got the all things	got the knowledge of all things
	So that all things	So all things
20{18}*	every thing else	everything else
	Gallilee	Galilee
	Yea, and he counted	Yea, he counted
	Because, to obtain the faith by which he could enjoy the knowledge of Christ Jesus the Lord, he had to suffer the loss of all things	because he had to suffer "the loss of all things" to obtain the faith by which he could enjoy the knowledge of Christ Jesus the Lord
	always have, and always will	always have attended and always will
	in order that the possessors	so the possessors
	will, through it, obtain all necessary knowledge and wisdom, until	will obtain all necessary knowledge and wisdom through it until

---

* Numbers in braces are erroneous paragraph numbers used in the 1835 edition.

Comparative Chart 2:
1835, 1876, 1891, and 1985
Editions of the Lectures on Faith

Although other editions exist besides the four cited here (notably the 1844 edition published soon after the Prophet's death, and the N. B. Lundwall edition published c. 1940), the textual changes in those editions are minimal. The Lundwall edition, for example, contains little to differentiate it from the 1891 edition. The 1844 edition, which was perhaps revised under Joseph Smith's direction, contains very few changes from the original publication of nine years earlier. No comparison of prefaces is made here, since the 1876 and 1891 editions had no prefaces and the 1985 edition contained only a partial reproduction of the 1835 preface as part of a historical background of the Lectures.

Because we have enclosed our own editorial notes in brackets, we have used «[ ]» to indicate the five occasions in the chart that brackets were actually part of the original material.

P	1835	1876	1891	1985
		Lecture 1		
1-10	No changes	------	------	------
11	assurance which we had	assurance which they had	------	------
	things which we had	things which they had	------	------
	dependant	dependent	------	------
12	Mark 16:16	------	------	(Mark 16:16; italics added.)
13-16	No changes	------	------	------
17	And that if the principle	And if the principle	------	------

P	1835	1876	1891	1985
18	mustard-seed	mustard seed	------	------
19	page 563,	page 540,	page 597,	page 563,[1] [end 1] Page 509 (Ether 12:13) in the 1981 LDS edition of the Book of Mormon.
	wrent	rent	------	------
	264th page;	251st page;	278th page;	264th page;[2] [end 2] Pages 245-46 (Alma 14:23-29) in 1981 edition.
	that it was	it was	------	------
	421st page,	403rd page;	443rd page;	421st page;[3] [end 3] Page 380 (Hel. 5:37-50) in 1981 edition.
	565th page.	541st page, second European edition.	599th page.	565th page.[4] [end 4] Page 511 (Ether 12:30) in 1981 edition.
20	No changes	------	------	------
21	Josh. 10:12	------	------	(Josh. 10:12-13.)
22	and worlds came	------	and the worlds came	and worlds came
	was in them	was in him	------	------
23	faith which was in man	faith which was in men	------	------
	prisons, lions, the human heart	prisons, the human heart	------	------
24	No changes	------	------	------

P	1835	1876	1891	1985

Lecture 1 Questions and Answers

P	1835	1876	1891	1985
1-3	No changes	------	------	------
4	rests; and «[s. I. P. 4.]» Thirdly	rests. Section i. 4. And, thirdly	------	------
5	the worlds	------	------	that the worlds
6	warned of things	------	------	warned of God of things
	should after receive	should afterwards receive	------	should after receive
7-10	No changes	------	------	------
11	page 264.	page 251.	page 278.	page 264:[5] [end 5] See note 2.
	Do. page 421.	Ibid. page 403.	Ibid. page 443.	Ibid. page 421:[6] [end 6] See note 3.
	Do. page 565.	Ibid. page 541.	Ibid. page 599.	Ibid. page 565:[7] [end 7] See note 4.
	themselves of their enemies	------	------	themselves upon their enemies
	mustard-seed	mustard seed	------	------
	Heb. 11:32. And what	Hebrews xi. 32 and the following verses: "And what	------	------
	I say more	------	------	I more say
	Gideon	------	------	Gedeon
	Jephthah	------	------	Jephthae
12-13	No changes	------	------	------

P	1835	1876	1891	1985

Lecture 2

P	1835	1876	1891	1985
1	No changes	------	------	------
2	perfection dwells	perfection dwell	------	------
	principle dwells	principle dwell	------	------
3-4	No changes	------	------	------
5	30th.	------	------	30th.[1] [end 1] See Joseph Smith Translation, Genesis 1:27-31; Moses 2:26-29.
6	And the Lord God said unto the Only Begotten, who was with him	------	"And I, God, said unto mine Only Begotten, which was with me	------
	and it was done	------	and it was so	------
7	And the Lord God said, Let them have dominion over the fish	------	"And I, God, said, 'Let them have dominion over the fishes	------
	creaps	creeps	creepeth	------
8	So God created man in his own image, in the image of the Only Begotten created he him; male and female created he them.	------	"And I, God, created man in mine own image, in the image of mine Only Begotten created I him; male and female created I them.	------
	And God blessed them, and God said unto them	------	And I, God, blessed them, and said unto them	------
	that moves upon the earth.	------	that moveth upon the earth.'	------

P	1835	1876	1891	1985
9	And the Lord God said unto man	------	"And I, God, said unto man	------
	in the which is the fruit	------	in the which shall be the fruit	------
10	Genesis 2:15, 16, 17, 19, 20:	------	------	Genesis 2:15-17, 19-20:[2] [end 2] Ibid. 2:18-22, 25-27; Moses 3:15-17, 19-20.
	And the Lord God	------	"And I, the Lord God,	------
	to dress it and to keep it.	to dress it and keep it.	to dress it, and to keep it.	------
	And the Lord God	------	And I, the Lord God,	------
	you may freely eat	------	thou mayest freely eat	------
	you shall not eat of it, neither shall you touch it;	------	thou shalt not eat of it;	------
	you may choose for yourself	------	thou mayest choose for thyself	------
	unto you	------	unto thee	------
	you eat thereof you shall	------	thou eatest thereof thou shalt	------
11	the Lord God	------	I, the Lord God	------
	should be brought	------	should come	------
	* * *And whatever	------	* * *And whatsoever	And . . . whatsoever
	was the name	------	should be the name	------
12	vail	veil	vail	------

P	1835	1876	1891	1985
13	hid themselves	------	went to hide themselves	------
	among the trees	------	amongst the trees	------
	And the Lord	------	And I, the Lord	------
	Where are you going?	------	Where goest thou?'	------
	your voice	------	thy voice	------
14	And the Lord	------	"And I, the Lord	------
	you that you were	------	thee thou wast	thee that thou wast
	Have you	------	Hast thou	------
	I told you that you should	------	I commanded thee that thou shouldst	------
	If so, you should	------	If so thou shouldst	------
	woman whom you gave me, and commanded	------	woman whom thou gavest me, and commandedst	woman whom thou gavest me, and commanded
15	And the Lord God	------	"And I, the Lord God,	------
	this which you have done?	------	this thing which thou hast done?	------
	I did eat.	------	------	I did eat."[3] [end 3] Ibid. 3:13-19; Moses 4:14-19.
16	multiply your sorrow, and your conception	------	multiply thy sorrow, and thy conception	------
	you shall bring	------	thou shalt bring	------
	your desire shall be to your husband	------	thy desire shall be to thy husband	------

140

P	1835	1876	1891	1985
	rule over you	------	rule over thee	------
17	And the Lord God said unto Adam,	------	"And unto Adam, I, the Lord God, said,	------
	you have hearkened	------	thou hast hearkened	------
	your wife	------	thy wife	------
	have eaten	------	hast eaten	------
	commanded you	------	commanded thee	------
	You shall not eat	------	Thou shalt not eat	------
	your sake	------	thy sake	------
	you shall eat	------	thou shalt eat	shalt thou eat
	your life	------	thy life	------
	to you	------	to thee	------
	you shall eat	------	thou shalt eat	------
	your face shall you	------	thy face shalt thou	------
	you shall return	------	thou shalt return	------
	you shall surely	------	thou shalt surely	------
	you were taken	------	wast thou taken	------
	dust you were	------	dust thou wast	------
	you shall return.	------	shalt thou return.' "	shalt thou return." [4] [end 4] Ibid. 3:22-25; Moses 4:22-25.
18-21	No changes	------	------	------
22	as the Lord	------	as I, the Lord	------
	toward	------	------	towards
	but he gave	------	and he gave	------

P	1835	1876	1891	1985
	commandment.	------	commandments of the Lord.	------
23	do you offer	------	dost thou offer	------
	but the Lord commanded me to offer sacrifices.	------	save the Lord commanded me.	------
24	And the angel said unto him,	------	"And then the angel spake, saying,	------
	who is full	------	------	which is full
	And you shall	------	And thou shalt	wherefore, thou shalt
	all that you do	------	all that thou doest	------
	you shall repent	------	thou shalt repent	------
	in his name forever	------	in the name of the Son for evermore	------
	Holy Spirit	------	Holy Ghost	------
	and bore record	------	which beareth record	------
	Father and the Son.	------	------	Father and the Son."[5] [end 5] Ibid. 4:1, 4-9; Moses 5:1, 4-9.
25	vail	veil	vail	------
26	God to them.	------	------	God to them.[6] [end 6] Ibid. 5:6-9, 17-25; Moses 5:19-23, 32-40.
	And Abel also brought	------	------	And Abel, he also brought,
	to his offering	------	unto his offering	to his offering
	very angry	------	very wroth	------

142

P	1835	1876	1891	1985
	are you angry	------	art thou wroth	------
	your countenance	------	thy countenance	------
	If you do well, will you not be accepted?	------	If thou doest well, thou shalt be accepted.	------
	if you do not well, sin lies	------	if thou doest not well, sin lieth	------
	satan desires to have you	------	Satan desireth to have thee	------
	you shall hearken	------	thou shalt hearken	------
	deliver you up	------	deliver thee up	------
	you according	------	thee according	------
27	and talked with his brother Abel.	------	and Cain talked with Abel, his brother.	------
	And while	------	And it came to pass, that while	------
	his brother Abel,	------	Abel, his brother,	------
	what he had done	------	that which he had done	------
	will now fall into	------	falleth into	------
28	But the Lord	------	------	"And the Lord
	Able, your brother?	------	Abel, thy brother?	------
	What have you done?	------	What hast thou done?	------
	your brother's	------	thy brother's	------
	you shall be cursed	------	thou shalt be cursed	------
	has opened	------	hath opened	------
	your brother's	------	thy brother's	------

P	1835	1876	1891	1985
	your hand	------	thy hand	------
	you till	------	thou tillest	------
	she shall not	------	it shall not	------
	yield unto you	------	yield unto thee	------
	also, you shall	------	shalt thou	------
29	also angry	------	wroth also	------
	was accepted, and mine was not	------	thou didst accept, and not mine	------
	you have driven	------	thou hast driven	------
	face of men	------	face of the Lord	------
	your face	------	thy face	------
	hid also;	------	hid;	------
	every one that finds	------	that he that findeth	------
	will slay	------	------	shall slay
	my oath	------	mine iniquities	------
	And the Lord	------	------	And I, the Lord,
	Therefore, whoever slays Cain,	------	Whosoever slayeth thee	------
	seven fold	seven-fold	sevenfold	seven-fold
	And the Lord	------	And I the Lord	------
30	and his posterity	and to his posterity	------	------
31-39	No changes	------	------	------

144

P	1835	1876	1891	1985
40	translated. 5:22,23.	translated (verses 22, 23).* [fn] According to the Old Testament. For Enoch's age, see Covenants and Command-ments, section iii. 24.	translated (verses 22, 23).* [fn] According to the Old Testament. For Enoch's age see Covenants and Command-ments, section 107. 49.	translated. (Vv. 22-23.)[7] [end 7] Orson Pratt, when he edited the Doctrine and Covenants in 1879, added this footnote: "According to [. . .] section 107.49."
41	987th,	------	987th,* [fn same as in 40 above]	987th,[8] [end 8] See note 7.
42-43	No changes	------	------	------
44	but of the true	but the true	------	------
45	afterward	afterwards	------	------
46-47	No changes	------	------	------
48	500	500 years	------	------
49	grand-father	grandfather	------	------
50	Selah	Salah	------	------
51-52	No changes	------	------	------
53	dubiety	doubt	------	------
	before mentioned	before-mentioned	------	------
54-55	No changes	------	------	------
56	enquiry	inquiry	------	------
	search	------	seach	search
	enquiry	inquiry	------	------
	enquire	inquire	------	------
	enquiry	inquiry	------	------
	persued	pursued	------	------

P	1835	1876	1891	1985

Lecture 2 Questions and Answers

P	1835	1876	1891	1985
1-2	No changes	------	------	------
3	omnicient	omniscient	------	------
4	No changes	------	------	------
5	counsellor	------	counselor	counsellor
	8th to the 18th.	9th to the 18th verses:	------	------
	the Lord your God	------	------	the Lord God
	his lambs	------	------	the lambs
	weighed	------	------	and weighed
	ballance	balance	------	------
	counsellor	------	counselor	counsellor
	shewed	showed	------	shewed
	ballance	balance	------	------
	are before him	-----	------	before him are
	streached	stretched	------	------
	vapors	------	vapours	vapour
6-7	No changes	------	------	------
8	existence of a God	existence of God	------	------
	dependant	dependent	------	------
9	beside Adam	besides Adam	------	------
10	thro'	through	------	------
11	Frst	First	------	------
12-21	No changes	------	------	------
22	Sixty five.	Sixty-five years.	------	------
23	No changes	------	------	------
24	Ho w	How	------	------

P	1835	1876	1891	1985
25-27	No changes	------	------	------
28	nnd	and	------	------
29	No changes	------	------	------
30	thirty five.	thirty-five years.	------	------
31-32	No changes	------	------	------
33	Eight hundred.	Eight hundred years.	------	------
34-46	No changes	------	------	------
47	translatedd	translated	------	------
	Gen. 5:23.	------	Genesis v. 23.* [fn] For Enoch's age, see Covenants and Commandments, Section 107. 49.	(Gen. 5:23.)[9] [end 9] Orson Pratt added this footnote: "For Enoch's age, [. . .] Section 107.49."
48-49	No changes	------	------	------
50	n e y five years	ninety-five years	------	------
51-52	No changes	------	------	------
53	translated?	------	translated?* [fn same as in 47 above]	translated?[10] [end 10] See note 9.
54-67	No changes	------	------	------
68	Seth, Enos, Cainan	Enos, Cainan	------	------
69-72	No changes	------	------	------
73	Gen. 5:32. 11:10.	Genesis v. 32.	------	------
74-75	No changes	------	------	------
76	Gen. 9:29	------	Genesis xi. 29	Gen. 9:29
77-78	No changes	------	------	------
79	Thirty. Gen. 11:14	Thirty years. Genesis xi. 16	------	Thirty years. Gen. 11:14

P	1835	1876	1891	1985
80	Gen. 11:16	Genesis xi. 14	------	Gen. 11:16
81-83	No changes	------	------	------
84	Twenty nine.	Twenty-nine years.	------	------
85	No changes	------	------	------
86	Gen. 12:4. 11:26.	Genesis xi. 26.	------	------
87	he were born	he was born	------	------
88-89	No changes	------	------	------
90	Gen. 21:13	Genesis xi. 13	------	------
91	No changes	------	------	------
92	years. Gen. 11:15.	years.	------	------
93-111	No changes	------	------	------
112	ninty	ninety	------	------
113-123	No changes	------	------	------
124	he were born	he was born	------	------
125-133	No changes	------	------	------
134	Selah	Salah	------	------
135-139	No changes	------	------	------
140	Who was it?	Who was he?	------	------
141-142	No changes	------	------	------
143	the earth was	------	------	was the earth
144-146	No changes	------	------	------
147	until persons receive	until a person receives	------	------
148	first lecture of the second section.	first lecture and of the second section.	first and second lectures.	------

P	1835	1876	1891	1985

Lecture 3

P	1835	1876	1891	1985
1	shown	shewn	------	------
	had no idea	have no idea	------	------
	«[New Translation.]»	------	------	(New Translation.)[1] [end 1] See Joseph Smith Tanslation, Romans 10:14-16.
2-6	No changes	------	------	------
7	eye has not seen	eye hath not seen	------	------
	God has prepared	God hath prepared	------	------
	God has revealed	God hath revealed	------	------
	Spirit searches	Spirit searcheth	------	------
	man knows	man knoweth	------	------
	no man knows but by the Spirit	knoweth no man but the Spirit	------	------
8	No changes	------	------	------
9	The Lord God	------	------	The Lord
	executes	executeth	------	------
	ever you had	ever thou hadst	------	------
	you are God	thou art God	------	------
	And you, Lord	And thou, Lord	------	------
	have laid	hast laid	------	------
	your hands	thine hands	------	------
	you shall remain	thou remainest	------	------
	they shall	they all shall	------	------
	as a garment	as doth a garment	------	------

P	1835	1876	1891	1985
	shall you fold	shalt thou fold	------	------
	you are the same	thou art the same	------	------
	your years	thy years	------	------
	comes down	cometh down	------	------
10	chapt. 2nd, commencing in the third line of the first paragraph:	------	Sec. 3, v. 2:	chapter 2, commencing in the third line of the first paragraph:[2] [end 2] See Doctrine and Covenants 3:2.
	God does not walk	------	------	God doth not walk
	neither does he turn	------	------	neither doth he turn
	or the left, or vary	------	------	nor the left; neither doth he vary
	has said	------	------	hath said
	strait	straight	------	strait
	chapt. 37:1.	------	Sec. 35, v. 1:	chapter 37, verse 1:[3] [end 3] Ibid. 35:1.
	same yesterday to-day	------	------	same today as yesterday
11	loves not, knows not God;	loveth not, knoweth not God,	------	------
	Acts, 10:34	Acts x. 34, 35	------	------
	fears God and works	feareth God and worketh	------	feareth him, and worketh
12-14	No changes	------	------	------
15	forever	for ever	------	------
16-18	No changes	------	------	------
19	be a greater	be greater	------	------

P	1835	1876	1891	1985
	fulfil	------	fulfill	------
20	No changes	------	------	------
21	unchangibleness	unchangeable-ness	------	------
22	can lie	cannot lie	------	------
23-26	No changes	------	------	------

Lecture 3 Questions and Answers

1-3	No changes	------	------	------
4	16	tenth	------	------
5-6	No changes	------	------	------
7	above mentioned	above-mentioned	------	------
8	No changes	------	------	------
9	before mentioned	before-mentioned	------	------
10	No changes	------	------	------
11	Job 11:7, 8:9	Job xi. 7, 8, 9	------	------
12-18	No changes	------	------	------
19	to day	to-day	------	------
20-24	No changes	------	------	------

Lecture 4

1	No changes	------	------	------
2	faith on	faith in	------	------
	weakness of man	weakness of men	------	------
3	made to man	made to men	------	------
4	No changes	------	------	------
5	Isaiah 46:9, 10.	------	------	Isaiah 46:9-10 (italics added):

151

COMPARATIVE CHART 2

P	1835	1876	1891	1985
	ancient time	------	------	ancient times
6	No changes	------	------	------
7	has declared this from the ancient time? Have not I	hath declared this from the ancient time? have not I	------	hath declared this from ancient time? . . . have not I
	Zeph. 5:5	Zephaniah iii. 5	------	------
	thy King comes	thy King cometh	------	------
8	forever: he has prepared	forever. He hath prepared	------	------
	executes	executeth	------	------
9	Ps. 89:15	Psalm lxxxix. 14	------	------
	his face	------	------	thy face
10	Into thy hand	Into Thine hand	------	------
11-12	No changes	------	------	------
13	sufficiently	sufficient	------	------
	with most unshaken	with the most unshaken	------	------
14-16	No changes	------	------	------
17	before mentioned	before-mentioned	------	------
	in as much	inasmuch	------	------
	exercised toward them	exercised towards them	------	------
	attribute toward them	attribute towards them	------	------
	into the midst	in the midst	------	------
18	No changes	------	------	------
19	to day and forever	to-day, and for ever	------	------

P	1835	1876	1891	1985

Lecture 4 Questions and Answers

P	1835	1876	1891	1985
1-3	No changes	------	------	------
4	in in his	in his	------	------
5	No changes	------	------	------
6	those attributes	------	these attributes	------
7-9	No changes	------	------	------
10	authoity	authority	------	------
11	No changes	------	------	------

Lecture 5

P	1835	1876	1891	1985
1	No changes	------	------	------
2	Fathe	Father	------	------
	and was ordained	and ordained	------	------
	a Mediator	mediator	------	------
3	No changes	------	------	------

Lecture 5 Questions and Answers

P	1835	1876	1891	1985
1-3	No changes	------	------	------
4	s. 2. P. 6.	------	------	Lecture 2:6:[1] [end 1] See Joseph Smith Translation, Genesis 1:27; Moses 2:26.
	And the Lord God	------	------	"And I, God,
	the Only	------	------	mine Only
	who was with him	------	------	which was with me
	and it was done	------	------	and it was so

P	1835	1876	1891	1985
	Gen 3:22.	------	------	Genesis 3:22:[2] [end 2] Ibid. Genesis 3:28; Moses 4:28.
	And the Lord	------	------	"And I, the Lord
5	No changes	------	------	------
6	thunders	------	------	thundereth
	incorruptible	------	------	uncorruptible
	corruptible men	corruptible man	------	------
	1 Chron. 29:4	1 Chronicles xxix. 11	------	------
	the earth and the heavens	------	------	the heaven and the earth
	bro't them	brought them	------	brought thee
	commenceing	commencing	------	------
	He stretches	He stretcheth	------	------
	hangs the earth	hangeth the earth	------	------
	binds up	bindeth up	------	------
	holds back	holdeth back	------	------
	spreads his cloud	spreadeth his cloud	------	------
	has compassed	hath compassed	------	------
	divides the sea	divideth the sea	------	------
	he smites	he smiteth	------	------
	has garnished	hath garnished	------	------
	has formed	hath formed	------	------
7	No changes	------	------	------
8	Jesus says	Jesus saith	------	------
	yet have you	yet hast thou	------	------

P	1835	1876	1891	1985
	has seen me has seen the Father	hath seen me hath seen the Father	------	------
	do you say	sayest thou	------	------
	Show us	------	------	Shew us
	Do you not believe,	Believest thou not	------	------
	dwells in me, he does the works	dwelleth in me he doeth the works	------	------
	Philip. 2.	Philippians ii. 2-8:	------	Philippians 2:5-8:
	likeness of man	------	------	likeness of men
	time past	times past	------	time past
	has in these	hath in these	------	------
	has appointed	hath appointed	------	------
9	Col. 1: 15, 16, 17.	------	Collossians i. 15, 16, 17:	Colossians 1:15-17:
	dominions, principalities	------	------	dominions, or principalities
	created the heavens	------	------	created the heaven
	Has in these	"Hath in these	------	------
	has appointed	hath appointed	------	------
10	in him dwells	in him dwelleth	------	------
	him that fills	------	------	him that filleth
11	Luke 1:33.	------	------	Luke 1:35:
	well pleased.	------	------	well pleased."[3] [end 3] Ibid. Matthew 3:45- 46.
12	as you know that you	as ye know that ye	------	------
	Rev.	Revelations	------	Revelation
	hidden mystery	------	------	hidden wisdom

P	1835	1876	1891	1985
13	my own self	------	------	mine own self
	not my own will	------	------	not mine own will
	who sent me	------	------	which hath sent me
	do my own will	------	------	do mine own will
14	proceeds	------	------	proceedeth
	you are sons, God has sent	ye are sons, God hath sent	------	------
15	No changes	------	------	------
16	Does the believer	Do the believers	------	------
	who shall believe	------	------	which shall believe
17-18	No changes	------	------	------

Lecture 6

1	personsmust	persons must	------	------
2	It was this	------	It is this	It was this
3	No changes	------	------	------
4	course that they are	course they are	------	------
	ensures	insures	------	------
5-8	No changes	------	------	------
9	Ps. 50:3,4,5.	Psalm i. 3, 4, 5:	Psalm l. 3, 4, 5:	------
	covenant unto	covenant with	------	------
10	No changes	------	------	------
11	endure us seeing	endure as seeing	------	------
12	uncertainty is, there faith	uncertainty are there faith	uncertainty are their faith	uncertainty are there faith

156

P	1835	1876	1891	1985
	do not exist	do no exist	do not exist	------
	Note. This lecture	This lecture	------	------

Lecture 7

P	1835	1876	1891	1985
1	lectures	lessons	------	------
2	we will, in a lecture	we shall, in a lecture	------	------
3	obey you.	------	------	obey you."[1] [end 1] Genesis 1:3. Joshua 10:12-13. 1 Kings 17:1; 18:1, 41-45. See Matthew 17:20; Luke 17:6.
4	eternty	eternity	------	------
5	undrstood	understood	------	------
6	No changes	------	------	------
7	please God.	------	------	please God."[2] [end 2] See Hebrews 11:6.
8	No changes	------	------	------
9	assimulated	assimilated	------	------
	saved--they must be like that individual or they cannot be saved: we think	saved. We think	------	------
	existance	existence	------	------
	interogation	interrogation	------	------
	Behold, now we are	Beloved, now are we	------	------
	not appear	not yet appear	------	------
	any man that has	every man that hath	------	------

P	1835	1876	1891	1985
	purifies himself	purifieth himself	------	------
	purify himself	purify themselves	------	------
10	first epistle, 1:15 and 16	------	------	first epistle «[of Peter]», 1:15-16
	who has called	which hath called	------	------
	Matthew, 15:48	Matthew v. 48	------	------
	Be ye perfect	"Be ye therefore perfect	------	------
	who is in heaven	which is in heaven	------	------
11	testimony, 4:12:	testimony, xiv. 12:	------	testimony, 14:12:[3] [end 3] John 14:12.
	these,	these shall he do,	------	------
	24:	24th verses:	------	24th verses:[4] [end 4] John 17:20-24.
	their words	------	------	their word
	lovedest	lovedst	------	------
12	Jesus done	Jesus had done	------	------
	he done	he had done	------	------
	who shall	------	------	which shall
	one in us.	------	------	one in us."[5] [end 5] John 17:20-21.
13-14	No changes	------	------	------
15	and the Son	and Son	------	------
	works which I do, shall they do	------	------	works that I do shall he do also

P	1835	1876	1891	1985
	shall they do, be cause I go to the Father?	shall they do, because I go to my Father."	------	shall he do; because I go unto my Father."[6] [end 6] See note 3.
16	prototype	------	proto ype	prototype
	assimulated	assimilated	------	------
17	endeavoring	------	------	endeavouring
	please God;	------	------	please God";[7] [end 7] See note 2.
	Romans 9:32.	------	------	(Romans 9:32.)[9] [end 8] See Romans 9:31-32.
	the things	those things	------	------
	of the Lord	from the Lord	------	------
	the dead	their dead	------	------
	2nd epistle, 1:1, 2 and 3 says,	second epistle, first chapter, second and third verses, says	------	second epistle «[of Peter]», first chapter, second and third verses, says
	has called us unto	hath called us to	------	------
	first epistle, 1:3,	------	------	first epistle «[of Peter]», first chapter, third
	who according	which according	------	------
	has begotten	hath begotten	------	------
18{16}*	No changes	------	------	------
19{17}*	the all things	the knowledge of all things	------	------

* Numbers in braces are erroneous paragraph numbers used in the 1835 edition.

P	1835	1876	1891	1985
20{18}*	Gallilee	Galilee	------	------
	Philipians	Philippians	------	------
	always have,	------	always have attended,	------
	every other necessary	every necessary	------	------

---

* Numbers in braces are erroneous paragraph numbers used in the 1835 edition.

Discussions
of the
Lectures on Faith

What Faith Is

Dennis F. Rasmussen

I first met the Lectures on Faith twenty-five years ago as a young missionary. I have returned to them often since. I have learned that to understand the Lectures on Faith we must be prepared to read and to ponder them prayerfully. We must seek to trace out their latent ideas. We must be patient. By sincere searching we may gain more and more of the deep wisdom they offer us.

The first lecture announces the three-fold division of the lectures taken together: Lecture 1 concerns the nature of faith; Lectures 2 through 6, the object of faith; and Lecture 7, the effects of faith. The first lecture introduces the topic and lays a basis for what follows. The later lectures expand and clarify the teaching of the first. My purpose is to provide some reflections concerning Lecture 1, which treats faith in its most general sense. To speak of faith in general, without reference to its object or effects, is to give but a preliminary and partial account. The teachings of the other lectures are essential to a proper understanding of the first lecture, for the part cannot be grasped without the whole. But the whole cannot be presented all at once. So the diligent student of the Lectures on Faith must read them all many times. Only in the course of this kind of study will their comprehensive unity and meaning become clear.

What, then, is faith? Lecture 1 quotes Hebrews 11:1, adding the word "assurance": "Now faith is the substance [assurance] of things hoped for, the evidence of things not seen"

(LF 1:8). In other words, faith sustains hope for things not yet obtained and grants assurance that they will be. What is the practical import of this assurance? What is the nature of faith? The lecture affirms that faith is "the principle of action in all intelligent beings" (LF 1:9). These few words provide a new viewpoint from which to study the nature of faith.

We may approach this viewpoint in terms of hope. Hope is confidence in the future, the time when the things not yet seen will appear. Hope, then, requires an awareness of time and a power to conceive what has not yet occurred. We say "tomorrow" or "next week" or "next year," and often fail to note the marvel: we can speak and think about what has not yet happened and does not yet exist. All the world is immersed in time, but only intelligent beings understand this, and they alone can hope. This power to look forward to the future is two-sided. We may face the future with hope but also with fear. Those creatures that cannot conceive the future as we can do not share our plans and purposes, but neither do they bear our worries and cares. To be filled with hopeless thoughts of the morrow is surely more painful than to have no awareness of the future at all.

But human beings do face the future, an unknown yet all-embracing realm toward which and into which every path of life leads. By means of our power to consider the future, we may introduce purpose and aim into the course of our lives. We may, if we will, guide our lives by thoughtfulness and hope. But hope alone is not enough. Faith gives confidence or assurance to hope that it can find the things it seeks. By giving assurance concerning the future, faith helps us to plan our present actions with an eye to the future. Faith sustains our imagination and strengthens our will. For faith is the principle of action. This means that faith is the beginning or origin of action. Because we are intelligent beings who possess faith as well as hope, the things we seek in the future can affect our present plans. These plans, when faith puts them into action, can in turn help to secure what we seek. As the very "substance of things hoped for," faith thus makes genuine hope possible. We may, perhaps, believe we can do something without hoping to do it. But we cannot hope to do something without believing we are able to do it. In the words of Mormon, "without faith there cannot be any hope" (Moroni 7:42).

We not only consider the future but also remember the past —both our own and that of others. The past contains the lessons mankind has learned. We ignore it at great risk. But of the two, past and future, the future must be regarded as the more vital. The idea of progress, so important in the gospel and in Western civilization where Christianity took root, is clearly a product of faith and hope. We keep the ideal of progress vivid and strong when we seek to go forward and do better than we have. If ever we begin to think more about past deeds than about future deeds, then progress has ceased to beckon us. But though we look to the future, we live in the present, which is the time for action, the day, as scripture says, in which our labors are to be performed (see Alma 34:32-33).

What, then, is action? An action occurs when an intelligent being living in a world of time carries out a choice or plan first conceived in his mind. The idea precedes the act. Even actions performed by habit, which seem to involve no aim, were not always so. They were once subject to choice, and they became habits by choice, even if the choice was simply a passive refusal to prevent them. To choose something actively means to pursue it as an end to be achieved in the future, even if that future reaches no further ahead of the present than a brief moment. An action is voluntary, chosen, done on purpose. The aims of actions may vary, but every action has an aim, some result intended. Because faith is the principle of action, action has faith as its source. Action is faith at work; without faith, there would be no action. In the words of the first lecture,

> If men were duly to consider themselves and turn their thoughts and reflections to the operations of their own minds, they would readily discover that it is faith, and faith only, which is the moving cause of all action in them; that without it both mind and body would be in a state of inactivity, and all their exertions would cease, both physical and mental (LF 1:10).

Faith, then, "is not only the principle of action, it is also the principle of power in all intelligent beings, whether in heaven or on earth" (LF 1:13). These words imply that even God himself acts by faith, and the lecture goes on to assert that

> we understand that the principle of power which existed in the bosom of God, by which he framed the worlds, was faith; and that it is by reason of this principle of power existing in the Deity that all created things exist; so that all things in heaven, on earth, or under the earth exist by reason of faith as it existed in him (LF 1:15).

Modern revelation declares that "the glory of God is intelligence" (D&C 93:36). The first lecture teaches that faith is the principle and power of intelligence in action. Insofar, then, as man is an intelligent being who acts by the principle of faith within him, he partakes of a divine principle. When God gave man dominion over the earth, he did so because man, as an intelligent being, had the power to act by faith, and thus to act like God. Man's task, within the sphere of his stewardship, is to continue the work of creation by the principle of faith, shaping the future in accordance with this principle.

In the foregoing I have tried to give an account of the teaching of the first lecture on faith. I want now to turn to what I called at the beginning its latent ideas about faith. In other words, I wish to discuss some of the ideas that seem to follow from the first lecture. We have seen that faith is "the principle of action in all intelligent beings." Faith prompts them to plan, to prepare, and then to act so as to obtain some purpose or end which lies yet in the future. But what end? Intelligent beings are equipped by the principle of faith with power to act and hence to realize the ends they hope for. Is there any final or ultimate end toward which all their actions ought to aim? Is one end just as much worth pursuing as any other, or, among all the ends which intelligent beings might imagine and pursue, is there one that includes all others? Is there some end that is proper for man to seek? The great thinkers of the ages have combined in agreement with the rest of mankind in their answer. All have answered, yes. There is an ultimate end for which all men naturally search. Its name is happiness. The right of men to pursue happiness is one of three rights called "inalienable" in the Declaration of Independence.

What is happiness? Here the agreement which answered the former question vanishes. Who could count the multitude of answers to the question, what is happiness? But is it not strange that there should be agreement about the name for man's highest end and none about its content? Some people today answer, no. They see nothing strange at all in this, and they encourage what they sometimes refer to as alternative experiments in living. They urge each man to find his happiness as he will, alleging that as men differ, so should their aims. All around us we find people who seem to believe such ideas, people crisscrossing the human landscape in every direction seeking their own kind of happiness. Unheard or unheeded are those who warn that most of these paths will lead to a wrong and bitter end. Unstudied is the gospel teaching that speaks of a strait gate and a narrow way. But the fact remains, happiness is not whatever anyone chooses to call it. Happiness is not wherever anyone tries to find it. Real happiness has its own unchanging nature, and the wise, at least, remain agreed on what it is. In the words of Aristotle, written over 2,300 years ago, happiness is "an activity of soul in accordance with virtue" (I:vii). This idea will sound familiar to Latter-day Saints, who believe in being virtuous, and who read in the Book of Mormon that life should be guided by "the great plan of happiness," and that "wickedness never was happiness" (Alma 42:8; 41:10). I want for a moment to emphasize just the first part of Aristotle's statement, because it too should be familiar to Latter-day Saints, and also because it can shed light on one of the profound ideas latent in the first lecture. Aristotle says that happiness is an activity. This means that happiness is not the sort of end that can be obtained and held. It is an end that literally must be lived; it is the highest kind of existence, the highest way of living for human beings.

We know from the teachings of Lehi that there are two kinds of beings, those that act and those that are acted upon

(2 Nephi 2:14). Man is a being who acts. He acts by faith, which is the principle of action within him. The final aim of all his action is happiness. But as Aristotle saw, happiness is not an object, not a thing to be acted upon, not something to be kept, hoarded, or defended against thieves. Happiness is activity. How could it be otherwise and still be a proper end for a being whose nature is to act? But happiness is not just any activity. It is "an activity of soul in accordance with virtue." Joseph Smith said almost the same thing: "Happiness is the object and design of our existence; and will be the end thereof, if we pursue the path that leads to it; and this path is virtue, uprightness, faithfulness, holiness, and keeping all the commandments of God" (*Teachings of the Prophet Joseph Smith* 255-256). In agreement with Aristotle, the Prophet taught that happiness can be achieved only through virtuous action. Drawing upon revelation as well as reason, he could give a fuller account of such action than the ancient philosopher could. But both men understood that happiness is man's highest end and that it depends on acting in the proper way.

The next question to be raised is how do we show that we are truly acting in accordance with virtue? What will indicate that our actions are right, so that we may look back and say with Nephi that "we lived after the manner of happiness" (2 Nephi 5:27)? Because faith is the principle of action, its presence will only be disclosed in some action. It shows itself in the deed. Imagine a very young boy at play. You can see by looking that he is small, that his hair is brown, that his eyes are blue. But can even the keenest eye tell by looking whether or not he can walk? No, because an ability or power cannot be seen or discovered in advance of the action in which it displays itself. So, too, faith is revealed in the action that it calls forth. Prior to that action, faith, like ability, remains hidden and unused. It exists as a capacity, as a potential action. It is there—it can be used or put to work—but that will require action.

In our actions we not only show others our faith, but we show it to ourselves as well. Returning for a moment to the young child, he himself does not know he can walk until he actually does. His power to walk is revealed to him too at the moment of action. But faith is more than an optimistic state of mind or a good feeling or a warm sense of security; it is the beginning of action; it is the power to act. As such it can never be found just by looking within. It cannot be found by looking at all. It can only be found by acting, because it only displays itself in action. The real test of our faith is how we act. There is deep wisdom, then, in a familiar idiom of Latter-day Saints. When we want to speak of someone's religious commitment, we do not usually say he is pious or observant or devout. Instead we say he is faithful, or, more commonly, we say he is *active*. A faithful member of the Church *is an active member*, because faith is the principle of action. Faith finally reveals itself in action and nowhere else. The Apostle James was being ironic when he wrote, "shew me thy faith without thy works." In fact, this is impossible. Everyone, like James, must say, if there be any doubt about it, "I will shew thee my faith by my works" (James 2:18).

The words of Aristotle speak of happiness as an activity of the soul. The soul, of course, directs the body, and thus far I have mentioned only activities that might be called physical or external. But there is an internal or mental activity of the soul that must also be mentioned if we are to understand correctly and fully what faith is. I will return to this inward work of faith after treating some other matters first.

I have said that we show our faith even to ourselves by our works. This should give both assurance and reassurance to those who are sometimes inclined to reflect or even to doubt. As faith is the principle of action, so the opposite of faith, which we usually call doubt, is the principle of inaction. Faith is not just a state of mind; doubt is not just a state of mind either. In the end it matters little what kind of reluctance I may happen to feel. What does matter is how I act. However uncomfortable it may be, a feeling of bewilderment or uncertainty, which may occasionally trouble the best of us, is no reliable measure of our faith or lack of it. The real measure is always the same. As King Benjamin taught, "if you believe all these things see that ye do them" (Mosiah 4:10). Turning this statement around, we may also say, if you do all these things, see (or recognize or acknowledge to yourself) that ye believe them. We need to trust what our own good deeds tell us about ourselves. The unexpected and amazed hero, after the crisis has passed, may truly say, "I can't believe I did it." The fact remains that he did. And he did because he could, even though he did not know it until the need of the moment led him to draw on a source of action deep within himself, a source whose full strength he had never before measured. None of us really knows in advance how much he can do. So we can rarely, if ever, say with complete certainty, "I did my best."

"Faith is the principle of action in all intelligent beings." Does it follow that faith is the principle of *all* their actions? If so, shall we be forced to say that faith leads to evil actions as well as good ones? To answer these questions we need to consider more closely what it means to be intelligent in the scriptural sense of this word.

Because intelligence, as scripture says, is identical with light and truth, it seeks these in all things (see D&C 93:36; 88:40). To be intelligent also includes insight into the rational ordering of things. It includes an understanding of logical structures, causes and effects, laws, and principles. But most of all, intelligence always embraces what is true, just, and virtuous. In matters of conduct it looks for the right way to join means and ends. It wants to choose what is good in its quest for happiness. Now faith in its widest possible sense is the principle of all actions of all intelligent beings, but only to the degree that these actions are truly intelligent and do in fact seek light and truth. Unfortunately, an intelligent being is capable of acting in unintelligent ways. He is capable of willfully rebelling against his own intelligence and following something else instead—appetite, passion, whim, momentary desire, and, at the extreme, evil itself. But when he does this, he no longer acts by means of the principle of faith as an intelligent being. To the degree that anyone seeks evil, he loses, to that same degree, his intelligence, for "light and truth forsake that evil one" (D&C 93:37). Anyone bereft of intelligence because he prefers darkness to light can have no faith by which to act, but only a degenerate desire that will lead finally not to happiness but to hell. If for a time he may claim to "take happiness in sin," the time will be short, and the illusory happiness will quickly turn, in Mormon's terrible words, into the "sorrowing of the damned" (Mormon 2:13).

Insofar as intelligence governs someone, he will seek by faith to obtain his highest end, which is happiness. Now since happiness is "an activity of soul in accordance with virtue," not just acting, but acting in a certain way is required for happiness. We perform the actions that will finally yield happiness only by choosing first to follow virtue. In the words of the 18th-century philosopher Immanuel Kant, "virtue (as the worthiness to be happy) is the supreme condition . . . of all our pursuit of happiness" (Book II:II). Only the virtuous, only those who seek the good, only those who keep God's commandments are worthy of happiness. And only those who are worthy of happiness can achieve it. This is not because God or anyone else would seek to withhold it, but because happiness is "an activity of soul in accordance with virtue." Happiness is not something which another can give or take away. Neither is it something that can be achieved when sought directly and solely for itself. It only comes when its proper condition is met. That condition is virtue. Happiness requires, happiness *is* a virtuous or moral way of acting. Everyone finally decides for himself, by how he acts throughout his life, whether or not he will be happy. Only the worthy can be, and only the worthy will be.

To the early Christians the apostle Peter declared, "add to your faith virtue" (2 Peter 1:5). We now need to clarify just how faith helps us develop virtue or the moral worthiness that is the condition of all true happiness. Faith, as the principle of activity, looks to the future. The future is a realm of ends, but some of them exclude each other. An action that will achieve one end, such as traveling, excludes another, that of staying home instead. In facing the future, then, faith is always confronted with choices.

It must seek one end or another, but it cannot seek all ends. And even though it sets for itself as its highest end the achievement of happiness, faith must still choose among various particular actions. But how can faith be sure it will choose the right one? Not knowing in advance all that an action involves, but hoping to reach happiness, how can faith choose wisely?

When we ponder this question, we see that faith needs something more than its highest end, happiness, to guide its choices and actions. Without in any way renouncing happiness as our daily and also our eternal goal, we see that by itself happiness is not a sure guide. We do not always clearly know in advance what will make us happy. We can look forward to the new day or to the distant future, hoping it will reward our search for happiness, but how it will do this lies beyond our own unaided powers. We cannot, then, act wisely upon the basis of what we think the future will bring. Neither can we follow those who advise us to forget the future and live only in the present, savoring its delights while we can. Were we to try this, we would soon find that all our actions have consequences, whether or not we intend them or seek to ignore them. Though we try not to look beyond the moment, our actions will carry us beyond it, and soon cause us to wish we had looked and considered what might follow from what we did. But even if we had, we still might have missed our aim. We cannot by ourselves foretell the future. And so we need to guide our lives by reference to something other than the happiness we hope to attain.

"Faith is the principle of action in all intelligent beings," and its final end is happiness. The immediate guide for faith, however, is not happiness, but virtue or worthiness to be happy. Such worthiness means, as we have seen, uprightness, goodness, holiness, obedience to God's commandments. So we must give up happiness as our direct end if we are to attain it as our final end. Like many other worthwhile things, happiness cannot be obtained as a direct end. Earning a diploma, mastering a skill, building a house, raising a child—these are worthy ends, but each one follows from certain kinds of activities and cannot be achieved except by means of those activities. To obtain the end we must undertake the proper activity, because the end cannot be separated from that activity. The end cannot be had directly, but it will follow if we do our work well. So faith understands those earnest words, "Do what is right; let the consequence follow" (*Hymns* #237). It is not for us to foretell the precise arrangement of things yet future. It is for us each day to follow steadfastly the guidance of virtue, full of hope and faith that as we do, as we make ourselves worthy of happiness, that end will follow. Faith gives us confidence that virtuous conduct and happiness can never long be kept apart. But for now, during the moment at hand, faith repeats the message of the Preacher, "Fear God, and keep his commandments: for this is the whole duty of man" (Eccl 12:13).

At its highest level faith as the principle of action thus becomes the principle of duty to keep the commandments of God. These have been given to us. We know what they require, we know how to obey them. The commandments give us what we need: a constant and ever-present standard by which to guide our lives. And as we seek to obey them, our faith once again supports our hope. Anyone who has a sense of duty to keep the commandments also has hope that duty can, indeed, be done. It would be pointless to speak of a duty that bids us to do what we cannot do. What we ought to do we can do, in spite of all appearances to the contrary. Such faith and hope sustained young Nephi as he said, "I will go and do the things which the Lord hath commanded, for I know that the Lord giveth no commandments unto the children of men, save he shall prepare a way for them that they may accomplish the thing which he commandeth them" (1 Nephi 3:7).

Some observers have claimed that a life of duty and virtue limits men and hampers their spontaneous powers. They bid men to leave their fetters behind and to follow their natural inclinations. But faith regarded as the call to virtue, to duty, to keeping the commandments, does not limit or bind us. It liberates our power to act. Alone and unguided, we all too often defeat our own best plans because we are divided against ourselves. We are halfhearted, torn by conflicting impulses. Undisciplined spontaneity only scatters and wastes our lives. But duty calls in an urgent voice that demands a response from our whole being. When heeded it gathers and magnifies all our powers like a lens focusing the rays of the sun. Nothing else can create the intensity of life that obedience to duty can. Such willingness to obey fills the soul with strength and allows the pure principle of faith to guide its course. Latter-day Saints, of all people, know first-hand what men and women filled with the spirit of obedience to duty can achieve. Our history is replete with examples of those whose faith became invincible because they never doubted that they could do what they were commanded to do.

When we think of action, we think first of outward deeds that can be seen, and up to this point I have sought to clarify the nature of faith in terms of such deeds. Emphasis on the outward deed prevents us from substituting mere good wishes for actual performance. It reminds us that we are not pure spirits but embodied spirits, and that we must teach our bodies as well as our hearts to be kind, our lips as well as our thoughts to be clean.

We have seen that faith never demands anything less than external acts or works. But it always demands something more. Important as outward works may be, they remain outward expressions of another, inward way of working. The inward works of faith are the true source and soul of all the outward works. For as a man "thinketh in his heart, so is he" (Prov 23:7). "What are we to understand by a man's working by faith?" asks Lecture 7. "We answer: we understand that when a man works by faith he works by mental exertion instead of physical force" (LF 7:3).

What does this mean? In what sense does faith involve a kind of inward action and how is this action related to outward deeds? Human faith as we encounter it in our everyday lives may be compared to art. We often use the phrase "work of art," as when we say, "that is a beautiful work of art." When we speak in this way we are describing something which is the result of external action. But what are we saying about it? We are saying that the object embodies a particular kind of action. What kind?

An action governed or directed by art. In other words, we are saying that the object has in some way captured what we might call art at work.

Now where does art dwell in the first place? Not in an object, but in an artist. Art is first of all a principle within an artist that guides him in fashioning an external object so as to embody in it his art. We often call the principle of art that some people have a gift. But it is not a visible thing, and there is a sense in which it possesses the artist just as much as he possesses it. Art acts within the artist as his master, an inward voice that guides and disciplines his outward work. Truly speaking, a man does not paint with his hand but with his soul. The brush, the palette, the hand, the body—these are all tools directed by the inward working of the artist's soul in accordance with his art. So the work of art is first of all an inward activity that later expresses itself in some outward object. No outward work of art, no object to delight the eye or ear, can be created unless that object emerges from a prior inward work of art, from the labor of the soul.

Now let us turn from the work of art to the work of faith. Whatever the specific outward action may be, the work of faith has its origin, like the work of art, in the principle that dwells and works within. The work of faith, like the work of art, begins in the soul. Faith as the principle of outer action is first of all the principle of inner action that provides the basis for the outward one. This fact needs to be remembered and constantly emphasized in an age such as ours, which tends so much to prize tangible results and observable consequences. The point is not that these are unimportant but that in order to have real worth they must follow from a virtuous inward action of the soul that intended them. That is why Aristotle spoke of happiness not just as an activity of the body, but as an activity of the soul in accordance with virtue. This virtuous inward activity is the "real intent" spoken of by Moroni: "For behold, God hath said a man being evil cannot do that which is good; for if he offereth a gift, or prayeth unto God, except he shall do it with real intent it profiteth him nothing" (Moroni 7:6). Inward acting, real intending, is the means by which we first seek the kingdom of God and his righteousness. It is a solitary task. It requires concern for matters that perhaps few others care about. It demands obedience to a rule of life that may not always or even often yield immediate outward benefits. It calls for commitments that reach far beyond what any counsel of mere prudence or common sense could recommend.

As a single example of the kind of commitment made by this inward activity of the soul in accordance with virtue, think of the act of promising. Only intelligent beings, beings capable of faith, can make a promise. But what is a promise? A promise is more than a spoken utterance and more than a written agreement, though these external things may manifest it. First and foremost, a promise is a self-chosen act of will that remains fixed and unchanging over a span of time reaching into the future. Some promises, such as legal contracts, have a specified period of duration. Other promises, such as those we call sacred covenants, have no temporal limit. They reach out into the future forever. How much faith and hope does it take to make and then to keep such covenants? When people make unbreakable covenants, they perform the ultimate act of faith. The principle of faith working within them rises far above all merely human considerations of circumstance, risk, and reward, and reveals what the English poet Gerard Manley Hopkins called "true virtue . . . that chastity of mind which seems to lie at the very heart and be the parent of all other good, the seeing at once what is best, the holding to that, and then of not allowing anything else whatever to be even heard pleading to the contrary" (406).

In a world filled with uncertain outcomes and merely provisional commitments, only being true to covenants, only keeping faith, can lift the soul beyond the reach of doubt and worry and lead it to the source of perfect confidence which is God. Before us all lies a journey that began at our birth and will go on till our death. We live in the time between and act each day as best we can. Some days bring gladness; others force upon us heavy burdens. At times we may question how our path can lead to happiness or if our faith has reached its limit. We know that strength is gained in struggles; we wonder if we can survive on our own. But so long as we seek to do good, so long as we choose the right, deep within us our faith is working, and our hope still lives. Let us believe this. Let us then continue to act as duty bids. As we do, our faith will be sufficient, and our happiness will be assured.

BIBLIOGRAPHY

Aristotle. *The Ethics of Aristotle: The Nicomachean Ethics*. Trans. J. A. K. Thomson. Rev. ed. New York: Penguin Books, 1976.

Hopkins, Gerard Manley. *A Hopkins Reader*. Ed. John Pick. Garden City, NY: Image Books, 1966.

Hymns. Salt Lake City: The Church of Jesus Christ of Latter-day Saints, 1985.

Kant, Immanuel. *Critique of Practical Reason*. Ed. and trans. Lewis White Beck. Chicago: Univ of Chicago, 1949.

Teachings of the Prophet Joseph Smith. Comp. Joseph Fielding Smith. Salt Lake City: Deseret Book, 1976.

Dennis F. Rasmussen is associate professor of Philosophy at Brigham Young University.

Chosen Vessels and the Order of the Priesthood

Joseph Fielding McConkie

*I*t is of God we speak and how one comes to know him. The subject commands attention. There is no knowledge of greater importance. Surely there is no salvation to be found in the worship of false gods. Certainly no benefit can accrue from spurious or delusive doctrine. Even that which is innocently ignorant is without the power to bless. Sincerity, however pure it may be, cannot remit sins, raise the dead, or create a celestial kingdom. Salvation is not the child of darkness, it is not the child of stern and heartless justice, nor is it the child of indulgent and intemperate mercy. Christ addressed the issue in his intercessory prayer: "*And this is life eternal,*" he said, "*that they might know thee the only true God, and Jesus Christ, whom thou hast sent*" (John 17:3; emphasis added). The bloodline must be pure—eternal life can only be the offspring of eternal truth.

Anciently it was said that all roads led to Rome. It was equally true that there was only one entrance to the Holy of Holies. This is true in spiritual matters as well. There is one path to exaltation. What is it? How then are we to approach the true and living God? What is the system that the heavens have ordained whereby we are to obtain a sure knowledge of the plan of salvation? Such are the questions to which the Prophet responds in the second lecture on faith.

179

My purpose here is to follow Joseph Smith's lead. Having become a perfect witness of God the Father and his Son, Jesus Christ, the Prophet proceeds to show us the way whereby we too can share that same knowledge. How fitting it is that Joseph Smith himself is the crowning example of the principle that he taught in the School of the Elders. He is God's witness, and it is through his testimony that we are encouraged to seek God's divine presence. Such is the system. We learn of God from those who know him (LF 2:35). If there were none who knew of God, if we had no testimonies of him, we would have little inclination to seek after him. It is because of the testimony of one who knows him that we seek to know him. Initially, we are all dependent on someone else's testimony. Thus, we grow spiritually as we do physically; both body and spirit are born dependant, both require careful nurturing, both are intended to grow to a state of maturity and independence, and then both are expected to assume a parenting role to others that the process may begin anew. All who obtain a knowledge of saving truths, a knowledge of God and his plan for the salvation of his children, have that knowledge because of the goodness and grace of others and therefore assume the obligation to extend that blessing to as many as they properly can.

Adam: Earth's First Apostle

It was not intended that man dwell in darkness. Long before the first of our race was placed upon the earth the Lord had given the command: "Let there be light" (Gen 1:3). Nor was it intended that Adam wander in doubt or uncertainty relative to the nature and purpose of his creation or to whom he was answerable for his conduct. "God conversed with him face to face: in his presence he was permitted to stand, and from his own mouth he was permitted to receive instruction. He heard his voice, walked before him, and gazed upon his glory, while intelligence burst upon his understanding and enabled him to give names to the vast assemblage of his Maker's works" (LF 2:18).

Obviously Adam's transgression did not deprive him of the knowledge with which he had previously been endowed (LF 2:19). Upon hearing God's voice, Adam, knowing his shame, sought to hide himself. Nor did the expulsion of Adam and Eve from the Garden of the Divine Presence bring an end to communion with their Father (LF 2:20). Their circumstance in the lone and dreary world immediately evoked the desire for divine assistance. Nor did their prayers go unheeded, for we read,

> and they heard the voice of the Lord from the way toward the Garden of Eden, speaking unto them, and they saw him not; for they were shut out from his presence. And he gave unto them commandments, that they should worship the Lord their God, and should offer the firstlings of their flocks, for an offering unto the Lord. And Adam was obedient unto the commandments of the Lord. And after many days, an angel of the Lord appeared unto Adam, saying, Why dost thou offer sacrifices unto the Lord? And Adam said unto him: I know not, save the Lord commanded me. And then the angel spake, saying, This thing is a similitude of the sacrifice of the Only Begotten of the Father, which is full of grace and truth. Wherefore, thou shalt do all that thou doest in the name of the Son, and thou shalt repent, and call upon God, in the name of the Son forevermore. And in that day, the Holy Ghost fell upon Adam, which beareth record of the Father and the Son (Moses 5:4-9).

The quotation clearly establishes two points: first, the Fall did not cause Adam and Eve to lose their knowledge of God; and second, "no sooner was the plan of redemption revealed to man and he began to call upon God, than the Holy Spirit was given, bearing record of the Father and Son" (LF 2:25). How then did the family of Adam obtain a knowledge of God? Adam and Eve communicated that knowledge to them (LF 2:31). How did Adam and Eve obtain that knowledge? God manifested himself to them in the Garden and he continued to speak to them after their transgression and expulsion from Eden (LF 2:30). Thus it was for Adam and Eve, as special witnesses, to plant the first seeds of testimony in the hearts of their children and their children's children for many generations. Thus man learned to have faith in God after the Fall.

Adam and Eve establish the pattern to be followed in all subsequent dispensations and in all generations. This pattern is that the posterity of Adam in all ages first learn of God or have the seeds of faith planted in their hearts by special witnesses chosen of God for that purpose. It is for one man to plant the seed in the heart of another. Most properly it is for parents to plant the seed in the hearts of their children, for previous to the time that any of "Adam's posterity had obtained a manifestation of God to themselves, Adam, their common father, had testified unto them of the existence of God and of his eternal power and Godhead" (LF 2:35).

Thus the whole human family partakes of the fruit of the tree of faith because father Adam planted the tree. Each dispensation in its turn has had its special witness or witnesses—its "Adams"—but in all cases it has been "human testimony, and human testimony only," that motivated man's initial investigation concerning God. It has been the belief exercised in "the testimony of their fathers," that aroused their minds to "inquire after the knowledge of God. That inquiry frequently terminated, indeed always terminated when rightly pursued, in the most glorious discoveries and eternal certainty" (LF 2:56).

Though one may plant the seed in the heart of another, each must nourish the seed for himself. The Prophet said

> that after any members of the human family are made acquainted with the important fact that there is a God who has created and does uphold all things, the extent of their knowledge respecting his character and glory will depend upon their diligence and faithfulness in seeking after him, until, like Enoch, the brother of Jared, and Moses, they shall obtain faith in God and power with him to behold him face to face (LF 2:55).

Chosen Vessels

"Thus the Gospel began to be preached, from the beginning, being declared by holy angels sent forth from the presence of God, and by his own voice, and by the gift of the Holy Ghost" (Moses 5:58; see LF 2:24, 30). Adam and his posterity had no reason to be in doubt as to the nature of that being in whom they were to exercise faith or as to what God expected of them. It is recorded that "all things were confirmed unto Adam, by an holy ordinance, and the Gospel preached, and a decree sent forth, that it should be in the world, until the end thereof" (Moses 5:58-59; LF 2:33-36). Further, we are told that the "same Priesthood, which was in the beginning, shall be in the end of the world also" (Moses 6:7). Adam, then, is the pattern; his dispensation the example; and the order or system of heaven is everlastingly the same.

Mormon testified,

> Wherefore, by the ministering of angels, and by every word which proceeded forth out of the mouth of God, men began to exercise faith in Christ; and thus by faith, they did lay hold upon every good thing; and thus it was until the coming of Christ. And after that he came men also were saved by faith in his name; and by faith, they became the sons of God (Moroni 7:25-26).

As to the matter of who it is the angels appear to, Mormon explained that they manifest themselves to "chosen vessels," teaching them the "word of Christ," so that those chosen ones can in turn bear testimony to all others.

> And the office of their ministry is to call men to repentance . . . by declaring the word of Christ unto the chosen vessels of the Lord, that they may bear testimony of him. And by so doing, the Lord God prepareth the way that the residue of men may have faith in Christ, that the Holy Ghost may have place in their hearts, according to the power thereof; and after this manner bringeth to pass the Father, the covenants which he hath made unto the children of men (Moroni 7:31-32).

Lecture 2 shows how Adam taught his descendants and they taught theirs, all the way to Abraham (LF 2:37-53). Let us look at our dispensation to find a similar example. With the appearance of that God known to Adam in Eden and his Only Begotten Son, our Lord and Savior Jesus Christ, to the youthful Joseph Smith, a dispensation was born. Though only a boy fourteen years of age, Joseph Smith then knew more about God and the truths of salvation than any other man on earth. He was earth's most competent witness on the nature and purposes of God. No other man could bear the testimony he bore, for he alone had stood in the divine presence. He was the vessel chosen in heaven from which the truths of salvation were again to be poured out to the generality of mankind.

When we speak of dispensations, as Elder Bruce R. McConkie explained, we speak

> of those designated portions of the earth's history when the Lord, through one man, gives his word to the whole world and makes all the prophets, and all the seers, and all the administrators, and all the apostles of that period subject to, and exponents of, what came through that individual. . . . Every prophet is a witness of Christ; every dispensation head is a revealer of Christ for his day; and every other prophet or apostle who comes is a reflection and an echo and an exponent of the dispensation head. All such come to echo to the world and to expound and unfold what God has revealed through the man who was appointed for that era to give his eternal word to the world. Such is the dispensation concept ("This Generation" 4-5).

Thus when we find the Lord saying to Joseph Smith, "this generation shall have my word through you" (D&C 5:10), he means our dispensation,[1] the period from the First Vision to the Second Coming. "Shall" means "must"; it is mandatory, it is the bold assertion that there are no options. You accept Joseph Smith's testimony or you are damned. "My word" means the

---

[1]The word "generation" is used with a wide range of meanings in the scriptures. For instance, it is used to describe an indeterminate period or age, as in the declaration that the priesthood is found in the Church "in all generations" (D&C 84:17), or in the Savior's statement that it is a "wicked and adulterous generation [that] seeketh after a sign" (Matthew 16:4). Similarly, it is used as a synonym for a dispensation, as in the statement that the Book of Mormon is given to prove that God will call prophets in this "age and generation, as well as in generations of old" (D&C 20:11). By contrast it is also used to describe more limited periods, for instance, the time necessary for children to grow to maturity and have offspring of their own (see D&C 98:28).

The question in the present text is how it can confidently be asserted that "generation" is being used as a synonym for "dispensation," when it is used with a different meaning in the previous verse. Such an interpretation conforms to a significant number of other texts. For instance, a revelation given on the day the Church was organized directed its members to "give heed" to all of Joseph Smith's words with the promise that the gates of hell will have no power over those who do so and cause the heavens to shake for their good (D&C 21:6-7). Indeed, we are told that we are to declare the things revealed to Joseph Smith for they are "glad tidings of great joy unto this generation" (D&C 31:3), obviously meaning dispensation.

"gospel of salvation; the word is the plan of salvation; the word is the mind and will and purposes of the Lord as pertaining to his children on earth; the word is all the truths and rights and powers and doctrines and principles that are needed by men so they can take the souls they possess and transform them into the kind of souls that can go where God and Christ are" (McConkie, "This Generation" 3).

Revelation is in no way limited only to the Prophet Joseph Smith, who was called to stand as the dispensation head. Our faith embraces "all that God has revealed, all that He does now reveal" and the promise that "He will yet reveal many great and important things pertaining to the Kingdom of God" (A of F #9). Classic illustrations include Joseph F. Smith's vision of the redemption of the dead (D&C 138) and Spencer W. Kimball's revelation extending the privilege of the priesthood and the temple to those of all races (OD #2). Yet, it was for Joseph Smith to lay the theological foundations of the Restored Church. He was the chosen vessel to whom the angels appeared to restore every key and power and authority necessary for men to work out their salvation and obtain their eternal inheritance. The revelations that came after the ministry of Joseph Smith, came to other chosen vessels to amplify, to expound, and to expand upon that which he received. No such revelations are ever given to those who have rejected the testimony of the dispensation head.

In our day the faithful Latter-day Saint stands in fast and testimony meeting and testifies that God lives, that Jesus is the Christ, that Joseph Smith is the great prophet of the Restoration, that whoever is presiding over the Church at the time is his lawful successor, and that this is the only true and living Church on the face of the whole earth. Had we attended a testimony meeting in the days of Adam, Enoch, Noah, or any of the other gospel dispensations, the nature of the testimonies would have been essentially the same. In Adam's day, for example, we might have listened to a testimony to this effect: "I know that God lives, that he will yet have a Son in the flesh who will work out an atoning sacrifice and thereby redeem us from the effects of the Fall. I know that Adam is the chosen vessel of the Lord, the one called and ordained to stand at the head of the Church in this dispensation and reveal to us the laws and ordinances necessary for our salvation."

The Order of the Priesthood

Although the words "Priesthood" and "order" are not used in Lecture 2, it is clear that the transmittal of the gospel message from Adam to later generations was patterned and orderly (LF 2:43-44, 52-53). The gospel, that is the revealed knowledge of God and his plan for the salvation of his children, by its very nature bespeaks system and order. There is no disorder in the kingdom of heaven. God does not get confused, he does not forget, he is not the author of contention, his ways are not capricious, he does not act with irregularity, his kingdom is not one of disunity, disarray, or dishevelment. He is a God of order. Indeed, we have been told that "he hath given a law unto all things, by which they move in their times and their seasons; and their courses are fixed, even the courses of the heavens and the earth, which comprehend the earth and all the planets" (D&C 88:42-43). He has done all this that man might be taught the gospel. Are we then to suppose that God forgot to ordain a system whereby this would be done—a system that would allow all men in all ages equal opportunity to hear the message of salvation and lay claim to the blessings of heaven?

Surely the system whereby the message of salvation is to be declared must be worthy of the principles it espouses. It must be a system of order, consistency, and unity. It must be a system of God's ordination, not man's. Pure water cannot be housed in impure vessels. What then is the system that God has ordained by which his gospel is to be taught? The scriptures, as we shall see, respond with plainness.

In response to the question of how the gospel is to be taught, let me cite two classic scriptural texts—one from the Book of

Mormon, the other from the Doctrine and Covenants. Alma, in the conclusion of a marvelous discourse on how we obtain salvation, testified: "I have spoken unto you plainly that ye cannot err, or have spoken according to the commandments of God" (Alma 5:43). In that which preceded this verse, Alma had indeed spoken with considerable plainness. That those carrying the gospel message are to be plain and straightforward is obviously part of their commission, for Alma continues, "For I am called to speak after this manner, according to the holy order of God, which is in Christ Jesus" (Alma 5:44).

Note particularly the language Alma uses to identify his commission to preach—ie, "the holy order of God." This is a phrase that we read frequently in the Book of Mormon. It is interchangeable with the phrase "the order of his Son," and has reference to the Melchizedek Priesthood. The same phrase is used in the revelations of our dispensation as the Lord describes the nature of the priesthood to us. We also find it in the Old Testament to the extent that the purity of that record has been retained. Section 84 in the Doctrine and Covenants describes the Melchizedek Priesthood as "the holiest order of God," and then states that this holy priesthood is to administer the gospel (see 84:18-19). In the JST Genesis we read that Melchizedek, the very man after whom the priesthood was named, was first "approved of God" and then he was

> ordained an high priest after the *order* of the covenant which God made with Enoch, it being after the *order of the Son of God*; which *order* came, not by man, nor the will of man; neither by father nor mother; neither by beginning of days nor end of years; but of God; and it was delivered unto men by the calling of his own voice, according to his own will, unto as many as believed on his name (14:27-29; emphasis added).

In Section 107:3-4, we learn that anciently the priesthood

> was called *the Holy Priesthood, after the Order of the Son of God.* But out of respect or reverence to the name of the Supreme Being, to avoid the too frequent repetition of his name, they, the church . . . called that priesthood after Melchizedek" (emphasis in original).

Mechizedek's name was used because he "was such a great high priest" (v 2).

Now the thrust of all this is that the doctrine of "order" is inseparable from the functioning of the priesthood and that priesthood is inseparable from the declaration of the gospel. This is why we have Joseph Smith saying, "Where there is a prophet, a priest, or a righteous man unto whom God gives His oracles, there is the kingdom of God; and where the oracles of God are not, there the kingdom of God is not" (*Teachings of the Prophet Joseph Smith* 272; hereafter *TPJS*). Now he didn't say where one believer is, there is the kingdom of God also. It takes more than the conviction of one individual to comply with the heavenly ordained order whereby the gospel is to be taught. Thus the very name of the priesthood (ie, the Holy Order) stands as a refutation of the protestant concept of "priesthood of all believers," which is the idea that to accept Christ grants one the authority to act in his name.

Returning to our text in Alma, we read the prophet saying, "I am commanded to stand and testify unto this people the things which have been spoken by our fathers concerning the things which are to come" (5:44). His testimony is that he had been "called . . . according to the holy order of God" and that he was "commanded" to declare certain things—specifically that which had been spoken by the fathers, that is the things recorded in the scriptures. "And this is not all," he added.

> Do ye not suppose that I know of these things myself? Behold, I testify unto you that I do know that these things whereof I have spoken are true. And how do ye suppose that I know of their surety? Behold, I say unto you they are made known unto me by the Holy Spirit of God. Behold, I have fasted and prayed many days that I might know these things of myself. And now I do know of myself that they are true; for the Lord God hath made them manifest unto me by his Holy Spirit; and this is the spirit of revelation which is in me. And moreover, I say unto you that it has thus been revealed unto me, that the words which have been spoken by our fathers are true, even so according to the spirit of prophecy which is in me, which is also by the manifestation of the Spirit of God. I say unto you, that I know of myself that whatsoever I shall

say unto you, concerning that which is to come, is true (Alma 5:45-48).

Alma then testifies about the coming of Christ:

> And now I say unto you that this is the order after which I am called, yea, to preach unto my beloved brethren, yea, and every one that dwelleth in the land; yea, to preach unto all, both old and young, both bond and free; yea, I say unto you the aged, and also the middle aged, and the rising generation; yea, to cry unto them that they must repent and be born again (Alma 5:49).

In summary, Alma did not assume the right to preach; rather he was called and ordained to the "holy order." With that ordination came the commandment to preach with plainness. That which he preached was that which he learned from the testimony of the fathers—that is, the witness of the scriptures and that which had been revealed to him through his study of them. Thus he had the confirming revelation about what the fathers had taught and additional revelation that enabled him to expound and expand upon that which the chosen vessels of times past had recorded. In a subsequent chapter we read that Alma

> began to declare the word of God . . . according to the revelation of the truth of the word which had been spoken by his fathers, and according to the spirit of prophecy which was in him, according to the testimony of Jesus Christ, the Son of God . . . and the holy order by which he was called" (Alma 6:8; see also 8:4, 24).

Our second example is a revelation directed to a young elder by the name of Orson Hyde. It is important to note that this revelation was given some three and half years before Elder Hyde was called to the Apostleship. It announced that he was "called by his ordination [to the priesthood] to proclaim the everlasting gospel, by the Spirit of the living God." It further stated that he was to reason with those to whom he preached, "expounding all scriptures unto them" (D&C 68:1). Elder Hyde was then told to be an "ensample" (v 2), meaning he was to be the pattern or model for all others who held the same priesthood.

> And this is the ensample unto them, that they shall speak as they are moved upon by the Holy Ghost. And whatsoever they shall

speak when moved upon by the Holy Ghost shall be scripture, shall be the will of the Lord, shall be the mind of the Lord, shall be the word of the Lord, shall be the voice of the Lord, and the power of God unto salvation. Behold, this is the promise of the Lord unto you, O ye my servants (D&C 68:3-5).

The revelation then directs "all the faithful elders of [the] church" to be of good cheer, to preach without fear, and to testify of the Christ, and it states that the promises given therein are directed to them (vv 6-7).

This is what Alma called the holy order—that is, when men have been properly called to the priesthood and commissioned to go forth to teach, they are to do so from the scriptures (or as Alma said, the things spoken by the fathers). Then with the Holy Ghost, they will be granted the power to expand the written word and to add scripture to scripture. The principle is succinctly stated in a revelation instructing the early missionaries of this dispensation: "And let them journey from thence preaching the word by the way, saying none other things than that which the prophets and apostles have written, and that which is taught them by the Comforter through the prayer of faith" (D&C 52:9).

A modern Apostle articulated this principle in this very instructive language:

> Those who preach by the power of the Holy Ghost use the scriptures as their basic source of knowledge and doctrine. They begin with what the Lord has before revealed to other inspired men. But it is the practice of the Lord to give added knowledge to those upon whose hearts the true meaning and intents of the scriptures have been impressed. Many great doctrinal revelations come to those who preach from the scriptures. When they are in tune with the Infinite, the Lord lets them know, first, the full and complete meaning of the scriptures they are expounding, and then he ofttimes expands their views so that new truths flood in upon them, and they learn added things that those who do not follow such a course can never know (McConkie, *The Promised Messiah* 515-16).

We must keep all the commandments of God. "But," as Joseph Smith observed, "we cannot keep all the commandments without first knowing them, and we cannot expect to know all, or more than we now know unless we comply with or keep those we have already received" (*TPJS* 256). If we are to receive more and thus know more, we must master and live by what we have been given. We reduce the realm of the unknown, not by wandering in it, but rather by feasting on and expanding our knowledge of that which God has already revealed. Hence, we have the commandment to teach from the scriptures with the attendant promise that by so doing we will be granted understanding that goes beyond the written word. This is the reason the canon of scripture can never be complete. To argue for a closed canon is to defeat the very purpose of scripture, it is to contend with the Spirit of truth, and offend the Holy Ghost.

The Book of Mormon has been criticized because its prophets quote so frequently from Bible texts. Well of course they do. It is the holy order of God. It is the manner after which their prophets were commanded to preach. Only if they didn't do so could it be argued that the Book of Mormon was not authentic scripture. Those prophets whose teachings are recorded for us in the scriptures are our patterns; chief among them is Christ himself. He commenced his mortal ministry with a quotation from Isaiah (Luke 4:16-21), constantly quoted the scriptures in his teaching (Matthew 19:4; Mark 12:10), challenged his detractors to search the scriptures (John 5:39), and even in his appearances as a resurrected being continued to expound "in all the scriptures the things concerning himself" (Luke 24:27, 44-45).

While he was among the Nephites, the glorified Christ not only quoted Old World scriptures, including the words of Moses, Isaiah, Habakkuk, Micah, and Malachi, but he "expounded all the scriptures unto them which they had received" (3 Nephi 23:6). That is, he expounded their own Nephite scripture, then "expounded all the scriptures [both the New World and the Old World scripture] in one." And then he commanded them to "teach the things which he had expounded unto them" (3 Nephi 23:14). Thus the inspired pronouncements of the fathers kindle the spirit of revelation in the resurrected Christ who speaks new scripture to the Nephites. They in turn were to teach the words Christ has spoken to them. By so doing they came to know the spirit of revelation and were able to amplify what he taught. Thus the gospel goes forth in ever widening circles until that glorious day when it will fill the whole earth as the waters do the seas. This is the pattern, Christ is the classic example, and the manner in which the scriptural prophets teach illustrates it. When Amulek, for instance, wanted to support Alma's teaching that "the word is in Christ unto salvation," he noted that Alma had quoted the prophets Zenos, Zenock, and Moses, and then he said, "And now, behold, I will testify unto you of myself that these things are true" (Alma 34:5-8). Thus in compliance with the holy order he taught those things which had been manifest to him by the spirit of revelation. In our day we have the Doctrine and Covenants as the perfect illustration of this principle. In literally hundreds of instances the Doctrine and Covenants picks up a phrase from the Old or New Testament and amplifies on it. Many of these revelations grow out of Joseph Smith's work on the Bible, which we now call the Joseph Smith Translation. That is, as he labored over the meaning and intent of the words of the biblical fathers, the spirit of revelation unfolded that meaning to him in the form of additional scripture for our dispensation. Such is and ever has been the system—the holy order of God. This is the way it was with Adam and those who followed in his family down to Abraham as outlined in Lecture 2:35-53.

A Word of Caution

As we emphasize the fact that the gospel is to be taught by chosen vessels, there is a tendency to say that only one chosen vessel, the president of the Church, can interpret and expound scripture. Some contend that no one but the head of the Church should declare or write doctrine. Let us briefly consider the implications of such a notion. If, for instance, we are to state that no one but the president of the Church can write scripture or can speak to the whole Church, what are we to do with the New

Testament? Of its twenty-seven books, it can be argued that only those written by Peter and John were written by "the prophet"; and it is highly doubtful that the writings of John and Peter were all done while they presided over the Church. Be that as it may, certainly Matthew, Mark, and Luke never presided over the Church; yet, we have accepted their writings as scripture. Paul, of course, is the major contributor to the New Testament, generally credited with fourteen of its books. No one argues that Paul presided over the Church. The discussion as far as Paul is concerned is whether or not he was a member of the Quorum of the Twelve. It seems evident that he was, but there is no clear proof even of this. As to James and Jude, according to the standard suggested, they obviously had no business writing "general" epistles either. And be there no mistake about the fact that they intended their writings to go to all the world. James addressed his epistle "to the twelve tribes . . . scattered abroad" (1:1); Jude addressed himself to all who have been "called," and "sanctified" (1:1).

This is not to suggest that there was no discipline in the meridian Church relative to who could write and preach. Certainly there was. The house of God in every dispensation must be a house of order. The writings of both Paul and John indicate that all within the faith, both men and women, were entitled to the spirit of prophecy and revelation—indeed, they were expected to be prophets or prophetesses (See 1 Cor 14:29-32; Rev 19:10). The commonality of prophets among the congregations of the meridian Saints is seen in the frequent warnings against false prophets that would arise among their number (see Matt 7:15; 24:11; 2 Peter 2:1; 1 John 4:1). Though it was believed to be within the providence of all to prophesy, some were specifically identified as holding the office of a prophet in the ecclesiastical hierarchy of the Church (see 1 Cor 12:28-29; Eph 2:19-20; 4:11).

Paul's doctrine was that when Saints met together they were all to share the fruits of their spiritual gifts. One could come having written an inspired hymn, another with doctrinal understanding, another speaking in tongues, another to interpret, and still another with the spirit of revelation. "All things to be done unto edifying" (1 Cor 14:26). "For ye may all prophesy one by one," Paul declared, "that all may learn, and all may be comforted" (v 31) that "all may be edified of all" (D&C 84:110), or as another modern revelation states, "that every man may have an equal privilege" (D&C 88:122). "And the spirits of the prophets are subject to the prophets," Paul said (1 Cor 14:32). That is, the doctrine espoused by any who truly have the spirit of prophecy will be in harmony with that doctrine revealed through those whose office it is to officially establish the doctrines of the kingdom. By way of illustration, Paul's epistle is regarded as scripture. His office and calling as an Apostle granted him the right to speak as one having authority, as a chosen vessel, to the Corinthian Saints. In turn all the members of the church in Corinth were entitled to that same spirit of prophecy that they might edify one another. In doing so they would teach no doctrines that were out of harmony with the inspired counsel or holy writ they had already received. Still they neither individually nor collectively had the authority to write an epistle of instruction to Paul or to some other branch of the Church. Thus their spirit of prophecy and revelation was subject to the prophets, the chosen vessels, who had been called of the Lord to preside over them. Concluding his thought, Paul said, "Wherefore, brethren, covet to prophesy, and forbid not to speak with tongues [nor, it might be added, forbid the expression of any other spiritual gift]. Let all things be done decently and in order" (1 Cor 14:39-40).

As to our own day, there are many revelations relative to proclaiming the gospel and teaching one another the doctrines of the kingdom. The revealed word tells us that the gospel and the priesthood were restored so "every man might speak in the name of God the Lord, even the Savior of the world" (D&C 1:20). As already quoted, whatever is spoken by any elder when moved upon by the Holy Ghost is scripture and is the mind and will and voice of the Lord. Joseph Smith said that God would not reveal anything to him that he would not reveal to the Twelve, and to the least and last Saint as soon as he was able to bear it (*TPJS* 149). He further declared that even those holding office in the Aaronic Priesthood were "to preach, teach, expound, exhort," with the scriptures by the spirit of revelation (D&C 20:46; 42:14).

To join the Church is, in a sense, to join a School of the Elders. To receive the priesthood is to accept the responsibility to teach and testify of those truths revealed to that vessel chosen as the instrument of restoration in the particular dispensation in which one lives. To those of our dispensation the Lord has said: "You shall declare the things which have been revealed to my servant, Joseph Smith, Jun." (D&C 31:4). Thus it is for us to teach the message of the restoration and to do it from those scriptures the Lord has given us for that purpose. We are without the right or the authority to preach any other gospel than that restored to us. Our commission is to "declare the word with truth and soberness," that is to faithfully declare the gospel as it has been revealed, without distortion of any sort to please either the speaker or the listener (see Alma 42:31).

Now just what does it mean to declare doctrine? Are we speaking of adding to, augmenting, and changing doctrinal concepts? Or, do we mean preaching and interpreting the doctrines now found in the standard works? Is the President of the Church the only General Authority who can declare doctrine in the sense that he alone writes doctrinal books; or is his position unique in that he alone can announce new doctrine and stand as the final arbiter upon differing doctrinal views? Certainly there is a difference between writing by wisdom and writing by commandment, as illustrated by the divine command to Oliver Cowdery: "If thou art led at any time by the Comforter to speak or teach, or at all times by the way of commandment unto the church, thou mayest do it. But thou shalt not write by way of commandment, but by wisdom" (D&C 28:4-5).

Surely it is not intended that only ordained prophets write all the inspired books, poetry, plays, or music in the Church. Neither is it intended that they give all the patriarchal blessings, deliver all the inspired addresses, teach all of the classes, or lead all of the choirs. Indeed, it may never be their lot to paint the great paintings, sculpt with inspiration, or design chapels and temples. The kingdom of God is to be built as the tabernacle in the wilderness or the temple in Jerusalem were, that is, by the revelation of God as it manifests itself through a prophet, and also a nation of artists and craftsmen. All who labor to build the house of the Lord, be it temporal or spiritual, be it ancient or modern, are to do so with the spirit of revelation. And it goes without saying, that as the greatest of temples awaits building, so the best of books, music, art, and all things that testify of our God still await the day of their earthly creation.

Conclusion

How then have men learned of God and what they must do to please him? From the days of Adam to our own, the only answer that can satisfy is revelation (LF 2:13). Unless God chooses to reveal himself as he did to Adam and has to his other chosen vessels through the centuries, men are forever without a sure and certain knowledge of him. They would therefore be unable to exercise faith in him for they can hardly exercise faith in uncertainty. Thus God has chosen to manifest himself and his plan for the salvation of his children to certain chosen vessels who stand as witnesses of him in all the world.

All but Adam first learned of God by human testimony (LF 2:30-31). Thereafter it is the right of every living soul through faith and obedience to obtain a personal manifestation of the verity of that testimony communicated to them. Thus they stand independent and become the source of first testimony to others (LF 2:34).

For our day, Joseph Smith was the chosen vessel through whom the dispensation was established and the pure knowledge of God was again restored to the earth. Those who listen in faith to his testimony come to know by the manifestation of the spirit of prophecy and revelation that he is a competent and reliable witness and that the authority of heaven rests with him. Having obtained such a testimony, members then become witnesses themselves and aid in taking the message of the restored gospel to the ends of the earth. The spirit of this divinely ordained system—outlined in Lecture 2 and known to us in the scriptures as the order of the priesthood—is beautifully captured in Parley P. Pratt's poetic tribute to the Prophet Joseph Smith:

> He has organized the kingdom of God—
>> We will extend its dominion.
> He has restored the fulness of the Gospel.
>> We will spread it abroad.
> He has laid the foundation of Nauvoo.
>> We will build it up.
> He has laid the foundation of the Temple.
>> We will bring up the topstone with shouting.
> He has kindled a fire.
>> We will fan the flame.
> He has kindled up the dawn of a day of glory.
>> We will bring it to its meridian splendor.
> He was a "little one," and became a thousand.
>> We are a small one, and will become a strong nation.
> He quarried the stone from the mountain.
>> We will cause it to become a great mountain and fill the whole earth (151-52).

BIBLIOGRAPHY

McConkie, Bruce R. *The Promised Messiah.* Salt Lake City: Deseret Book, 1978.

———. "This Generation Shall Have My Word Through You." *Hearken, O Ye People.* Salt Lake City: Randall Book, 1984. 3-15.

Pratt, Parley P. "Proclamation." *Millennial Star* (Mar 1845) 5:149-53.

Teachings of the Prophet Joseph Smith. Comp. Joseph Fielding Smith. Salt Lake City: Deseret Book, 1976.

Joseph F. McConkie is professor of Ancient Scripture at Brigham Young University.

A Discussion of Lectures 3 and 4

The Imperative and Unchanging Nature of God

Rodney Turner

I n the winter of 1834-35, the Prophet Joseph Smith instructed the "school of the Elders" in Kirtland, Ohio, on the subject of faith. The first of the seven discussions subsequently published in the Doctrine and Covenants defined faith, while the second established the fact that God was its ultimate source and object. We will now treat the third and fourth lectures concerning God's character, perfections, and attributes, and how those divine qualities relate to one's ability to exercise a saving faith. In doing so, a certain amount of interweaving of the ideas in the two lectures will occur.

Thirty-nine verses from the Bible and two from the Doctrine and Covenants are quoted to "prove" the premises of these lectures. In the Lectures on Faith, God's moral nature is extrapolated from the Bible, not the Book of Mormon or other modern scriptures. An even stronger argument can be made using these latter-day sources. However, we must understand that such proof is textual, not empirical. No wholly spiritual or other-worldly proposition can, in the scientific sense, be demonstrated. This is necessarily the case. If the validity of scripture was, like gravity, self-evident, there would be no need for faith, virtue, or the witness of the Holy Spirit. Hence Moroni's admonition to those who have read the Book of Mormon to "ask God . . . if these things are not true" (Moroni 10:4). If the validity of the Book of

Mormon were self-evident, there would be no necessity to "ask God." Likewise, had mankind's knowledge of the premortal first estate been retained, the exercise of moral agency in this second estate would have been significantly compromised.[1] Likewise, if the consequences of good or evil were immediate, again there would be no need for faith in God's eventual justice. In mortality, to protect the unworthy, and therefore the unprepared, actual proof of spiritual realities must be merited. Hence, Moroni's statement: "Ye receive no witness until after the trial of your faith" (Ether 12:6).

True Faith Versus False Faith

But the trial of faith is only as valid as the faith itself. A vain or false faith can only produce erroneous results. Still, many religious people view faith pragmatically as an end in itself: faith in faith. It does not matter what you believe as long as you believe in *something*. This utilitarian approach to faith is the equivalent of whistling past the graveyard—a psychological crutch for limping through a dark world. The notion that one god, or one religion, is as good as another is an attempt to democratize the principle of faith. But faith has no saving power if it is directed toward false gods or false religious concepts and practices. Jesus taught: "This is life eternal, that they might know thee the *only true* God, and Jesus Christ whom thou hast sent" (John 17:3; emphasis added). No matter how fervent one's supposed faith, to be ignorant of that God and his will is to be without a valid hope of salvation. A faith compounded from religious error is the ultimate "vanity of vanities" (Eccl 1:2).

"If men do not comprehend the character of God, they do not comprehend themselves. . . . *It is the first principle of the gospel to know for a certainty the Character* [sic] *of God*" (*Teachings of the Prophet Joseph Smith* 343, 345; hereafter

---

[1] Scripture teaches that the physical universe is a witness for Christ. See Moses 6:63; Alma 30:44; Hel 8:24; D&C 88:41-47.

TPJS). These remarks by Joseph Smith, alluding to God's material character as a resurrected being, summarize the central issue of religion. God is the key to man's true identity; to know who and what God is, is to know who and what we are. Conversely, ignorance of God is ignorance of oneself.

False gods beget false religions. The primary reason contemporary Christianity is riddled with misconceptions about the gospel of Jesus Christ is that it is blind to the essential truth about the God it purports to worship. The gospel is an extension of God's nature. It is precisely what it is because God is what he is. How can we understand the gospel if we do not understand the God who authored it?

God's Existence

Faith cannot exist in a vacuum; a measure of knowledge—real or imagined—must precede it. We must know *about* before we can believe *in*. We cannot have faith in someone or something of whom, or of which, we have no knowledge (LF 2:18; 3:6). Paul asked: "How shall they believe in him of whom they have not heard?" (Rom 10:14). Contrary to the views of most social anthropologists, the origin of belief in a supreme being was not human reason, but divine revelation. Man did not rationalize God into existence; man did not invent God as an explanation for the then- mysterious workings of nature. Rather, the Almighty appeared to Adam and Eve "and it was through this means that the thought was first suggested to their minds that there was a God" (LF 2:31). The almost universal belief in God originated with the patriarch of the human family.

The "great first cause" has never been identified; indeed, there probably never was such a "cause." God not only exists, he has always existed. He—like his priesthood—is "without beginning of days or end of years" (Alma 13:7; Moses 1:3). He is "God over all, from everlasting to everlasting" (LF 3:19). In this timeless sense, "God" is not one solitary being, but the sum total of all those men and women who achieve a fulness of exaltation. President Brigham Young spoke to this point: "How many Gods there are, I do not know. But there never was a time when there were not Gods and worlds, and when men were not passing through the same ordeals that we are now passing through. That course has been from all eternity, and it is and will be to all eternity" (*Journal of Discourses* 7:333; hereafter *JD*). William W. Phelps, a close associate of Joseph Smith, reflected this sentiment in verse:

> If you could hie to Kolob in the twinkling of an eye,
> And then continue onward with that same speed to fly,
> Do you think that you could ever, through all eternity,
> Find out the generation where Gods began to be?
> (*Hymns* #284).

However, in speaking *only* of the Father of Jesus Christ, the Prophet Joseph Smith said: "We have imagined and supposed that God was God from all eternity. I will refute that idea, and take away the veil, so that you may see." The Prophet then explained that the Father once lived as a mortal on another earth and "worked out his salvation with fear and trembling"—presumably under *his* Father and *his* God (*TPJS* 345, 347). When understood in their contexts, the statements of Brigham Young and Joseph Smith are in perfect harmony. While we know of no identifiable personage who has always existed *as God*, yet God—at least in *principle*—has always existed. As far as has been revealed, "God" simply *is*.

The Material Nature of God

Zophar, one of Job's "comforters," asked: "Canst thou by searching find out God? Canst thou find out the Almighty unto perfection?" (Job 11:7). The answer is no (LF 3:7). God's divine nature cannot be discovered by human reason. His *genuine* nature was no more a product of human reason than was belief in his existence. Indeed, reason at its presumed best (as represented by the ancient philosophers and the Christian creedmakers) defined God as a totally transcendent, formless, immaterial, spirit essence, which definition Parley P. Pratt once called "a pious name for atheism." This type of "piety" suited the unembodied spirit Lucifer perfectly: unable to overthrow the Almighty, he sought to redefine him out of existence.

Unfortunately many have wrested the Bible into a game of "Trivial Pursuit." In spite of the preponderence of passages describing God in anthropomorphic terms, one brief verse in John, "God is a Spirit" (4:24), is seized upon to *prove* the contrary.[2] However, the Son of Man came into the world to manifest both the spiritual and material natures of the Father. The resurrected Lord told Mary Magdalene: "I ascend unto my Father, and your Father; and to my God, and your God" (John 20:17). The evening of the same day he invited his astonished disciples to: "Behold my hands and my feet, that it is I myself: handle me, and see; for a spirit hath not flesh and bones, as ye see me have" (Luke 24:39).

Yet Christian theologians ignored the plain doctrines of these scriptures and twisted the identities of the Father and the Son into a philosophical pretzel—endowing the Son of God with two totally distinct natures—one divine, one human. His divine nature was with the Father in heaven at the same time his human, incarnate, nature was with mankind on earth! Unable either rationally or scripturally to explain how God can be absolutely one supreme being of immaterial essence, and yet be absolutely three distinct persons (one having a corporeal body of flesh and bone),[3] the theologians resolved the dilemma by begging the question and declaring the doctrine an incomprehensible mystery. Thus the subjective creeds of men were given precedence over God's objective revelation of himself. Thanks to the learned philosophers who chose to ignore the plain teachings of Jesus and Paul,

---

[2] The JST reads: "For unto such hath God promised his Spirit" (John 4:26).

[3] Catholic doctrine is to the effect that the resurrected corporeal body of Christ became transcendently spiritual—though still real—when (as recorded in Acts 1:9) he ascended into heaven.

Athens' "Unknown God" remains unknown (see Acts 17:22-23; *JD* 6:318).

False Gods

Ancient Gods

What ungodly gods Satan, the "god of this world" (2 Cor 4:4), has concocted! Sin, ignorance, and devilish revelation filled the ancient world with a pantheon of sightless, soulless idols. Because these dumb horrors were symbols of power rather than principle, religious morality as we think of it played a very minor role in the overall scheme of things. The result was a nightmare of fanaticism, cruelty, and depravity: torture, human sacrifice, prostitution, and incest figured prominently in the work of the devil's "priesthoods."

For example, in homage to the Mother Goddess of Western Asia (who went by many names: Aphrodite, Astarte, Artemis, Diana, Venus, etc), "sanctified harlotry" in her temples was widespread (see Frazer 330-32).

The cruel gods of the ancient world were fashioned in the image of their cruel worshippers. But inhumane acts were not limited to the idolatrous nations of antiquity. The histories of Christianity, Islam, Hinduism, and other contemporary world religions are rife with devilish chapters of fanaticism, torture, murder, and immorality. Only God knows the full catalogue of crimes committed in his name.

Modern Gods

If the gods of Greece and Rome—tempered somewhat by philosophy—were somewhat less immoral than those of earlier millennia, still they were far from patterns of piety. The Olympian myths ascribe to Zeus (or Jupiter in the Latin myths) and his celestial entourage many of the same weaknesses and vices common to mankind. The ten commandments were not an issue for these gods and the men they ruled. Ritual, not righteousness, was the central issue.

Such is often the case even now among the world's religions, sects, and cults. Millions of Christians and billions of non-Christians not only continue to worship false gods (Hinduism has thirty million deities), but often with a credulous emphasis on man-contrived rituals. They flourish along a continuum from the very simple and prosaic to the most outlandish and bizarre. Light the candles, burn the incense, bang the gongs, bathe in sacred rivers, parade the images, intone the mystical formulas, and pray the prayers—all this serves to meet the demands of whatever gods there be. And so confusion abounds as a result of mankind's efforts—eagerly abetted by the god of this world—to fashion gods in his own kaleidoscopic image.

For others, God is either dead, irrelevant, or his existence is highly questionable. Some prominent scientists, intellectuals, and even religionists are secular humanists whose creed states:

> As secular humanists . . . we find that traditional views of the existence of God either are meaningless, have not yet been demonstrated to be true, or are tyrannically exploitative. Secular humanists . . . find insufficient evidence for the claim that some divine purpose exists for the universe. They reject the idea that God has intervened miraculously in history or revealed himself to a chosen few, or that he can save or redeem sinners. They believe that men and women are free and are responsible for their own destinies and that they cannot look toward some transcendent Being for salvation. We reject the divinity of Jesus, the divine mission of Moses, Mohammed, and other latter-day prophets and saints of the various sects and denominations (Kurtz 17-18).

For such thinkers, man has not simply created a god in his own image; man is his god. Man is the author of moral law and the determiner of what is morally acceptable. Science has presumably emancipated mankind from the ancient myths that kept it in bondage to foolish illusions about the supernatural. There is no supernatural, metaphysical, or spiritual opposition to temporal or physical reality. All reality is circumscribed by the natural order—the experiential order that can be weighed, measured, analyzed, and controlled by man.

The secular humanists believe that, while man, of necessity, must work in harmony with such manifest natural laws as gravity and electromagnetism, he does not need a corresponding moral order, and indeed it does not exist. Man—individually and collectively—will provide the moral framework for human happiness and security. Such is the position of secular humanism, pure existentialism, and naturalism. These philosophies permeate much of higher education in Europe and America today.

The One and Only True God

As we are indebted for the idea of his existence to a revelation which God made of himself to his creatures, in the first instance, so in like manner we are indebted to the revelations which he has given to us for a correct understanding of his character, perfections, and attributes. Because without the revelations which he has given to us, no man by searching could find out God (LF 3:7).

Regardless of who or what men worship, the fact remains that they can only be as moral as their gods. Likewise, their faith is only as valid and their salvation is only as assured as their gods and religions are true. A false faith may have a certain pragmatic value in time, but it is of very questionable worth in eternity.

Christ declared the creeds an abomination because they produced an abominable harvest of religious tares choking and obscuring the wheat of truth—especially the truth about the literal fatherhood of God upon which the doctrine of eternal marriage and exaltation is based. For if God is not an exalted man, he can have no children to aspire to a like glory. But he is the Man of all men, the measure by which they will be judged. To the extent that any life falls short of his perfection, it is a less successful, less significant, and less glorious life than a life can be. We will look now at the character and some attributes of the one and only true God as listed in Lectures 3 and 4, and will show how latter-day revelations and prophets support the teachings of the Lectures.

An Almighty God

> *For unless God had power over all things . . . men could not be saved (LF 4:12).*

Nothing exists outside of God. As Paul told the Athenians: "For *in* him we live, and move, and have our being" (Acts 17:28; emphasis added). His Spirit emanates from his presence "to fill the immensity of space" (D&C 88:12). His dominions are co-extensive with all matter, space, and time. And matter, space, and time are subject to his will; he can compress, expand, or modify them as he sees fit. The Almighty is as omniscient, omnipotent, and omnipresent as it is possible to be.

To know all that can be known is to possess all the power that can be possessed. Knowledge is the source of power. Knowing all things enables the Almighty to organize, control, and sustain all things. His faith in himself is absolute: "There is nothing that the Lord thy God shall take in his heart to do but what he will do it" (Abr 3:17).

The seventh lecture on faith states: "Faith, then, works by words; and with these its mightiest works have been and will be, performed" (LF 7:3). God's own works are works of pure faith, unadulterated by physical effort on his part. He *speaks* and "the power of his voice" causes all creation to obey: "Yea, and if he say unto the earth—Move—it is moved. Yea, if he say unto the earth—Thou shalt go back, that it lengthen out the day for many hours—it is done. . . . And behold also, if he say unto the waters of the great deep—Be thou dried up—it is done" (Hel 12:13, 16). Jehovah told Abraham: "I stretch my hand over the sea, and it obeys my voice; I cause the wind and the fire to be my chariot; I say to the mountains—Depart hence—and behold, they are taken away by a whirlwind, in an instant, suddenly" (Abr 2:7).

Truly, the Almighty is a miracle-worker whose ways and works remain a yet-to-be-revealed mystery to the most knowledgeable of mortals. The recognition of this fact is one definition of humility. Unfortunately this quality is sadly lacking in a growing number of self-ordained "intellectuals" who persist in defining the Creator's moral and intellectual character in their own finite image. Joseph Smith noted: "It is the constitutional disposition of mankind to set up stakes and set bounds to the works and ways of the Almighty" (*TPJS* 320). In other words, men seek to shrink God down to their own intellectual size, to de-miracle-ize the Miracle Worker. But Moroni wrote: "God has not ceased to be a God of miracles" (Mormon 9:15). As long as God is God, there will be miracles.

Having the power to organize, control, and sustain all things, the Lord can also sanctify, immortalize, and exalt all things. Our faith in God is contingent upon God's faith in himself. The motivating confidence we have in the reality of those as-yet-unexperienced immortal wonders which "eye hath not seen, nor ear heard, neither have entered into the heart of man" (1 Cor 2:9), together with our hope of attaining them, rests upon our unshakeable trust in that divine power resulting from God's own perfect faith and knowledge.

The Moral Attributes of God

Jesus said: "There is none good, but one, that is, God" (Matt 19:17; *TPJS* 303). In every way, the Most High is infinitely more than man at his best. Because of the vast gulf created by that essential, but cataclysmic, event called the Fall, the noblest of men only approximate his glory. Being holy, God's ways are not our ways, and his thoughts are not our thoughts. And yet the Lord is a man of passions. He *really* loves, and he *really* hates. He does not speak in monotones. His reactions are not impersonal, mechanical, or contrived. He *feels*. And those feelings run the gamut from love and compassion to wrath and judgment.

He is responsive to the ever-changing circumstances stemming from the moral agency he has given his children. The Redeemer told some Saints in Missouri: "I, the Lord, was angry with you yesterday, but today mine anger is turned away" (D&C 61:20). He also said: "I command and men obey not; I revoke and they receive not the blessing" (D&C 58:32).

The Lord, not man, is the ultimate determiner of what is right and wrong. Joseph Smith wrote:

> That which is wrong under one circumstance, may be, and often is, right under another. . . . God said, "Thou shalt not kill"; at another time He said, "Thou shalt utterly destroy." This is the principle on which the government of heaven is conducted—by revelation adapted to the circumstances in which the children of the kingdom are placed. Whatever God requires is right, no matter what it is, although we may not see the reason thereof till long after the events transpire (*TPJS* 256).

It is for the Lord with his "all-searching eye" to judge men; it is not for myopic men to judge the Lord, or even to presume to judge in his stead. To do so is "the greater sin" (D&C 64:9).

God Is Unchanging

> *For without the idea of unchangeableness in the character of the Deity, doubt would take the place of faith (LF 3:21).*

God is "the same yesterday, today, and forever" (1 Nephi 10:18; Heb 13:8). He "changes not"; he is ever the same, and "his course is one eternal round" (D&C 3:2). That course is centered in his never-ending work: "to bring to pass the immortality and eternal life of man" (Moses 1:39). Mormon testified: "For I know that God is not a partial God, neither a changeable being; but he is unchangeable from all eternity to all eternity" (Moroni 8:18). Consequently, the principles of life and salvation emanating from him are likewise unchanging. It is because God is unchanging that men must change. They must repent and put off "the natural man" (Mosiah 3:19) if they are to achieve sanctification and become one with God's unchanging nature.

Because God is ever the same, his government—wherever it may be found in the eternities—is ever the same. It is government by unchanging principles—government by priesthood. The plan of salvation reflects heaven's government and is likewise ever the same. As there is but one God, so is there but one priesthood, and one plan of salvation. Favoritism is not shown one eternity or one world over another anymore than it is shown one person over another.

If God Changed

Since God's fundamental nature cannot be improved upon, it follows that his nature must remain what it has always been if he is to remain a perfect God (see Alma 42:15; 3 Nephi 12:48). To modify or abandon any essential attribute of that nature would inevitably diminish him and alter the very meaning of God. He would forfeit perfection. Not that he would cease to exist as an organized intelligence, or that he would be dethroned (for who or what could dethrone him?),[4] but he would no longer be the God he has always been.[5] He would be transformed into a new and different deity ruling over new and different realities. Such an eventuality would have an unimaginable impact on the moral character of eternity. The very nature of truth and law would be altered. Certitude would be lost, because a god who abandoned one attribute could abandon another. Shock-waves of uncertainty would rumble from world to world destroying the very foundation of faith as we know it.

Applying this purely theoretical argument to the aggregate of the gods in eternity, if one of them were to modify or discard even a single attribute, the perfect unity that makes all gods one god would be violated (see D&C 38:27). To restore that unity, such a fallen being would, like Lucifer, have to be cast down (see Isa 14:12-15).

---

[4] "God" is a general or generic title as well as a specific one. In LDS thought it may pertain to one Being or to all of those achieving any degree of divinity—from the lowest to the Most High—even as the Melchizedek priesthood pertains to one or all of those ordained to any office therein. A renegade individual such as Lucifer (D&C 76:25-27) is subject to being cast down by the Gods. However, in saying that God would cease to be God, Alma is speaking of God in the collective or universal sense rather than in any relative sense of the word.

[5] That God is ever the same is stated six times in the Book of Mormon (1 Nephi 10:18; 2 Nephi 2:4; 27:23; 29:9; Mormon 9:9; Moroni 10:19), twice in the Doctrine and Covenants (20:12; 35:1), and once—in reference to Christ—in the Bible (Heb 13:8).

A God of Truth

For without the idea that he is a God of truth . . . men could not have the confidence in his word necessary to exercise faith in him (LF 3:22).

For without the idea of the existence of this attribute [truth] . . . all would be confusion and doubt (LF 4:16).

Truth is the sum of reality or, as John Jaques wrote, "the sum of existence" (*Hymns* #272). God is omniscient in part because he is omnipresent via his Spirit throughout all reality or existence. He is above, in, through, and round about all things (D&C 88:41). He possesses a fulness of truth, being the very "Spirit of truth" (D&C 93:26). He is the Supreme Intelligence whose wisdom excelleth that of all other organized intelligences combined (see Abr 3:19; also *TPJS* 353). He is the totality of that light and truth constituting his immortal glory (see D&C 93:36).

Unlike his rebellious son Lucifer (who was "a liar from the beginning"—D&C 93:25), God, by nature and by definition, "cannot lie" (Enos 1:6; Ether 3:12; D&C 62:6). A lie is a contradiction of the truth. A God of truth cannot be a self-contradiction. Nor does he deal in illusions. His "Spirit speaketh the truth and lieth not. Wherefore, it speaketh of things as they really are, and of things as they really will be" (Jacob 4:13).

The Lord is a holy being because he is a *whole* being. He is, in every sense, the *mature* Man. His integrity is absolute. Zion —unity in all things—is his supreme objective (see Moses 7:31). It results from each being bound to each in one grand kingdom of light and truth. Because "truth embraceth truth" (D&C 88:40), it can be added upon, but never discarded. Unlike the theories of men, there is no cause to fear that time and circumstance will negate an eternal truth, or that new facts will prove one false. Rest assured, the truths God has made known to us are constant, compatible, and in accordance with "things as they are, and as they were, and as they are to come" (D&C 93:24).

A God of Mercy

For without the idea of the existence of this attribute [mercy] in the Deity, the spirits of the Saints would faint in the midst of the tribulations, afflictions, and persecutions which they have to endure for righteousness' sake (LF 4:15).

God is a merciful God: gracious, compassionate, slow to anger, patient, and long-suffering. If he were not, human nature —a relative compound of ignorance, immaturity, instability, and impotence—would render the hope of eternal life an impossible dream. The gulf between divinity and humanity, holiness and unholiness, is so vast that any faith we might muster would eventually be swallowed up in paralyzing doubt. How could we ever become acceptable to a flawless God with his "all-searching eye" (Mosiah 27:31)? How could we ever be at ease, much less happy, in his presence? But because of our faith in the redemptive power of Christ, we can "come boldly unto the throne of grace, that we may obtain mercy, and find grace to help [us] in time of need" (Heb 4:16).

Without divine mercy, heaven would be hell. Moroni understood this point: "Behold, I say unto you that ye would be more miserable to dwell with a holy and just God, under a consciousness of your filthiness before him, than ye would to dwell with the damned souls in hell. For behold, when ye shall be brought to see your nakedness before God, and also the glory of God, and the holiness of Jesus Christ, it will kindle a flame of unquenchable fire upon you" (Mormon 9:4-5; compare Alma 12:14-15; Mosiah 27:31).

Paradoxically, it is his very holiness which makes mercy essential if we are "to be received into the kingdom of the Father to go no more out, but to dwell with God eternally in the heavens" (3 Nephi 28:40). For salvation depends far more upon what God is and does, than upon what we, of ourselves, are or can do. Hence, Nephi's words: "It is by grace [mercy] that we are saved, after all we can do" (2 Nephi 25:23). We are hopelessly lost unless a higher nature overwhelms and transforms our fallen natures.

This higher nature—with its attendant powers—is found in Jesus Christ. Elder James E. Talmage wrote:

> Without Him mankind would forever remain in a fallen state, and as to hope of eternal progression would be inevitably lost. The mortal probation is provided as an opportunity for advancement; but so great are the difficulties and the dangers, so strong is the influence of evil in the world, and so weak is man in resistance thereto, that without the aid of a power above that of humanity no soul would find its way back to God from whom it came. The need of a Redeemer lies in the inability of man to raise himself from the temporal to the spiritual plane, from the lower kingdom to the higher (26-27).

When we have demonstrated all of the faith, repentance, and obedience required of us, it will still be insufficient; we must still rely "wholly upon the merits of him who is mighty to save" (2 Nephi 31:19). Jesus Christ is the embodiment of God's indispensible mercy. The Father can be merciful only because the Son atoned for the sins of his fallen brothers and sisters.

Divine mercy is not limited to those moral and spiritual issues which dictate our destiny in some future life; he is merciful in the here and now. His invisible hand is extended to us far more often than we realize. Only at the last judgment when the full account of God's dealings with mankind—collectively and individually—are revealed, will we learn the full extent of his providential care. But that this care is available to us all is unquestionable. Alma testified: "I do know that whosoever shall put their trust in God shall be supported in their trials, and their troubles, and their afflictions, and shall be lifted up at the last day (Alma 36:3; compare 38:5). We are never alone, even when we feel abandoned. God is not some remote, disinterested "force" in the universe. Jehovah, in the person of Jesus Christ, left his high mountain and joined his people in the low valley of mortal trials, temptations, and suffering (see Mosiah 3:7; Alma 7:11-12; Heb 4:15).

Human nature being what it is, there is a danger that God's mercy will be interpreted as divine weakness or indifference (see Rom 2:4-6). This would be a fatal error. We must not be slothful simply because God is merciful. The Almighty has infinite patience, but he will not extend it to us infinitely. "For the Spirit of the Lord will not always strive with man. And when the Spirit ceaseth to strive with man then cometh speedy destruction" (2 Nephi 26:11). There comes a day when—where repentance is concerned—there is "time no longer" (D&C 88:110). We are given adequate opportunity to reveal our true selves to ourselves, to establish what we everlastingly are. God can do no more; he will not coerce us into being what we do not choose to be. The last judgment is the finish line. When we reach it, the race with ourselves is over, and "the night of darkness wherein there can be no labor performed" (Alma 34:33) will descend upon mankind's day of probation.

A Law-abiding and Just God

For without the idea of the existence of the attribute justice in the Deity, men could not have confidence sufficient to place themselves under his guidance and direction (LF 4:13).

Whether by necessity or design, the fact remains that God operates within a framework of law. And law—to be law—must be constant and consistent. It must be dependable. There is a network of independent, but harmoniously interlocking systems of law governing all things, organic and inorganic, in the numberless kingdoms filling the immensity of space: "And unto every kingdom is given a law; and unto every law there are certain bounds also and conditions. All beings who abide not in those conditions are not justified. . . . [God] hath given a law unto all things, by which they move in their times and their seasons; and their courses are *fixed*" (D&C 88:38-39, 42-43; emphasis added; compare Abr 3:6-10).

Law did not create God; God created law. The Almighty did not begin his career as a cosmic Columbus who stumbled upon supposedly self-existing natural laws. If there was "a great first cause" of all things, he was it. He is, as President Spencer W. Kimball said: "The Creator who originated every law" (5).

The Prophet Joseph Smith is quoted as saying that God, "finding he was in the midst of spirits and glory, because he was more intelligent, saw proper to *institute laws* whereby the rest could have a privilege to advance like himself" (*TPJS* 354).

Justice—the righteous, impartial application of law—is God's quintessential attribute. Whereas mercy, redeeming grace, is contingent upon an infinite atonement, justice is a non-contingent principle. From the divine perspective, God—to be God— need not always be merciful, but he must always be just. He gives the unrepentant sinner justice, but not mercy (see Alma 42:13). Were God to cease to be just, he would become an arbitrary monarch, ruling by will and whim without regard for truth and law. Lucifer aspired to be just such a monarch. Had he succeeded, the chaotic scenes of blood and horror Satan has promoted on this earth would doubtless become eternity-wide. In time, all reality would dissolve itself into one vast hell, and death would envelope all things (see 2 Nephi 9:9). Of course, this will never happen, but if it did, the cruel gods of the ancient world would come alive at last.

In the administration of his laws and their attendant blessings, the Lord is "no respecter of persons" (Acts 10:34; Moroni 8:18; D&C 1:35). He is blind to gender, color, race, material wealth, social position, and intellectual attainments. All such purely temporal factors are swallowed up in his glory. All stand equal before his law; there is no double standard. Heaven's blessings are based on obedience, not favoritism (see D&C 130:19-20). He is not merciful to a predestined or chosen few; all have access to his grace regardless of when they learn of his will. "All men are privileged the one like unto the other; . . . he denieth none that come unto him, black and white, bond and free, male and female" (2 Nephi 26:28, 33). Being no respecter of persons means that all are equally blessed or deprived according to principles of law.

Although Jesus Christ labors in every possible way to save mankind, he will not forever continue to do so. In time, even God finally gives up on the incorrigible among us. He told Joseph

Smith: "I will take vengeance upon the wicked, for they will not repent; for the cup of mine indignation is full; for behold, my blood shall not cleanse them if they hear me not" (D&C 29:17; compare 133:51-52). The Prophet warned: "God . . . passes over no man's sins, but visits them with correction, and if His children will not repent of their sins He will discard them" (*TPJS* 189). The democratic notion that one individual's deeds are as noble and deserving as any other's is clearly false. We hear much about the sacredness of life, but life is only as sacred as we make it. The life of a murderer or rapist is a defiled life and will remain so unless there is repentance. To equate such a life with that of a virtuous person is a mockery of reason.

While the Lord is impartial, yet heaven has its "favorites" (LF 6:4). They are spoken of as the "noble and great" (Abr 3:22-23), the "chosen" (D&C 121:40), the "sanctified" (D&C 20:34), and so forth. They constitute what Elder Matthew Cowley called "the aristocracy of righteousness" (253). But they are not born aristocrats, they are exalted by merit, not by chance. "Behold, the Lord esteemeth all flesh in one; he that is righteous is favored of God" (1 Nephi 17:35). We read that "Nephi was more faithful in keeping the commandments of the Lord—therefore he was favored of the Lord, for the Lord heard his prayers and answered them" (Mosiah 10:13). And James wrote: "The effectual fervent prayer of a righteous man availeth much" (James 5:16).

Justice is a minority voice in this world. Although moral agency is a gift of God, because of wickedness it comes at a high price and continues to take a fearsome toll among the innocent. But the Lord hears the cries of the oppressed. They are assured of eventual deliverance via divine judgments. One of the greatest evidences of true conversion is the ability to accept injustices with the grace with which Jesus accepted them (see 1 Peter 2:19-25).

Faith embodies the conviction that, despite any notions to the contrary, when the members of the spirit family of the Almighty stand before him at the last judgment, "every nation, kindred, tongue, and people shall see eye to eye and shall confess before God that his judgments are just" (Mosiah 16:1).

A God of Love

> And lastly, but not less important to the exercise of faith in God, is the idea that he is love (LF 3:24).

"God is love" (1 John 4:8). Every act of God is an act of love. Every act is dictated by his benign wisdom. Love encapsulates all godly virtues even as it sums up all human duties. Jesus equated love with doing good to all men, friend and enemy alike (see Matt 5:44). Paul wrote the Romans: "Love is the fulfilling of the law" (13:10; compare Gal 5:14.)

Agape or divine love is a quality of the spirit. It is more than mere sympathy or concern, it is a personal, emotional identification with someone or something outside one's self. It is garnished with a profound sense of compassion. God could be holy, just, unchanging, impartial—even merciful—and still remain dispassionate. But love weeps (see 3 Nephi 17:21-22; Moses 7:28-40; John 11:35). It is acquainted with grief. It was personified in Jesus. He not only died for love's sake, but was its greatest living exemplar. Both as a mortal and as a resurrected being, he involved himself in the pains of a sick and suffering humanity (see D&C 133:53). He was a caring Christ.

The Lord expresses his love for us as much as we permit him to. As with any parent, the Father's love can be rejected and rendered impotent. The question then, is not does God love us, but do we love God? For while God is a loving Father, he is not an indulgent one. He practices law-abiding love. So it is a false idea that love forgives all and conquers all. If it did, the sacrifice of the Son of God would bring the whole human race to its knees, and there would be no need for perdition. But goodness has its limits; its ability to triumph over evil is not absolute. The sin of sins is not only to reject, but to betray, the sacrifice of love offered up by the Father in the person of his Beloved Son (see D&C 76:35; 132:27).

As spirit is drawn to Spirit, so is love drawn to Love (see D&C 88:40). John wrote: "We love him, because he first loved us" (1 John 4:19). Above all other attributes, it is the love of the Father and the Son that ultimately draws the souls of men and women to them "without compulsory means" (D&C 121:46). It is a compelling power. Few men have experienced such visions, revelations, and angelic visitations as were granted Joseph Smith. If ever a man would seem unneedful of others it was he. And yet the Prophet remarked: "When persons manifest the least kindness and love to me, O what power it has over my mind" (*TPJS* 240). The pure love of Christ is at the very heart of the Father's plan of salvation. It illuminates every divine attribute in the sanctified until they are ablaze with light and truth and become one with love as God is one with love.

A Happy God

To the character and attributes listed in Lectures 3 and 4, I would add the characteristic that God is a happy God and that happiness is man's goal. Lehi taught, "men are, that they might have joy" (2 Nephi 2:25). Alma called the gospel "the great plan of happiness" (Alma 42:8, 16). Benjamin assured the obedient that they would "dwell with God in a state of never-ending happiness" (Mosiah 2:41).

The Father—the happiest of men—endowed his Beloved Son with a "fulness of joy" (3 Nephi 28:10). He is in the business of "happifying" his children by sharing his own nature with them. Heber C. Kimball remarked:

> I am perfectly satisfied that my Father and my God is a cheerful, pleasant, lively, good-natured Being. Why? Because I am cheerful, pleasant, lively, and good-natured when I have His Spirit. That is one reason why I know; and another is—the Lord said, through Joseph Smith, "I delight in a glad heart and a cheerful countenance." That arises from the perfection of His attributes; He is a jovial, lively person, and a beautiful man (*JD* 4:222).

Our individual capacity for happiness was first developed in the premortal estate. It was there that we learned the rudiments of joy from the gods set over us. As we partook of their spirit, we experienced a measure of the happiness righteousness produces. In this world of oppositions, joy is veiled; it cannot be experienced in its fulness—a fulness of joy comes only with resurrection (see D&C 93:33; 101:36). But, from time to time we can—like Elder Kimball—partake of the joy of the Spirit. Indeed, we not only have the opportunity, but the obligation, to do so. A perpetually unhappy Saint is an oxymoron, a self-contradiction. President Spencer W. Kimball remarked: "If you are not happy today, you may never be happy" (*Teachings of Spencer W. Kimball* 173). "Happiness," said the Prophet Joseph, "is the object and design of our existence" (*TPJS* 255). Righteousness alone can bring it to pass. To the degree that each of us acquires the divine nature, we will enter into "the joy of the Lord" (see D&C 51:19). Consequently, when all is said and done, each of us will be as happy as we have chosen to be, which is to say, we will be as much one with God as we have chosen to be.

Conclusion

The Lectures on Faith testify that the great plan of salvation is compatible with, and a reflection of, the virtues and powers of the one and only true God. To that testimony I add my own. We have every reason to exercise faith in him unto salvation. Our gracious Father has revealed himself through his Son, his Spirit, his prophets, and his scriptures. To that extent we know him. And, to the extent that we know him, we know ourselves (see *TPJS* 343). It only remains for us to magnify that knowledge until we are perfected and glorified in him.

BIBLIOGRAPHY

Cowley, Matthew. *Matthew Cowley Speaks*. Salt Lake City: Deseret Book, 1954.

Durant, Will. *Our Oriental Heritage.* Vol 1 of *The Story of Civilization.* 10 vols. New York: Simon and Schuster, 1954-67.

Frazer, James G. *The Golden Bough.* Abridged ed. in 1 vol. New York: Macmillan, 1922, 1931.

Hymns. Salt Lake City: The Church of Jesus Christ of Latter-day Saints, 1985.

Journal of Discourses. 26 vols. 1854-86.

Kimball, Spencer W. "Absolute Truth." *Ensign* (Sep 1978) 8:3-8.

Kurtz, Paul. *A Secular Humanist Declaration.* N.p.:n.p. 1980. Pamphlet reprinted from *Free Inquiry* (Win 1980) vol 1.

McConkie, Bruce R. *Mormon Doctrine.* 2nd ed. Salt Lake City: Bookcraft, 1979.

Pratt, Orson. *The Great First Cause or the Self-Moving Forces of the Universe.* Liverpool: Franklin R. James, 1851.

————. "The Pre-existence of Man." *The Seer* (Aug 1853) 1:113-21.

Talmage, James E. *Jesus the Christ.* Salt Lake City: The Church of Jesus Christ of Latter-day Saints, 1981.

Teachings of the Prophet Joseph Smith. Comp. Joseph Fielding Smith. Salt Lake City: Deseret Book, 1976.

The Teachings of Spencer W. Kimball. Ed. Edward L. Kimball. Salt Lake City: Bookcraft, 1982.

Rodney Turner is emeritus professor of Ancient Scripture, Brigham Young University.

The Supreme Power over All Things:The Doctrine of the Godhead in the Lectures on Faith

Robert L. Millet

N ot long before his death, Elder Bruce R. McConkie wrote the following concerning the fifth Lecture on Faith:

> Using the holy scriptures as the recorded source of the knowledge of God, knowing what the Lord has revealed to them of old in visions and by the power of the Spirit, and writing as guided by that same Spirit, Joseph Smith and the early brethren of this dispensation prepared a creedal statement on the Godhead. It is without question the most excellent summary of revealed and eternal truth relative to the Godhead that is now extant in mortal language. In it is set forth the mystery of Godliness; that is, it sets forth the personalities, missions, and ministries of those holy beings who comprise the supreme presidency of the universe. To spiritually illiterate persons, it may seem hard and confusing; to those whose souls are aflame with heavenly light, it is a nearly perfect summary of those things which must be believed to gain salvation (*A New Witness* 72).

After many years of concentrated study of the Lectures on Faith, and particularly Lecture 5, I have come to appreciate Elder McConkie's assessment; I believe the doctrines taught therein to be true and the concepts presented—though difficult and in some cases seemingly at odds with more traditional discussions of God and the Godhead—to be deep, penetrating, and, when fully grasped, soul inspiring. I believe them to be in harmony with other doctrines found in the standard works and the teachings of living apostles and prophets.

Because the Prophet was not at liberty to reveal all he knew, we are under solemn obligation to read, study, teach, and take seriously that which God *did* see fit to make known to the Latter-day Saints through him. Because Joseph Smith was given the mind of Deity, and because he was given the unique power and authorization of "expounding all scriptures" (see D&C 24:5, 9) unto the people of this dispensation, it is both fitting and proper that as we search and prayerfully consider matters pertaining to the Godhead, we give solemn and ponderous thought to insights provided by "the choice seer" of the last days.

God and the Godhead: Some Preliminary Observations

The nature of God—his character and attributes and perfections—has been treated at length by others in this symposium. I would like here to simply draw attention to a few matters which have some doctrinal bearing on a more detailed discussion of the Godhead.

First of all, it is important to note that there is no distinction made in the lectures between faith in God the Father and faith in his Son, Jesus Christ. This is as it should be, for faith in one is faith in the other. "Christ and his Father are one," wrote Elder McConkie.

> They possess the same powers, are of the same character, embody the same attributes, and stand as beacons to all others with reference to the same eternal perfections. The words and acts of one are the words and acts of the other. The Father was in Christ manifesting himself to the world. Hence, faith in the Son is faith in the Father. And as Christ is the way to the Father, faith centers in him and in his redeeming sacrifice and goes thereby to the Father, who is the Creator (*A New Witness* 185).

Secondly, a careful study of all of the lectures reveals a profoundly deep concept of God. These teachings relative to God—despite some claims to the contrary—are neither primitive nor Protestant. We are made privy to a divine Being who is omnipotent, omniscient, and omnipresent:[1] he has all power, all knowledge, and is, by the power of his Spirit, everywhere present. At the same time, we are given insights into a Being who can be approached, a God who communicates freely with his people and reveals himself to those who, like Enoch, the brother of Jared, and Moses, seek after him with diligence and faithfulness (see LF 2:55). Most profoundly, we come face to face with the reality later taught in the King Follett Sermon—that men and women can mature spiritually to the point where they can become even as their exalted Sire (see LF 5:2-3; 7:8-9, 16). As indicated, these lectures are not primitive: they contain doctrinal pronouncements and allusions which would normally be associated with the mature Joseph Smith in Nauvoo. These lectures are not Protestant: indeed, we learn of a truly infinite Being—a totally independent Being (see LF 2:2) who possesses every godly attribute in perfection (see LF 3:12-24; 4:3-16, 19; 5:1). But in no way do we encounter the utterly transcendent Deity of the creeds. God's infinity does not preclude either his immediacy or his intimacy.

The Father: A Personage of Spirit

"There are two personages," Joseph Smith explained, "who constitute the great, matchless, governing, and supreme power

---

[1] I should distinguish here between an LDS view of God's omnipotence, omniscience, and omnipresence, and that held by many in Catholicism or Protestantism. We do not believe in the utterly transcendent Being of the creeds, nor do we subscribe to the notion of a creation *ex nihilo*. God has all power but works within established parameters. "Whatever His wisdom indicates as necessary to be done God can and will do. The means through which He operates may not be of infinite capacity in themselves, but they are directed by an infinite power. A rational conception of His omnipotence is power to do all that He may will to do" (Talmage 44). Latter-day Saints attest to God's corporeality and thus his inability to be, in person at least, everywhere at the same time. He is able, however, through his holy Spirit (also called the Light of Christ) to be in and through all things.

over all things, by whom all things were created and made. . . . They are the Father and the Son" (LF 5:2). The Father and the Son are indeed the central members of the heavenly hierarchy, but as the Prophet later observed in the same lecture, the Holy Spirit is also a vital part of this eternal presidency. "These three are one," he stated; "or, in other words, these three constitute the great, matchless, governing, and supreme power over all things, by whom all things were created and made. And these three constitute the Godhead and are one" (LF 5:2).

Again quoting from the Prophet: "They are the Father and the Son: *the Father being a personage of spirit*, *glory*, and *power*, possessing all perfection and fulness. *The Son*, who was in the bosom of the Father, is *a personage of tabernacle*" (LF 5:2; emphasis added). This is a perplexing passage, perhaps one of the two most enigmatic passages of Lecture 5,[2] a segment of the lecture which seems to have resulted in confusion on the part of members and may have contributed eventually to the deletion of the Lectures on Faith from the Doctrine and Covenants in 1921. The problem lies in the fact that the Prophet appears to be teaching that God the Father is a "personage of spirit" while Jesus is "a personage of tabernacle." The latter proposition is, of course, no problem. It is the notion of the Father as a personage of spirit which is unsettling. Let us consider some possible explanations for this statement.

We cannot avoid the possible conclusion that Joseph Smith simply did not understand the corporeal or physical nature of God at the time the Lectures on Faith were delivered in the winter of 1834-35. His knowledge of things—like that of all men and women —was often incremental, and his development in understanding was thereby accomplished in "line upon line" fashion. When he left the grove of trees in 1820, Joseph Smith, Jr. did not have the doctrinal grasp or spiritual maturity that he would have when he died a martyr's death in Carthage some 24 years later.

---

[2]The other troublesome passage deals with the role of the Holy Spirit as the "mind" of the other two members of the Godhead (LF 5:2), and will be discussed below.

As a result of the First Vision, Joseph knew that the heavens were no longer sealed; that Satan was more than myth or metaphor; and that the Father and Son were separate and distinct personages. There is no mention in any of his known accounts of the First Vision of the fact that God has a body of flesh and bones (Backman, *Joseph Smith's First Vision* 155-67). The earliest reference in a sermon by Joseph Smith on the corporeality of God seems to be 5 January 1841. On that occasion William Clayton recorded the Prophet as saying: "That which is without body or parts is nothing. There is no other God in heaven but that God who has flesh and bones" (Ehat and Cook, *Words of Joseph Smith* 60; hereafter *Words*).[3] Six weeks later "Joseph said concerning the Godhead [that] it was not as many imagined—three heads and but one body; he said the three were separate bodies" (*Words* 63). On 9 March 1841 he spoke of the ministries of Jesus as the Mediator and the Holy Ghost as the witness or Testator. He then declared that "the Son had a Tabernacle and so had the Father" (*Words* 64). Finally, it was on 2 April 1843 in Ramus, Illinois that Joseph the Prophet delivered instructions on this matter which are the basis for D&C 130:22-23: "The Father has a body of flesh and bones as tangible as man's; the Son also; but the Holy Ghost . . . is a personage of Spirit" (see *Words* 173).

A second possibility is that Joseph Smith did indeed understand that God has a body but that the passage in Lecture 5 under consideration has simply been misunderstood. If so, what could the phrase mean? To begin with, we should note that the complete expression is not "a personage of spirit," but rather "a personage of *spirit*, *glory*, and *power*." This may well be intended more as a description of God's divine nature—a statement regarding his exalted and glorified status—than of his physical being. The word "spirit," as used for example in Moses 1, is a synonym for glory or power: his Spirit is his glory. Thus the account indicates that after a marvelous vision "the *presence* of God withdrew from

---

[3] Quotations from *Words of Joseph Smith* have been modernized and corrected in this article.

Moses, that his *glory* was not upon Moses" (v 9). When Satan came tempting and taunting, the Lawgiver found that he was still possessed of sufficient spiritual power and discernment to distinguish between the true God of glory and the "god of this world" (v 20; see also 2 Cor 4:4). "Blessed be the name of my God," Moses exulted, "for *his Spirit* hath not altogether withdrawn from me" (Moses 1:15; emphasis added). To speak of the spirit, glory, and power of the Father is to speak of his greatness, of his omnipotence, of his majesty. Thus it is that later in this lecture the Prophet says, "The Father and the Son possess the same mind, the same wisdom, glory, power, and fulness—filling all in all. *The Son, being filled with the fulness of the mind, glory, and power, or in other words, the spirit, glory, and power, of the Father*, possesses all knowledge and glory" (LF 5:2; emphasis added). Please note that the phrase "spirit, glory, and power" is used here to describe that which makes the Son one with the Father—the attributes of Godhood. Note the equation of spirit with *light* in the following verse from the Doctrine and Covenants: "For the word of the Lord is truth, and whatsoever is truth is light, and whatsoever is light is Spirit, even the Spirit of Jesus Christ" (D&C 84:45).

Elder Bruce R. McConkie has suggested that the phrase "a personage of spirit" has reference to God's *spiritual* nature—the fact that he is a resurrected and immortal being and as such is not subject to death, ie, a spiritual body. "They are the two personages who came to Joseph Smith in the spring of 1820"; he also wrote:

> They are exalted men. Each is a personage of spirit; each is a personage of tabernacle. Both of them have bodies, tangible bodies of flesh and bones. They are resurrected beings. Words, with their finite connotations, cannot fully describe them. A personage of tabernacle, as here used, is one whose body and spirit are inseparably connected and for whom there can be no death. A personage of spirit, as here used and as distinguished from the spirit children of the Father, is a resurrected personage. Resurrected bodies, as contrasted with mortal bodies, are in fact spiritual bodies (*A New Witness* 72-73; see also Penrose 12-13; 1 Cor 15:44; D&C 88:27; Alma 11:45).

It is interesting to read the catechism following Lecture 5. In response to the question, "What is the Father?" the answer is given: "He is a personage of glory and of power." Note the rather obvious omission of any reference to the Father as *a personage of spirit.* I suggest that there is no reference to his being a personage of spirit because to say such is repetitious; we have already established that he is a personage of power and glory, which in the mind of Joseph Smith is the same as saying that he is a personage of spirit. It is also worth noting in the catechism that in the scriptures cited to establish the Father as a personage of power and glory, all of them speak of his attributes and his exaltation. Noticeably absent is John 4:24—the one passage from the Bible that might have been used to establish clearly that God is a spirit. "God is a spirit," the King James Version has Jesus explaining, "and they that worship him must worship him in spirit and in truth." But of course Joseph Smith would not cite this passage from the King James Bible, since he had previously learned by revelation—some time between November 1831 and 16 February 1832 (Matthews 96)—that this verse was a mistranslation. The inspired translation reads as follows: "And the hour cometh, and now is, when the true worshippers shall worship the Father in spirit and in truth; for the Father seeketh such to worship him. For unto such hath God promised his Spirit. And they who worship him, must worship in spirit and in truth" (JST John 4:25-26). One cannot help but wonder whether the inspired revision did not have some impact on the Prophet's thought regarding the nature of God; that is to say, if he did not know of the corporeality of God at the time of the First Vision, did he know it by the time he had translated these verses in John?[4]

I am indebted to my colleague Professor Milton Backman for bringing to light an important document—a description of

---

[4] At an even earlier date (Nov-Dec 1830), the Prophet's inspired revision of Genesis resulted in the following scripture: "In the day that God created man, (in the likeness of God made he him,) *in the image of his own body,* male and female created he them, and blessed them, and called their name Adam, in the day when they were created, and became living souls, in the land, upon the footstool of God" (JST Gen 6:9; emphasis added; see also Moses 6:8-9).

Mormonism by a Protestant clergyman in Ohio. Truman Coe, a Presbyterian minister who had for four years lived among the Saints in Kirtland, published the following regarding the Mormons in the 11 August 1836 *Ohio Observer*: "They contend that the God worshipped by the Presbyterians and all other sectarians is no better than a wooden god. *They believe that the true God is a material being, composed of body and parts*; and that when the Creator formed Adam in his own image, he made him about the size and shape of God himself" (Backman, "Truman Coe's 1836 Description of Mormonism" 347, 354; emphasis added). If a non-Mormon had observed as early as 1836 that the Latter-day Saints were teaching that God has a body, it is certainly not inconceivable that such things were known by Joseph Smith a year or so earlier at the time of the School of the Elders. It is interesting to note in D&C 93:33 the Lord states that "man is spirit." This would appear to be a reference to man's eternal nature, and certainly not an allusion to his physical person. Perhaps the phrase "personage of spirit" also has reference to God as a being who is from everlasting to everlasting.

The Son: A Personage of Tabernacle

Jesus Christ the Son is described in Lecture 5 as having been "in the bosom of the Father . . . a personage of tabernacle, made or fashioned like unto man, being in the form and likeness of man, or rather man was formed after his likeness and in his image. He is also the express image and likeness of the personage of the Father, possessing all the fulness of the Father, or the same fulness with the Father" (LF 5:2). The section of this lecture dealing with Christ is a statement of the Incarnation, a re-affirmation of what the Book of Mormon prophets knew as "the condescension of God" (see 1 Nephi 11; Mosiah 3:1-11; 7:26-28). He who had been in the bosom of the Father—who had been the Lord God Omnipotent, the Holy One of Israel and the God of Abraham, Isaac, and Jacob—came to earth; he chose to "descend from his throne divine" (*Hymns* 193) to accomplish his mission of mercy. The Son is called a "personage of tabernacle" here because his assignment on earth pertained to the redemption and regeneration of the flesh. Thus Elohim is designated as the Father, a being of spirit, glory, and power, while Jesus Christ is called the Son, "because of the flesh" (LF 5:2). These words are in harmony with the doctrines of the condescension of God in the Book of Mormon. Abinadi thus prophesied that because Jesus the Messiah would dwell "in the flesh he shall be called the Son of God" (Mosiah 15:2). King Limhi explained to Ammon concerning Abinadi:

> And because he said unto them that Christ was the God, the Father of all things, and said that he should take upon him the image of man, and it should be the image after which man was created in the beginning; or, in other words, he said that man was created after the image of God, and that God should come down among the children of men, and take upon him flesh and blood, and go forth upon the face of the earth—and now, because he said this, they did put him to death (Mosiah 7:27-28).

The language of Lecture 5 regarding the relationship of the Father to the Son is also highly reminiscent of the language of the 93rd section of the Doctrine and Covenants. In this revelation, for example, Christ explained that he is called "the Father because [Elohim] gave me of his fulness, and *the Son because I was in the world and made flesh my tabernacle*, and dwelt among the sons of men" (D&C 93:4; emphasis added). Further, in regard to the divine indwelling relationship that exists between the Father and the Son—the manner in which in the resurrection the fulness of the glory of the Father came to be centered in the Son—the revelation continues with an excerpt from the record of John. It is stated that Christ was called the Son of God "because he received not of the fulness at the first," but that in the resurrection "he received a fulness of the glory of the Father; and he received all power, both in heaven and on earth, and the glory of the Father was with him, for he dwelt in him" (D&C 93:14, 16-17).

The divine Sonship of Christ—the fact that Jesus possessed the powers of immortality while he dwelt in the flesh—is also affirmed in Lecture 5. Jesus "descended in suffering below that which man can suffer; or, in other words, he suffered greater sufferings and was exposed to more powerful contradictions than any man can be" (LF 5:2). The conclusion: Jesus of Nazareth was more than man, for the full act of propitiation required a God (see Mosiah 3:7, 9; Alma 34:11). Our Lord is "he that ascended up on high, as also he descended below all things, in that he comprehended all things, that he might be in all and through all things, the light of truth" (D&C 88:6). In the words of Paul, "he that descended is the same also that ascended up far above all heavens, that he might fill all things" (Eph 4:10). How is it that Christ "was exposed to more powerful contradictions than any man can be"? Simply stated, the ministry of Messiah was a life filled with irony. During the hours of atonement, for example, he who had remained sinless became, as it were, the great sinner. In the language of Paul, God the Father "made him to be sin for us, who knew no sin" (2 Cor 5:21). To the Galatian Saints, Paul taught that "Christ hath redeemed us from the curse of the law, being made a curse for us" (Gal 3:13). He who deserved least of all to suffer suffered the most—more than mortal mind can fathom. He who had brought life—the more abundant life (John 10:10)—subjected himself to the powers of death and darkness.

Notwithstanding all the sufferings and the infinite opposition faced by the Infinite One, the Prophet testified that the Savior "kept the law of God and remained without sin, showing thereby that it is in the power of man to keep the law and remain also without sin. And also that by him a righteous judgment might come upon all flesh, that all who walk not in the law of God may justly be condemned by the law and have no excuse for their sins" (LF 5:2). Jesus never took a backward step nor a moral detour. He "was in all points tempted like as we are, yet without sin" (Heb 4:15; see also 1 Peter 2:22). As the Sinless One, he is thus the perfect Prototype (see LF 7:9), the standard against which all others are judged. The standard of perfection is fixed. It is in place. It is irrevocable. Because God himself is the embodiment of "truth, justice, judgment, mercy, and an infinity of fulness, from everlasting to everlasting" (D&C 109:77), he could not expect less from his children. What is possible, however, is not always probable. Though the standard is set and the example a matter of history, the Prophet recognized that ultimate perfection is a matter toward which men and women reach even beyond this life (*Words* 345, 358). "Where is the man that is free from vanity?" Joseph Smith asked on a subsequent occasion. "None ever were perfect but Jesus," he taught, "and why was he perfect? because he was the Son of God, and had the fulness of the Spirit, and greater power than any man" (*Words* 72). Similarly, Elder Bruce R. McConkie declared in an address at Brigham Young University:

> We have to become perfect to be saved in the celestial kingdom. But nobody becomes perfect in this life. Only the Lord Jesus attained that state, and he had an advantage that none of us has. He was the Son of God, and he came into this life with a spiritual capacity and a talent and an inheritance that exceeded beyond all comprehension what any of the rest of us was born with. Our revelations say that he was like unto God in the premortal life and he was, under the Father, the creator of worlds without number. That Holy Being was the Holy One of Israel anciently and he was the Sinless One in mortality. He lived a perfect life, and he set an ideal example. This shows that we can strive and go forward toward that goal, but no other mortal—not the greatest prophets nor the mightiest apostles nor any of the righteous saints of any of the ages—has ever been perfect, but we must become perfect to gain a celestial inheritance. As it is with being born again, and as it is with sanctifying our souls, so becoming perfect in Christ is a process ("Jesus Christ and Him Crucified" 399-400).

Christ is the Way, the Truth, and the Life (John 14:6). To the Nephites he said: "I am the law, and the light. Look unto me, and endure to the end, and ye shall live" (3 Nephi 15:9).

The Holy Spirit: The Mind of the Father and Son

Though the Prophet began the fifth lecture by stating that the Father and Son were the supreme power over all things, he also observed that the Holy Spirit is the third member of the eternal presidency and that these three—the Father, Son, and

Holy Spirit—"constitute the great, matchless, governing, and supreme power over all things, by whom all things were created and made. And these three constitute the Godhead and are one" (LF 5:2). It is true, as some have pointed out, that the Prophet did not refer in Lecture 5 to the Holy Spirit as a *personage*. Some have further suggested that this doctrine was not clarified until the administration of President Joseph F. Smith (Alexander, "The Reconstruction of Mormon Doctrine" 25-26; also *Mormonism in Transition* 272-306). As we will discuss later, what Joseph Smith knew and taught and what the Saints understood may be two different matters. One of the earliest references to the personage status of the Holy Spirit in the documents now available to us is from a sermon delivered some six years later, on 9 March 1841, a portion of which I cited earlier. In speaking of the separate and severable functions of the members of the Godhead, Joseph Smith explained that "the Son had a tabernacle and so had the Father, but the Holy Ghost is a personage of spirit without tabernacle" (*Words* 64). The most famous statement in Latter-day Saint theology regarding the mission of the Spirit is that recorded by Willard Richards in Ramus, Illinois:

> The Father has a body of flesh and bones as tangible as man's; the Son also. But the Holy Ghost is a personage of spirit. And a person cannot have the personage of the Holy Ghost in his heart. He may receive the gift of the Holy Ghost; it may descend upon him but not tarry with him (*Words* 173).

On 11 June 1843 Wilford Woodruff recorded the following remarks by the Prophet:

> There is much said concerning God the Godhead. And the scripture says there are Gods many and Lords many. The teachers of the day say that the Father is God, the Son is God, and the Holy Ghost is God and that they are all in one body and one God. Jesus says or prays that those that the Father had given him out of the world might be made one in us as we are one, but if they were to be stuffed into one person that would make a great God. If I were to testify that the world was wrong on this point it would be true. Peter says that Jesus Christ sat on the right hand of God. *Any person that has seen the heavens opened knows that there are three personages in the heavens holding the keys of power* (*Words* 214; emphasis added).

Finally, perhaps the most explicit statement as to the role and mission of the Holy Ghost is recorded by George Laub. According to Brother Laub, Joseph Smith taught on 16 June 1844 that God, Christ, and the Holy Ghost are separate persons but that they "all agree in one or the self same thing. But the Holy Ghost is yet a spiritual body and waiting to take to himself a body as the Savior did, or as God did, or the Gods before them took bodies" (*Words* 382).

The matter in Lecture 5 is complicated somewhat by the unusual manner in which the Prophet describes the work of the Spirit. Jesus Christ is said to have "received a fulness of the glory of the Father, *possessing the same mind with the Father, which mind is the Holy Spirit* that bears record of the Father and the Son" (LF 5:2; emphasis added). Not only is the Holy Spirit not accorded personage status in this reference, but he seems to be relegated to some type of mystical connecting link between the other two members of the Godhead. The Son is said to be "filled with the fulness of the *mind*, glory, and power, or in other words, the *spirit*, glory, and power, of the Father." The Son is "filled with the fulness of the *mind* of the Father, or . . . the *Spirit* of the Father, which Spirit is shed forth upon all who believe on his name and keep his commandments" (LF 5:2; emphasis added). It appears to me that the difficulty here is heightened by the lack of distinction between what we would call the Light of Christ and the Holy Ghost. Joseph Smith is speaking in the broadest of terms and simply refers to the Holy Spirit as the mind of God. "It is true," stated President Charles W. Penrose, "that the Holy Spirit conveys the mind of God; that is, I am speaking now of this universal spirit which is the life and the light of all things, which is in and through and round about all things, and God says he made the world by the power of that spirit. That is his agent; but the personage, the Comforter, which Jesus Christ said he would send when he went away, that was a personage of the Trinity" (Penrose 16). Elder Bruce R. McConkie likewise wrote that the Savior

possesses the same mind with the Father, knowing and believing and speaking and doing as though he were the Father. This mind is theirs by the power of the Holy Ghost. That is, the Holy Ghost, who is a personage of spirit (a spirit man!), using the light of Christ, can give the same mind to all men, whether mortal or immortal. The saints who are true and faithful in all things have, as Paul said, "the mind of Christ" (1 Corinthians 2:16), which means also that they have the mind of the Father (*A New Witness* 75).

It would not be difficult to suppose that at the time the Lectures on Faith were delivered the Prophet Joseph Smith had not yet learned of the personage status of the Holy Ghost and thus made no doctrinal distinction between the Spirit's person and powers. There is, however, one major difficulty with drawing the conclusion that the personage status of the Holy Ghost was not taught until after the turn of this century—Joseph Smith himself made a statement just eleven days before his death that disproves such a proposition. "I have always [taught]," Thomas Bullock quoted Joseph Smith as saying, "in all congregations when I have preached, it has been the plurality of Gods. It has been preached fifteen years. I have always declared God to be a distinct personage, Jesus Christ a separate and distinct personage from God the Father. The Holy Ghost was a distinct personage and or spirit, and these three constitute three distinct personages and three Gods" (*Words* 378). Rather than contradicting the Prophet— rather than concluding that Joseph did not preach something when he said he had—I choose to believe, with Elders Penrose and McConkie, that Joseph Smith did know the difference even though that difference is not clear in the records we have. Or it may have been that he thought it unnecessary to make that distinction every time he spoke because he had made it before. As we shall discuss shortly, there was, no doubt, a significant chasm between what the Prophet knew and what the Saints knew, as well as between what the Prophet knew and what he taught.

Becoming Heirs of the Heavenly Kingdom

In Lecture 5 Joseph Smith lifted our vision of man's eternal possibilities. Simply stated, he taught at this early date that man may become even as God. He instructed the School of the Elders that the Saints "who keep [the Lord's] commandments shall grow from grace to grace and become heirs of the heavenly kingdom, and joint-heirs with Jesus Christ. They will possess the same mind, being transformed into the same image or likeness, even the express image of him who fills all in all, being filled with the fulness of his glory and becoming one in him, even as the Father, Son, and Holy Spirit are one" (LF 5:2). We see reflected once again the doctrine of D&C 93, wherein Christ's pathway to Godhood is laid out, and the Saints are taught *how* to worship and *what* to worship. The essence of true worship is emulation, the imitation of the works and labors of Christ (McConkie, *The Promised Messiah* 568-69). Just as their prototype received divine assistance from the Father as he gave of himself to his fellow men (ie, he received "grace for grace"); just as Christ "received not of the fulness" of the glory of the Father at the first, but "continued from grace to grace"—grew line upon line, developed from one level of spiritual grace to a higher; and just as Christ received in the resurrection the fulness of the Father, so may all men and women follow such a path and grow in spiritual graces until they inherit all that the Father has (see D&C 93:12-20).

To say that men may possess "the same mind" as God, that they may be "transformed into [his] same image or likeness," or that they may partake "of the fulness of the Father and the Son through the Spirit" (LF 5:2, 3), is to say that men may come unto God in more than metaphorical fashion. To be a "joint-heir with Christ" is to be a co-inheritor with him, to possess on equal standing with the Holder of the birthright.[5] Elder McConkie has stressed that the fifth Lecture on Faith teaches "that we, as fallible, weak, mortal men—subject to all the ills, difficulties, and vicissitudes of life—have power to advance and progress and become

---

[5] Thus those who are entitled to membership in the "Church of the Firstborn" are not simply those who are members of the Lord's earthly church, but rather those who with Christ become joint-heirs to all the Father has; they are entitled to all of the blessings of the Firstborn and thus inherit them as though they were the firstborn. As such they are not just sons and daughters of Jesus Christ but sons and daughters of God, meaning the Father (see McConkie, *Doctrinal New Testament Commentary* 2:471-75; see also D&C 76:58).

like our exalted and eternal Father and his beloved Son." It thus sets forth "the same doctrine that concludes, 'As God now is, man may become.' This thing was announced, in principle, in the School of the Prophets and did not have to wait for a King Follett sermon, although, I suppose, the Saints did not fully grasp what was involved in this language initially" (McConkie, "The Lord God of Joseph Smith" 5). "Here then is Eternal life," the Prophet would teach at the theological peak of his ministry,

> to know the only wise and true God. You have got to learn how to be a God yourself and to be a king and priest to God, [the] same as all have done, by going from a small capacity to another, from grace to grace, until the resurrection, and sit in everlasting power as they who have gone before. . . . How consoling to the mourner when they are called to part with a wife, mother, father, daughter, relative, to know that although the earthly tabernacle shall be dissolved that they shall be heirs of God and joint-heirs of Jesus Christ, to inherit the same power . . . the same as those who are gone before" (*Words* 350).

Again I am eager to affirm that the Lectures on Faith are not primitive; I do not see them as being out of harmony in any way with what Joseph the Prophet later taught; they are certainly not something beyond which he and the Church later evolved. All the Lectures on Faith, and Lecture 5 in particular, contain much that is meaty, much that requires pondering and prayer and comparison and contemplation. They "were given to the saints and not the world, to enable the apostles, elders, and righteous people of the kingdom to fulfill the same plea made by the prophets of old—'Lord, Increase our faith'" (McConkie, "Lord, Increase Our Faith" 5).

The Knowledge of God:
The Prophets and the People

"Brother Joseph," observed Wilford Woodruff,

> used a great many methods of testing the integrity of men; and he taught a great many things which, in consequence of tradition, required prayer, faith, and a testimony from the Lord, before they

236

could be believed by many of the Saints. His mind was opened by the visions of the Almighty, and the Lord taught him many things by vision and revelation that were never taught publicly in his days; for the people could not bear the flood of intelligence which God poured into his mind (*Journal of Discourses* 5:83-84; hereafter *JD*).

Five months before his death, Joseph Smith lamented that

> there has been a great difficulty in getting anything into the heads of this generation. It has been like splitting hemlock knots with a corn-dodger for a wedge, and a pumpkin for a beetle. Even the Saints are slow to understand.
>
> I have tried for a number of years to get the minds of the Saints prepared to receive the things of God; but we frequently see some of them, after suffering all they have for the work of God, will fly to pieces like glass as soon as anything comes that is contrary to their traditions: they cannot stand the fire at all. How many will be able to abide a celestial law, and go through and receive their exaltation, I am unable to say, as many are called, but few are chosen (*History of the Church* 6:184-85; hereafter *HC*).

We simply are unable to gauge how much the Prophet knew —how much God had revealed to him personally—using only the basis of what the Saints knew. It would be a serious historical error to suppose that because the average member of the Church did not understand the nature of the Godhead—whether, for example, the Father had a corporeal body or whether the Holy Ghost was a personage—that Joseph the Prophet did not understand, and that the Lectures on Faith reflect that lack of understanding. This would also apply to some of the leaders of the Church, even some of the first Apostles. Because Parley P. Pratt failed to distinguish the Light of Christ from the personage of the Holy Ghost in his masterwork, *Key to the Science of Theology*,[6] does not reflect one way or another on what Joseph Smith comprehended or what he intended in the School of the Elders. Few would argue against the proposition that Parley's

---

[6]See Alexander's discussion in *Mormonism in Transition* (280-81). See also Parley P. Pratt's *An Answer to Mr. William Hewitt's Tract Against the Latter-Day Saints*, wherein even Elder Pratt gives evidence that he was struggling to understand the corporeality of God the Father.

brother, Orson, was one of the great theological minds of this dispensation. And yet we find Orson Pratt, as late as 1855, still wondering about the personage status of the Holy Ghost *(JD* 2:337-38), when, in fact, Joseph Smith had revealed clearly, as early as 1841, that the Holy Ghost was a personage of spirit as has already been noted above. The fact that the people did not fully grasp the intricacies of the doctrines is totally unrelated to what their leader was able to grasp and thus is unrelated to what he taught and what he intended to be understood. We must not be guilty of setting bounds for God or his prophet-leaders, subscribing them on the basis of our present view of things.

Conclusion

In my view the Lectures on Faith have not received the positive attention they ought to have received by the Latter-day Saints. They were, in fact, acknowledged by the members in 1835 as the "doctrine of the Church of the Latter Day Saints." I find the doctrine and scope of the Lectures to be stimulating and the perspective to be harmonious with traditional theology of the 20th-century Church. Like the Book of Mormon, I find their contents to be profound, even though they come from an early period in the Church's history. Truly "one of the flaws in the reasoning of some . . . is an over-reliance upon a linear view of history, an acceptance of the principle that phenomena evolve from previously existing circumstances. Such is certainly not the case in all situations; many events or movements"—and, without question, many doctrines—"[are] more revolutionary than evolutionary" (Millet 189). The Lectures on Faith are illustrative of this phenomenon: they come from a formative period of our history but make known truths which, when carefully studied and fully appreciated, would be considered a part of the mature Joseph Smith and the Nauvoo Church. Whether Joseph Smith himself literally wrote every word in Lecture 5 is immaterial to me; the Lectures were at least in part written by the Prophet and wholly approved by him in preparation for their inclusion in the first edition of the Doctrine and Covenants (*HC* 2:180).

"In my own judgment," said President Joseph Fielding Smith, "these Lectures on Faith are of great value and should be studied. . . . They were not taken out of the Doctrine and Covenants because they contained false doctrine, and I consider them to be of extreme value in the study of the gospel of Jesus Christ" (194). Perhaps Elder McConkie voiced my own feelings best when he spoke of Lecture Five to a Brigham Young University audience in 1972. "In my judgment," he said, "it is the most comprehensive, intelligent, inspired utterance that now exists . . . in one place defining, interpreting, expounding, announcing, and testifying what kind of being God is. It was written by the power of the Holy Ghost, by the spirit of inspiration. It is, in effect, eternal scripture; it is true" ("The Lord God of Joseph Smith" 4).

BIBLIOGRAPHY

Alexander, Thomas G. *Mormonism in Transition.* Chicago: Univ of Illinois, 1986.

———. "The Reconstruction of Mormon Doctrine: From Joseph Smith to Progressive Theology." *Sunstone* (Jul-Aug 1980) 5:24-33.

Backman, Milton V., Jr. *Joseph Smith's First Vision.* 2nd ed. Salt Lake City: Bookcraft, 1980.

———. "Truman Coe's 1836 Description of Mormonism." *BYU Studies* (Spring 1977) 17:347-55.

Ehat, Andrew F., and Lyndon W. Cook. *The Words of Joseph Smith.* Salt Lake City: Bookcraft, 1980.

History of the Church. 7 vols. Salt Lake City: Deseret Book, 1978.

Hymns. Salt Lake City: The Church of Jesus Christ of Latter-day Saints, 1985.

Journal of Discourses. 26 vols. 1854-86.

McConkie, Bruce R. *Doctrinal New Testament Commentary.* 3 vols. Salt Lake City: Bookcraft, 1965-73.

———. "Jesus Christ and Him Crucified." *Devotional Speeches of the Year, 1976.* Provo, UT: Brigham Young Univ, 1977. 391-405.

———. "The Lord God of Joseph Smith." *Speeches of the Year, 1971-1972.* Provo, UT: Brigham Young Univ, 1972.

———. "Lord, Increase Our Faith." *Speeches of the Year, 1967-1968.* Provo, UT: Brigham Young Univ, 1968.

———. *A New Witness for the Articles of Faith.* Salt Lake City: Deseret Book, 1985.

———. *The Promised Messiah.* Salt Lake City: Deseret Book, 1978.

Matthews, Robert J. *A Plainer Translation: Joseph Smith's Translation of the Bible, A History and Commentary.* Provo, UT: Brigham Young Univ, 1975.

Millet, Robert L. "Biblical Criticism and the Four Gospels: A Critical Look." *To Be Learned Is Good If . . . .* Ed. Robert L. Millet. Salt Lake City: Bookcraft, 1987. 187-204.

Penrose, Charles W. *Conference Report* (Apr 1921) 9-17.

Pratt, Parley P. *An Answer to Mr. William Hewitt's Tract Against the Latter-Day Saints.* Manchester: W. R. Thomas, 1840.

Smith, Joseph Fielding. *Seek Ye Earnestly.* Salt Lake City: Deseret Book, 1970.

Talmage, James E. *Articles of Faith.* Salt Lake City: The Church of Jesus Christ of Latter-day Saints, 1984.

Robert L. Millet is associate professor and chairman of Ancient Scripture at Brigham Young University.

A Discussion of Lecture 6

Great Faith Obtained Only Through Personal Sacrifice

Robert J. Matthews

*I*t is an honor to be involved with this symposium which is sponsored by the Religious Studies Center and is focused on the Lectures on Faith. It is certainly an important subject and it is appropriate that Brigham Young University should present a symposium and prepare a publication on this topic. The Lectures on Faith are the greatest and most profound treatises on faith that we know of. Although the seven lectures are systematically arranged in a logical way, they are not easy reading, but are worth the effort. The spiritual understanding that is available from the Lectures on Faith justifies many re-readings and invites an intense study for anyone who sincerely wants to know what faith really is. The lectures are a valuable clarification and bringing together of what the scriptures teach about faith in God and in the Lord Jesus Christ.

The orderly progress of ideas in the Lectures on Faith makes them one of our greatest possessions for explaining a systematic theology. The catechism for Lecture 1 defines "theology" as a "revealed science." We do not ordinarily think of theology or of religion as a "science," but it can be so regarded. And if the concepts are given by revelation, theology is the truest of sciences. President Brigham Young called it a "celestial science" (*Journal of Discourses* 6:318; hereafter *JD*). He also said:

We want every branch of science taught in this place that is taught in the world. But our favourite study is that branch which particularly belongs to the Elders of Israel—namely, theology. Every Elder should become a profound theologian—should understand this branch better than all the world (*JD* 6:317).

I am reminded also that the complete title to Elder Parley P. Pratt's popular work, *Key to Theology*, is actually *The Key to the Science of Theology*. In that light I would define the Lectures on Faith as lessons in the revealed science of theology. They are in a class by themselves and are literally "designed to unfold to the understanding the doctrine of Jesus Christ" in a rational, scientific manner (LF 1:1).

The earlier presentations in this symposium have emphasized what faith is and what it rests upon. It has been shown that in order to exercise true faith in God we need to know something of his perfect character and attributes. When we learn of the perfections and attributes of Deity, we are then able to develop unshaken confidence in God, because our minds can be at rest and be assured that God can and will fulfil all his promises. When we become men and women of faith, we can have this unshaken confidence and trust because the scriptures guarantee that the true God is perfect and is therefore an unchangeable, complete, and living God.

Such is the message of the first five of the Lectures on Faith. I have been asked to discuss the content of Lecture 6, which is a sobering task, and I feel a great need for the help of the Holy Ghost in order to present it in the proper perspective and spirit. I cannot speak for the Church or for the University, but I believe what I have written is correct. So that this paper will continue the unity and purpose of this symposium, it is necessary to quote briefly from two of the preceding lectures. First, from Lecture 4:2:

Let us here observe that the real design which the God of heaven had in view in making the human family acquainted with his attributes was that they might be enabled to exercise faith in him through the idea of the existence of his attributes. . . . The God of heaven, understanding most perfectly the constitution of human nature and the weakness of men, knew what was necessary to be revealed and what ideas needed to be planted in their minds to enable them to exercise faith in him unto eternal life.

And also paragraph 3 of Lecture 5:

From the foregoing account of the Godhead, which is given in his revelations, the Saints have a sure foundation laid for the exercise of faith unto life and salvation through the atonement and mediation of Jesus Christ. By his blood they have a forgiveness of sins. . . . As the Son partakes of the fulness of the Father through the Spirit, so the Saints are, by the same Spirit, to be partakers of the same fulness, to enjoy the same glory . . . through the love of the Father, the mediation of Jesus Christ, and the gift of the Holy Spirit. They are to be heirs of God and joint-heirs with Jesus Christ.

The sixth lecture, building on the foundation established by the earlier ones, introduces two major items: first, the necessity of each person's knowing (not merely believing or hoping) that his/her life is acceptable to God; and second, the necessity of our being willing to sacrifice all earthly possessions and honors as the means to obtain the knowledge of and the approval of the Lord Jesus Christ. We will discuss these items in that order.

Knowing That One's Life Is Acceptable to God

In the sixth Lecture on Faith, paragraphs 2 and 3, we read the following:

It is essential for any person to have an actual knowledge that the course of life which he is pursuing is according to the will of God to enable him to have that confidence in God without which no person can obtain eternal life. It was this that enabled the ancient Saints to endure all their afflictions and persecutions and to take joyfully the spoiling of their goods, knowing (not believing merely) that they had a more enduring substance.

Having the assurance that they were pursuing a course which was agreeable to the will of God, they were enabled to take not only the spoiling of their goods and the wasting of their substance joyfully, but also to suffer death in its most horrid forms, knowing (not merely believing) that when this "earthly house of this tabernacle [was] dissolved, we have a building of God, an house not made with hands, eternal in the heavens" (2 Cor 5:1).

What is there about living in this mortal fallen world that makes this kind of knowledge so important and necessary? We read from the next paragraph:

> Such was and always will be the situation of the Saints of God. Unless they have an actual knowledge that the course they are pursuing is according to the will of God, they will grow weary in their minds and faint. For such has been and always will be the opposition in the hearts of unbelievers and those who know not God against the pure and unadulterated religion of heaven (the only thing which ensures eternal life). They will persecute to the uttermost all who worship God according to his revelations, receive the truth in the love of it, and submit themselves to be guided and directed by his will. And they will drive them to such extremities that nothing short of an actual knowledge of their being the favorites of heaven and of their having embraced that order of things which God has established for the redemption of man will enable them to exercise that confidence in him necessary for them to overcome the world and obtain that crown of glory which is laid up for them that fear God (LF 6:4).

The matter is stated even more clearly in paragraph 5:

> For a man to lay down his all—his character and reputation, his honor and applause, his good name among men, his houses, his lands, his brothers and sisters, his wife and children, and even his own life also, counting all things but filth and dross for the excellency of the knowledge of Jesus Christ—requires more than mere belief or supposition that he is doing the will of God. It requires actual knowledge, realizing that when these sufferings are ended, he will enter into eternal rest and be a partaker of the glory of God.

The foregoing is so plain, so well stated, and so reasonable that I feel confident that anyone who reads it will understand it and will almost automatically want to have that same knowledge and testimony. It just naturally follows that after we learn of the perfect character and nature of God, what kind of a being he is, there wells up within our own hearts an intense desire, a craving and thirsting, a longing to be in harmony with him. That is why repentance, followed by baptism for the remission of sins and the laying on of hands for the baptism of fire or the Holy Ghost, accompany true faith in the Lord Jesus Christ. These are sequential steps that inch us along the pathway towards having our own lives conform to the revelations and commandments of God. Such a course of life feeds the soul, and comforts and gives it rest. Only a very calloused nature would not long for that unity and joy that come as a result of our knowing that we have the Lord's specific, precise, and particular approval.

Faith begins by hearing the word of God as it is preached by an authorized person through the testimony of the Holy Spirit. That Spirit kindles a desire for repentance and urges us to remove from our lives every deed and thought that would be offensive to God. Repentance brings unity and wholeness, whereas sin is fractious and divisive. "Wickedness never was happiness," and it jars the spirit of man (Alma 41:10). We cannot do wrong and feel right. These principles operate in everyone's life because we all came from God in the beginning and are his sons and daughters. Sometimes it takes a little longer for some of us to be touched and moved by the principles of eternal life, but we can be certain that sooner or later every human being will be so touched. With some it may be at the day of judgment, when it is too late to gain full benefit.

An example of how the preaching of the gospel and the workings of the Spirit move a people to repent and to seek divine approval is shown in Alma 22. Aaron begins teaching the king of the Lamanites by telling him what kind of a being God is and about the creation of the world and of Adam. Then he teaches the king about the fall of man and the plan of redemption through Jesus Christ. "And Aaron did expound all these things unto the king" (v 14).

The effect these teachings and the testimony of Aaron had on the king's mind illustrates the doctrine we are examining in Lecture 6:

> And it came to pass that after Aaron had expounded these things unto him, the king said: What shall I do that I may have this eternal life of which thou hast spoken? Yea, what shall I do that I may be born of God, having this wicked spirit rooted out of my breast, and receive his Spirit, that I may be filled with joy, that I may not be cast off at the last day? Behold, said he, I will give up

all that I possess, yea, I will forsake my kingdom, that I may receive this great joy.

But Aaron said unto him: If thou desirest this thing, if thou wilt bow down before God, yea, if thou wilt repent of all thy sins, and will bow down before God, and call on his name in faith, believing that ye shall receive, then shalt thou receive the hope which thou desirest.

And it came to pass that when Aaron had said these words, the king did bow down before the Lord, upon his knees; yea, even he did prostrate himself upon the earth, and cried mightily, saying:

O God, Aaron hath told me that there is a God; and if there is a God,and if thou art God, wilt thou make thyself known unto me, and I will give away all my sins to know thee, and that I may be raised from the dead, and be saved at the last day (Alma 22:15-18).

It is not difficult to see that the king wanted to be in favor with God. He didn't know a great deal about the scriptures or of the science of theology, but when he heard the gospel properly taught, his soul hungered for righteousness.

We have a similar example with Enos, who said his "soul hungered" because he had often heard his father Jacob speak "concerning eternal life, and the joy of the saints," and these things "sunk deep into [his] heart" (Enos 1:3-4). He had great strugglings in the spirit, a "wrestle" (v 2) he called it, until he gained a remission of his sins and obtained the voice of the Lord to his mind. Then he said "my guilt was swept away" (v 6), and "my soul did rest" (v 17). When he asked how it was done, the Lord said, "thy faith hath made thee whole" (v 8).

By reading the accounts of the Lamanite king and of Enos, we obtain a glimpse of what they felt. But what about we who live now? How can we feel what they felt and gain what they gained?

The great question for us, therefore, is: How do we today go about getting that individual assurance and actual knowledge that we are pursuing a course of life that is acceptable to the will of God? The answer is that we have to do the same things that were required in earler dispensations. The gospel has not changed. Faith is the same, the requirements are the same, and the rewards are the same. There are no special sales, no bargain days.

Being Willing to Sacrifice All Things

There is greater clarity given to us on the need to be willing to sacrifice all things than we have perhaps realized. We read in Lecture 6:7:

> Let us here observe that a religion that does not require the sacrifice of all things never has power sufficient to produce the faith necessary unto life and salvation. For from the first existence of man, the faith necessary unto the enjoyment of life and salvation never could be obtained without the sacrifice of all earthly things. It is through this sacrifice, and this only, that God has ordained that men should enjoy eternal life. And it is through the medium of the sacrifice of all earthly things that men do actually know that they are doing the things that are well pleasing in the sight of God. When a man has offered in sacrifice all that he has for the truth's sake, not even withholding his life, and believing before God that he has been called to make this sacrifice because he seeks to do His will, he does know, most assuredly, that God does and will accept his sacrifice and offering and that he has not sought nor will he seek His face in vain. Under these circumstances, then, he can obtain the faith necessary for him to lay hold on eternal life.

Why Faith and Knowledge Are Dependent upon Sacrifice

A major consideration at this point is *why* perfect faith can be obtained only by the willingness to sacrifice all earthly things. The quick answer may be: "God has so ordered it." No doubt this is true, but we may want to understand more about it. A large factor inherent in the willingness to sacrifice all earthly possessions is the knowledge that the plan of redemption neither begins nor ends with this mortal life. It began in the premortal world and extends to the postmortal one. This plan is founded in God's wisdom, God's knowledge, and God's power. Through the fall of Adam all mankind have become subject to two deaths—the physical death of the body, which is caused by the separation of the body and the spirit; and the spiritual death, which is caused by the separation of the person from the things of God, that is, to "die" as to things of righteousness.

Because of these two deaths, all human beings are cut off from a knowledge of God; they have no conscious memory of God, and no memory of a premortal life, nor any understanding of a postmortal one after this mortal probation. Our knowledge in this natural, mortal, fallen state is earthbound. Our affections, interests, ambitions, and desires are centered on this present mortal life. The natural man knows none of the things of God. Neither can he know them for they are only obtained by the Holy Ghost (1 Cor 2:14). As we learn the first principles of the gospel, the Holy Ghost gives us a testimony of the reality of God, of heaven, and of Jesus Christ. As we advance in righteousness, there comes a time when we will be asked to consecrate all that we have for the kingdom of God on earth. What better test of our faith and testimony is there than to be asked to forego our honors, possessions, reputations, and such things, to gain a future inheritance in a time and place which as natural man we didn't even know existed, nor did we know that the willingness to sacrifice all things is the way to get there.

In view of the conditions that exist with the natural, mortal world, it is obviously the right thing for the Lord to require of those of us who would partake of the fulness of salvation to consecrate all that we have to his work, and to be willing to serve him at all costs. Anything short of that would not be a complete and adequate test of our confidence and faith in the Almighty God. Nor could anything less measure the progress we have made in overcoming the natural man. It is in this way that mortality serves most effectively as a probationary and preparatory state.

Why the Miraculous Is Necessary in the Gospel

Due to the nature of fallen man, a true revealed religion must of necessity be miraculous in its nature. The knowledge, blessings, communications, and powers of a heavenly, divine system have to be extra-terrestrial. The power and the knowledge to save fallen mankind must come from outside the earth itself;

outside of us ourselves. It cannot originate with us. It must come from God, or there can be no salvation or redemption in it. Hence God tests his children by asking them to do something entirely outside of the natural style of mortality. All of the commandments of God are that way. Baptism, ordination, faith, sacrifice, prayer, repentance, obedience to specified commandments, personal cleanliness of thought, etc.—all are contrary to what comes naturally to us. Acts of obedience are responses that we must learn and do deliberately; they cannot happen by chance, happenstance, or accident. And obeying the commandments is not the kind of thing we would do naturally. Doing what comes naturally does not lead to celestial glory and godhood. Only by doing what is not natural, because of our faith, do we find salvation. We wouldn't consistently keep all the commandments if we didn't have faith, and that is why we can see the truth of Paul's declaration, "Without faith it is impossible to please [God]" (Heb 11:6).

Natural man, with the natural, unregenerated mind, is given to rationalization and to discounting the validity of divine revelation and the importance of obedience, and even the need for a redemptive sacrifice and death of a God. Rationalization thus becomes the great usurper, the eroder and the robber of our faith. This is demonstrated very clearly in the book of Helaman just previous to the time of Jesus' birth. Even though so many "signs . . . [had been] wrought among the people," those who did not believe in the gospel said: "It is not *reasonable* that such a being as Christ shall come" (16:18-23; emphasis added). The unbelievers' idea of "reasonableness" caused them to miss the message of redemption through Jesus Christ.

The Role of Revelation and Testimony

It is totally clear from the content of the Lectures on Faith that there can be no true religion among men and women on this earth without revelation and testimony from God. Without revelation from heaven, mankind would not know what kind of being God is, and any ideas about his attributes and perfections could only be guesswork. The God of heaven must reveal himself, or he must remain forever unknown. First, as we have seen, we could not exercise true faith in a God we knew nothing about. True faith cannot take root and thrive in ignorance. Second, our faith would not be strong and unshaken unless we knew by continuing revelation that our lifestyle was pleasing to God. It would simply be impossible for any of us to exercise the kind of pure faith that is described in these lectures in the absence of direct, immediate, and personal revelation.

Such necessary revelation does not often come by an angelic visitor or personal open vision, but it comes most often by the personal manifestations and whisperings of the Holy Ghost. The Prophet Joseph Smith explained, "the Holy Ghost is a revelator," and "no man can receive the Holy Ghost without receiving revelations" (*Teachings of the Prophet Joseph Smith* 328; hereafter *TPJS*). Revelation and testimony come to us through the Holy Ghost and are miraculous occurrences, outside the normal realm of man's five natural senses.

A religion without revelation is but a philosophical network of human ideas, no matter how ingenious and astute it may be. Without revelation its adherents and believers could not know whether the God they worshiped even existed—much less whether or not he was pleased with the way they worshipped him or even whether he cared. When it comes to the matter of man's relationship to God, not to have any revelation from him leaves everything to supposition and opinion. This is the idea given in Doctrine and Covenants 93:19, wherein the Lord says: "I give unto you these sayings that you may understand and know how to worship, and know what you worship, that you may come unto the Father in my name, and in due time receive of his fulness."

As we have discovered in the Lectures on Faith, revelation from God must cover several subject areas. First, it must reveal that there *is* a God. Second, it must reveal the traits of his character and attributes, and show that these attributes are perfect in him. Third, it must reveal what God wants man to do and what he wants him not to do. And fourth, it must assure us that what we are doing is what God would have us do. Receiving this last revelation is the basic message of the sixth lecture.

For a person to receive a direct, individual and personal revelation from God is an experience not obtained merely for the asking. To be told by the Almighty God, the Creator of the Universe, that he has noticed us and that he is pleased by our service and obedience is a blessing worth years of search and toil. Such a reward is the theme of both the parable of the "treasure hid in a field" and that of the "pearl of great price" (Matt 13:44, 45-46). The message of both parables is that giving all that we have would not be giving too much to gain such favor with God. Heaven, knowing the proper price to place on all its goods, has so ordained that the kind of faith that is powerful enough to enable us to lay hold on eternal life is available only on the basis of our being willing to sacrifice all earthly goods and honors.

There are records in the scriptures of those who have made this kind of sacrifice. Jesus is the greatest example. He said to the Nephites:

> I am the light and the life of the world; and I have drunk out of that bitter cup which the Father hath given me, and have glorified the Father in taking upon me the sins of the world, in the which I have suffered the will of the Father in all things from the beginning (3 Nephi 11:11).

Saul of Tarsus, later known as Paul, was a learned man, accepted within his own Pharisee group, valiant above those his own age, and had position, power, and influence. He was determined to prevent Christianity from destroying the religion of the Jews. He was not an evil man; he simply did not understand. And in his error he viewed the doctrine of Christ as an enemy to the revelations God had given to Moses and to Abraham. What did the Lord require of Paul? The same thing that he requires of all who seek salvation and a place with him in eternity. He required total obedience and the willingness to sacrifice all things. When Paul was first converted by a vision of Jesus on the road to Damascus, he little knew what awaited him. At that time the Lord said in a vision to Ananias, who had some doubts about Paul's reputation: "[Paul] is a chosen vessel unto me, to bear my name before the Gentiles, and kings, and the children of Israel: for I will shew him how great things he must suffer for my name's sake" (Acts 9:15-16).

Paul had many visions, many revelations and many trials, and suffered intense persecution and hardship, including imprisonment, whippings, character assassination, loss of friends, privation, and illness. Yet he stayed true to his testimony and came off victorious. In speaking of himself and of his companions who were thus tried and tested to the uttermost, Paul wrote:

> We are troubled on every side, yet not distressed; we are perplexed, but not in despair; persecuted, but not forsaken; cast down, but not destroyed (2 Cor 4:8-9).

Later, while in a Roman prison, he wrote:

> But what things were gain to me, those I counted loss for Christ. Yea doubtless, and I count all things but loss for the excellency of the knowledge of Christ Jesus my Lord: for whom I have suffered the loss of all things, and do count them but dung, that I may win Christ (Philip 3:7-8).

Why was Paul willing to continue on in the face of so much opposition? It was because he knew what God required, and that the God of heaven had accepted his efforts, and that his salvation was sure. We read from 2 Timothy 4:6-8, as Paul wrote from a prison cell in Rome:

> For I am now ready to be offered, and the time of my departure is at hand. I have fought a good fight, I have finished my course, I have kept the faith: Henceforth there is laid up for me a crown of righteousness, which the Lord, the righteous judge, shall give me at that day: and not to me only, but unto all them also that love his appearing.

Paul knew that his life was acceptable to God and that his calling and election were sure.

Paul's convert, Timothy, whom he affectionately called "my own dear son in the faith," was a man like Paul, dedicated

252

to the work of the Lord above his own interests. Paul, writing to the Church at Philippi, said of Timothy:

> For I have no man likeminded, who will naturally care for your state. For all seek their own, not the things which are Jesus Christ's. But ye know the proof of him, that, as a son with the father, he hath served with me in the gospel (Philip 2:20-22).

The Book of Mormon also is a record of faithful disciples who sacrificed all things. We read of Nephi, that righteous, wondrous prophet-son of Helaman who lived just before the advent of Jesus among the Nephites, that he was absolutely single-minded to God. In return for his obedience, the Lord trusted him and gave him power in the ministry and promised to bless him forever. We read from Helaman 10:3-5:

> And it came to pass as he was thus pondering—being much cast down because of the wickedness of the people of the Nephites, their secret works of darkness, and their murderings, and their plunderings, and all manner of iniquities—and it came to pass as he was thus pondering in his heart, behold, a voice came unto him saying:
> Blessed art thou, Nephi, for those things which thou hast done; for I have beheld how thou hast with unwearyingness declared the word, which I have given unto thee, unto this people. And thou hast not feared them, and hast not sought thine own life, but hast sought my will, and to keep my commandments.
> And now, because thou hast done this with such unwearyingness, behold, I will bless thee forever; and I will make thee mighty in word and in deed, in faith and in works; yea, even that all things shall be done unto thee according to thy word, for thou shalt not ask that which is contrary to my will.

There can be no question that after receiving this revelation, Nephi knew his life was acceptable to God and he would be saved.

These valiant souls (Jesus, Paul, Timothy, and Nephi, among many others) gave all that they had, their time, talents, possessions, and desires, to the building up of the kingdom of God on the earth. Some of them also gave their lives. And they knew that God was aware of their struggles and would not forget them.

But not all the heroes were in olden times. Those who lay in Richmond Jail, Liberty Jail, and Carthage Jail suffered in like manner as did the former prophets. And the Latter-day Saints who were driven out of Missouri and out of Illinois suffered as much in cold weather, prison, loss of family, loss of goods, and in death, as did the Former-day Saints in the lions' dens and the arenas of Rome.

It was in this light that the Prophet Joseph Smith viewed the sufferings of the Latter-day Saints in the early days of this Church:

> Such inhumanity, and relentless cruelty and barbarity as were practiced against the Saints in Missouri can scarcely be found in the annals of history (*TPJS* 126).

We also read in the Prophet's epistle to the Church, written 25 March 1839 from Liberty Jail, Missouri:

> And now, beloved brethren, we say unto you, that inasmuch as God hath said that He would have a tried people, that He would purge them as gold, now we think that this time He has chosen His own crucible, wherein we have been tried; and we think if we get through with any degree of safety, and shall have kept the faith, that it will be a sign to this generation, altogether sufficient to leave them without excuse; and we think also, it will be a trial of our faith equal to that of Abraham, and that the ancients will not have whereof to boast over us in the day of judgment, as being called to pass through heavier afflictions; that we may hold an even weight in the balance with them; but now, after having suffered so great sacrifice and having passed through so great a season of sorrow, we trust that a ram may be caught in the thicket speedily, to relieve the sons and daughters of Abraham from their great anxiety, and to light up the lamp of salvation upon their countenances, that they may hold on now, after having gone so far unto everlasting life (*TPJS* 135-136).

We now continue from Lecture 6:8:

> It is in vain for persons to fancy to themselves that they are heirs with those, or can be heirs with them, who have offered their all in sacrifice, and by this means obtained faith in God and favor with him so as to obtain eternal life, unless they in like manner offer unto him the same sacrifice and through that offering obtain the knowledge that they are accepted of him.

Trials and Tests Are Custom-made

We do not mean to imply by all these examples that only martyrs will be saved or that only those who are driven out of their homes or who lose their farms, businesses, and health to a mob are saved. What we find in the revelations and in the teachings of the brethren is that the Lord requires such undivided allegiance, that a person who expects to inherit a celestial glory must be willing to sacrifice all things if called upon to do so. The gospel provides a way for a person to show that willingness by solemn oath and covenant, in the Lord's own way and according to his plan of redemption. This is a covenant of total consecration. The Prophet Joseph Smith has said:

> When we consecrate our property to the Lord it is to administer to the wants of the poor and needy, for this is the law of God; it is not for the benefit of the rich, those who have no need; and when a man consecrates or dedicates his wife and children, he does not give them to his brother, or to his neighbor, for there is no such law. . . . For a man to consecrate his property, wife and children, to the Lord, is nothing more nor less than to feed the hungry, clothe the naked, visit the widow and fatherless, the sick and afflicted, and do all he can to administer to their relief in their afflictions, and for him and his house to serve the Lord. In order to do this, he and all his house must be virtuous, and must shun the very appearance of evil (*TPJS* 127).

The Lord's plan of redemption requires men and women to consecrate all their belongings and abilities to the service of God. This they do by covenant. The Lord may then test them to see how sincere they are and how much they are willing to sacrifice.

We cannot say what, in the economy of God, he will require of any one of us individually. There is a universal requirement of all mankind to "endure to the end," and we also know that "where much is given much is required." Some commandments pertain to everyone. Some individual tests, however, are "tailor-made" and suited to the particular person and circumstances. When a person has been obedient to the first principles and the universal requirements, it appears that the Lord then devises more searching, individualized tests for a specific purpose in relation to a specific individual. The most popular example of this is the commandment God gave to Abraham to offer his son Isaac as a sacrifice. It seems to have had at least two immediate purposes. One was to test Abraham's faith and obedience; and the other was to give Abraham experience whereby he would learn something about himself and about godliness that he had not understood sufficiently before. We read from President John Taylor:

> I heard the Prophet Joseph say, in speaking to the Twelve on one occasion: "You will have all kinds of trials to pass through. And it is quite as necessary for you to be tried as it was for Abraham and other men of God, and (said he) God will feel after you, and He will take hold of you and wrench your very heart strings, and if you cannot stand it you will not be fit for an inheritance in the Celestial Kingdom of God" (*JD* 24:197).

And again from another talk by President Taylor:

> I heard Joseph Smith say and I presume Brother Snow heard him also—in preaching to the Twelve in Nauvoo, that the Lord would get hold of their heart strings and wrench them, and that they would have to be tried as Abraham was tried. . . . And Joseph said that if God had known any other way whereby he could have touched Abraham's feelings more acutely and more keenly he would have done so. It was not only his parental feelings that were touched. There was something else besides. He had the promise that in him and in his seed all the nations of the earth should be blessed; that his seed should be multiplied as the stars of the heaven and as the sand upon the sea shore. He had looked forward through the vista of future ages and seen, by the spirit of revelation, myriads of his people rise up through whom God would convey intelligence, light and salvation to a world. But in being called upon to sacrifice his son it seemed as though all his prospects pertaining to posterity were come to naught. But he had faith in God, and he fulfilled the thing that was required of him. Yet we cannot conceive of anything that could be more trying and more perplexing than the position in which he was placed (*JD* 24:264).

Speaking also of the test given to Abraham, President George Q. Cannon said:

> Why did the Lord ask such things of Abraham? Because, knowing what his future would be and that he would be the father of an innumerable posterity, he [sic] was determined to test him. God did

not do this for His own sake for He knew by His foreknowledge what Abraham would do; but the purpose was to impress upon Abraham a lesson and to enable him to attain unto knowledge that he could not obtain in any other way. That is why God tries all of us. It is not for His own knowledge for He knows all things beforehand. He knows all your lives and everything you will do. But He tries us for our own good that we may know ourselves; for it is most important that a man should know himself.

He required Abraham to submit to this trial because He intended to give him glory, exaltation and honor; He intended to make him a king and a priest, to share with Himself the glory, power and dominion which He exercised. And was this trial any more than God himself had passed through? (89).

We Receive No Witness Until After the Trial of Our Faith

There is always a spiritual reward and benefit from obeying any commandment of God, and there is always a divine reason for that commandment, although the one so commanded may not be able to comprehend it until later. If we fail the small tests, we may never have the opportunity to take the large ones. Consequently, we may not realize what was really taking place. I think this is the point the prophet Moroni was making when he said, "dispute not because ye see not, for ye receive no witness until after the trial of your faith" (Ether 12:6). One of the lessons we learn from the scriptures is that trials are not always a penalty for sins. Sometimes, as with Abraham, Job, or Joseph Smith, trials have an educational purpose and are designed to "give experience, and shall be for thy good" (see D&C 122:7).

Sacrifice Is an Educational Experience

A significant reason for the Lord's requiring the willingness to sacrifice all things is the experience it gives those who do it. It is not only necessary that we have confidence in God, but there is also a dimension to be gained about ourselves through the experience and the discipline of making a sacrifice. Our own acts tell us something about ourselves. Sacrificing all that we have in obedience to the Lord's commandments greatly increases our own self-confidence. We know for ourselves that we *can* keep the commandments—we have done it. This has a powerful effect upon our attitude about ourselves. Notice the language of the Lord given in Doctrine and Covenants 97:8-9:

> Verily I say unto you, all among them who know their hearts are honest, and are broken, and their spirits contrite, and are willing to observe their covenants by sacrifice—yea, every sacrifice which I, the Lord, shall command—they are accepted of me. For I, the Lord, will cause them to bring forth as a very fruitful tree which is planted in a goodly land, by a pure stream, that yieldeth much precious fruit.

In speaking on this same subject—of a person's knowing and being aware that he or she has been obedient, even at a cost—President David O. McKay said that "spirituality is the consciousness of victory over self" (351).

Anciently, King David understood something of the importance of sacrifice, when on one occasion a friend wanted to give him oxen to sacrifice to the Lord. David's reply was:

> I will surely buy it of thee at a price: neither will I offer burnt offerings unto the Lord my God of that which doth cost me nothing. So David bought the threshingfloor and the oxen for fifty shekels of silver (2 Sam 24:24).

The concept of customized tests is very important. We do not all have the same tests, and we can benefit from what Elder Boyd K. Packer said on this theme in the October 1980 General Conference:

> Our lives are made up of thousands of everyday choices. Over the years these little choices will be bundled together and show clearly what we value.
>
> The crucial test of life, I repeat, does not center in the choice between fame and obscurity, nor between wealth and poverty. The greatest decision of life is between good and evil.
>
> We may foolishly bring unhappiness and trouble, even suffering upon ourselves. These are not always to be regarded as penalties imposed by a displeased Creator. They are part of the lessons of life, part of the test.

Some are tested by poor health, some by a body that is deformed or homely. Others are tested by handsome and healthy bodies; some by the passion of youth; others by the erosions of age.

Some suffer disappointment in marriage, family problems; others live in poverty and obscurity. Some (perhaps this is the hardest test) find ease and luxury.

All are part of the test, and there is more equality in this testing than sometimes we suspect.

It is possible to be both rich and famous and at the same time succeed spiritually. But the Lord warned of the difficulty of it when He talked of camels and needles (see Matt 19:24) (21).

Elder Neal A. Maxwell spoke along the same lines to some students at Brigham Young University:

God knows what his children can become and tries them to help them reach their potential. . . . In time each person will receive a "customized challenge" to determine his dedication to God ("Link Truths" 11).

Trials and adversities may often be blessings in disguise and are part of the "sacrifice of all things" required for the development of true faith. Several great prophets of this dispensation have spoken on this subject. President Harold B. Lee said the following in addressing Church Office employees at the annual Christmas Devotional in the Tabernacle on Temple Square on 13 December 1973:

We are tested, we are tried. . . . We don't realize perhaps the severity of the tests that we are going through. In [the early days of the Church], there were murderings, there were mobbings. . . . [The Saints] were driven out into the desert, they were starving and they were unclad, they were cold. We are the inheritors of what they gave to us. But what are we doing with it? Today we are basking in the lap of luxury, the like of which we've never seen before in the history of the world. It would seem that probably this is the most severe test of any . . . we've ever had in the history of this Church (4-5).

And President Ezra Taft Benson (then President of the Council of the Twelve) told the Regional Representatives on 30 September 1977:

Every generation has its tests and its chance to stand and prove itself. Would you like to know of one of our toughest tests?

Hear the warning words of President Brigham Young: "The worst fear I have about this people is that they will get rich in this country, forget God and His people, wax fat, and kick themselves out of the Church and go to hell. This people will stand mobbing, robbing, poverty and all manner of persecution and be true. But my greatest fear is that they cannot stand wealth."

Ours then seems to be the toughest test of all for the evils are more subtle, more clever. It all seems less menacing and it is harder to detect. While every test of righteousness represents a struggle, this particular test seems like no test at all, no struggle, and so could be the most deceiving of all tests.

Do you know what peace and prosperity can do to a people—it can put them to sleep (2).

Sacrifice Seen in Perspective

In this paper we have spoken much of sacrifice and the spiritual influence it has on those who do it and the loss to those who do not. In one sense, however, there is no lasting sacrifice as President George Q. Cannon explained:

If we expect to attain the fulfillment of the promises God has made to us, we must be self-sacrificing. There is no sacrifice that God can ask of us or His servants whom He has chosen to lead us that we should hesitate about making. In one sense of the word it is no sacrifice. We may call it so because it comes in contact with our selfishness and our unbelief (89).

And Elder Bruce R. McConkie said:

Sacrifice pertains to mortality; in the eternal sense there is none. Sacrifice involves giving up the things of this world because of the promises of blessings to be gained in a better world. In the eternal perspective there is no sacrifice in giving up all things—even including the laying down of one's life—if eternal life is gained through such a course (664).

We conclude and summarize this discussion by quoting excerpts from Lecture 6:9-12:

In the last days before the Lord comes, he is to gather together his saints who have made a covenant with him by sacrifice.
. . . Those who do not make the sacrifice cannot enjoy this faith, because men are dependent upon this sacrifice in order to obtain this faith. Therefore, they cannot lay hold upon eternal life,

because the revelations of God do not guarantee unto them the authority so to do; and without this guarantee faith could not exist.

All the Saints of whom we have account in all the revelations of God which are extant obtained the knowledge which they had of their acceptance in his sight through the sacrifice which they offered unto him. And through the knowledge thus obtained, their faith became sufficiently strong to lay hold upon the promise of eternal life. . . .

But those who have not made this sacrifice to God do not know that the course which they pursue is well pleasing in his sight. For whatever may be their belief or their opinion, it is a matter of doubt and uncertainty in their mind; and where doubt and uncertainty are, there faith is not, nor can it be. For doubt and faith do not exist in the same person at the same time. So persons whose minds are under doubts and fears cannot have unshaken confidence, and where unshaken confidence is not, there faith is weak. And where faith is weak, the persons will not be able to contend against all the opposition, tribulations, and afflictions which they will have to encounter in order to be heirs of God and joint-heirs with Christ Jesus. But they will grow weary in their minds, and the adversary will have power over them and destroy them.

Making a serious study of the Lectures on Faith is a sobering experience. I can assure you that one cannot examine and absorb these lectures and afterwards be flippant or indifferent about what God requires of us in this life. To study these lectures and to prepare a paper on them is a deep spiritual experience.

BIBLIOGRAPHY

Benson, Ezra Taft. "Our Obligation and Challenge." Address given at Regional Representative Seminar, 30 Sep 1977.

Cannon, George Q. *Gospel Truth*. Ed. Jerreld L. Newquist. Salt Lake City: Deseret Book, 1987.

Journal of Discourses. 26 vols. 1854-86.

Lee, Harold B. Address given at Christmas Devotional for LDS Church Employees, 13 Dec 1973.

"Link Truths, Students Told Wednesday." *Daily Universe* (7 Oct 1983) 37:11.

McConkie, Bruce R. *Mormon Doctrine*. 2nd ed. Salt Lake City: Bookcraft, 1979.

McKay, David O. "Choose You This Day Whom Ye Will Serve." *Improvement Era* (May 1949) 52:270-71, 350-51; also in *Conference Report* (Apr 1949)10-17.

Packer, Boyd K. "The Choice." *Ensign* (Nov 1980) 10:20-22; also in *Conference Report* (Oct 1980) 26-30.

Pratt, Parley P. *The Key to the Science of Theology*. 3rd ed. Salt Lake City: Deseret Book, 1966.

Teachings of the Prophet Joseph Smith. Comp. Joseph Fielding Smith. Salt Lake City: Deseret Book, 1976.

Robert J. Matthews is dean of Religious Education and professor of Ancient Scripture at Brigham Young University.

Fruits of Faith

Ardeth G. Kapp

I pray earnestly that my message, with a specific focus on Lecture 7 from the Lectures on Faith, may increase understanding of the fruits of faith and point our hearts toward earnestly seeking the greatest of all the gifts of God.

An ancient writer once asked the question:

> "Who is man . . . that he should take his place before thy face. . . . How can the clay and the potter sit together; or who understands thy wonderful plan of God?" And he supplies the answer: "For eternal glory he has chosen me, and for that he teaches me. . . ." the Way of Light itself is "the spirit of the understanding of all the Plan. . . . Without thee nothing came into existence—and he instructed me in all knowledge" (Nibley 33).

It is through the gospel of Jesus Christ, the plan of salvation, that the way is provided for each of us one day to sit down with the potter, the Creator, even God our Father and his Son Jesus Christ and to be one with them and to be like them, the ultimate fruit of faith.

I would like to discuss and illustrate some principles which relate to the fruits of faith as presented in the seventh lecture:

First, faith brings an eternal perspective to our mortal life;

Second, salvation is the result of faith; and

Third, perfection comes through faith.

Faith Brings an Eternal Perspective to Our Mortal Life

Faith Is the First Principle in the Science of Theology

In Lecture 7:5-6, we read:

> It is only necessary for us to say that the whole visible creation as it now exists is the effect of faith. It was faith by which it was framed, and it is by the power of faith that it continues in its organized form. . . . So, then, faith is truly the first principle in the science of theology, and, when understood, it leads the mind back to the beginning, and carries it forward to the end, or, in other words, from eternity to eternity. . . . All the blessings of eternity are the effects of faith.

Expanding this concept further, we read in paragraph 20:

> From this we may extend as far as any circumstances may require, whether on earth or in heaven, and we will find it the testimony of all inspired men or heavenly messengers that all things that pertain to life and godliness are the effects of faith and nothing else. All learning, wisdom, and prudence fail, and everything else as a means of salvation but faith.

Power by Which God Operates

Faith is literally the power by which God himself operates in earthly and heavenly affairs. Miracles are the fruits of faith; faith precedes the miracle. Behind each miracle is divine power, and that power is faith.

As a young girl who had just had a serious mastoid operation, I overheard the doctors explain to my parents that I would not only lose my hearing but also my equilibrium and thus the ability to walk. With my name on the prayer roll in the temple and my father's hands placed on my head, assisted by another Melchizedek Priesthood bearer, I knew that with faith in God I would be healed.

We read in the scriptures, "And neither at any time hath any wrought miracles until after their faith; wherefore they first believed in the Son of God" (Ether 12:18). Truly, as the Lord Jesus said: "All things are possible to him that believeth" (Mark 9:23). "For if there be no faith among the children of men God can do no miracle among them; wherefore, he showed not himself until after their faith" (Ether 12:12).

Faith is a principle, a key of power, that opens the door to our progress. The abundance of life and salvation can come to us only through our faith. It is the source of our feeling of well-being, of courage, and of peace both in this life and in the world to come. If we begin with Adam and look through the history of the generations of this earth, we see his descendants (ourselves included) receiving blessings and privileges according to the degree of faith that they possess. We read in Lecture 7:17, "Every man [has] received according to his faith: according as his faith was, so were his blessings and privileges. And nothing was withheld from him when his faith was sufficient to receive it."

By the Power of Faith the Heavens Are Opened

The restoration of the gospel of Jesus Christ began with the faith of one young boy. He had studied the scriptures. He had implicit trust in the words of God: "If any of you lack wisdom, let him ask of God. . . . But let him ask in faith, nothing wavering" (James 1:5-6). Of that scripture he recorded, "Never did any passage of scripture come with more power to the heart of man than this did at this time to mine" (JS-H 1:12). One beautiful spring morning in a grove of trees near his home, Joseph Smith knelt in prayer. He prayed vocally for the first time in his life and asked God a specific question. His prayer of faith unlocked the heavens. By the power of faith, the Father and his Son Jesus Christ appeared to Joseph Smith, called him by name, and instructed him. That same invitation to ask God in faith is extended to each of us today; and because of the restoration of the gospel of Jesus Christ, we know of the nature of God, the love of God, the reality of God and the great plan of salvation provided for us, his children, to return and once again dwell with him.

Some time ago, I was asked to speak to a group of young women on an early morning in the high Uinta mountains. At the conclusion of my remarks, I reminded them that the Prophet Joseph Smith went into a grove of trees and prayed in faith. I made the following suggestion:

"Each one of you, sometime before returning home, find a quiet spot in nature where you can experience reverence for life all around you, and talk with your Father in heaven and share with him the things that are in your heart. He is always there, and he will hear you.". . . Two weeks later, in a fast and testimony meeting, [in her own ward,] Becky [the assistant youth camp director] stood [to bear] her testimony. . . . "Something about the feelings I had that special morning made me want to be alone for a while. [So I] found a private spot where there was a little opening in the trees. When I knelt down on the ground, thick with pine needles, I didn't know for sure what to say, so I closed my eyes and said, 'Heavenly Father, do you know I am here?' I waited and waited, and I could hear the wind in the trees. Then I opened my eyes and saw the sun coming through the leaves, and I felt all warm inside." She paused a moment and then, in a reverent whisper, added, "You may not think it was anything, but I know he knew I was there" (Kapp, *Miracles* 39-40).

Becky, like the Prophet, had faith in God. She felt her request was appropriate. She had simply asked, "Do you know I'm here?" and she received an immediate answer. When she left the mountains, she was never the same again. She knew more about God than she had ever known before. She could better understand the testimony of the Prophet Joseph Smith, that God did hear and answer his prayer.

Do we know he knows we are here? Have we asked? From Becky's communication with God and by the power of faith, she learned for herself that God is real. He cares about us, his children. He hears our prayers. He answers with a message to our spirit that speaks louder than words. While others may not be impressed or believe, we can *know* he knows we are here by the power of our faith. And with that assurance, we have the first requirement necessary to develop the faith that leads to salvation—we know for ourselves that God lives.

Our Need for Greater Faith

We live in a time when people's hearts are failing them and they need greater faith in God and a deeper understanding of his eternal purposes. The burdens of life can be lifted through faith in the Lord Jesus Christ, but without faith people are unsettled, unsure, and unsaved. Skepticism, cynicism, and doubt run rampant as the world ripens in iniquity and would, if possible, destroy faith and its fruits like hoards of black crickets devouring tender shoots. In the absence of faith, the darkest clouds of fear and depression close in and put out the light.

These are no ordinary times. President Ezra Taft Benson, speaking recently to the youth of the Church, stated, "While our generation will be comparable in wickedness to the days of Noah, when the Lord cleansed the earth by flood, there is a major difference this time: God has saved for the final inning some of His stronger and most valiant children, who will help bear off the kingdom triumphantly. . . . You are the generation that must be prepared to meet your God" (Benson 73).

Our young Latter-day Saints are showing evidence of the quality of faith that will carry them through difficult times and prepare them to meet their God. Rosanna, a young girl from Anchorage, Alaska, one of many thousands of young women of the Church who wrote a message tied to a balloon and set it aloft on 11 October 1986, shared her testimony:

> I am 15 years old and a member of The Church of Jesus Christ of Latter-day Saints. I know that God lives and loves us. Jesus Christ is the Savior of the world. I love them with all my heart. If I could wish for anything for the world, I would wish that everyone had a sure knowledge that God lives and that he hears and answers prayers. I'm thankful for the answers I've received to my prayers. You too can receive answers to your prayers. All you have to do is ask. No matter who you are or what you have done, God will listen (*The Rising Generation* 44).

With faith in God and a knowledge that he listens to the prayers of his children, this young woman, with hundreds of others, is bearing strong testimony. Their faith will keep them on course as they walk the straight and narrow path leading to salvation.

Salvation Is the Result of Faith

Lecture 7:17, reads:

> Salvation is the effect of faith. . . . All the heavenly beings work by this principle; and it is because they are able so to do that they are saved, for nothing but this could save them. And this is the lesson which the God of heaven has been endeavoring to teach to the world by the mouth of all his holy prophets. Hence we are told that "without faith it is impossible to please him [God]" (Heb 11:6), and that salvation "is of faith, that it might be by grace; to the end the promise might be sure to all the seed" (Rom 4:16).

The understanding of grace is essential to our faith as we face our own limitations and weaknesses. The Bible Dictionary of the LDS edition of the scriptures explains grace as "an enabling power that allows men and women to lay hold on eternal life and exaltation after they have expended their own best efforts" (BD 697).

Again from the seventh lecture we read that the plan of salvation is offered to every child of God and is referred to as a "system of faith" that "begins with faith . . . continues by faith, and every blessing which is obtained in relation to it is the effect of faith, whether it pertains to this life or that which is to come" (LF 7:17).

What is the relationship between faith and salvation? The answer is found in the teachings of the Savior. Lecture 7:16 explains what Jesus proposed to the human family when he provided a means to save them. "He proposed to make them like unto himself, and he was like the Father, the great prototype of all saved beings. For any portion of the human family to be assimilated into their likeness is to be saved, and to be unlike them is to be destroyed. On this hinge turns the door of salvation."

Our diligent effort to plant the seed of faith and nourish it daily is the most significant thing we can pursue in this life. It gives us life. It is the very breath of life. It is the purpose of life.

Elder Bruce R.McConkie states, "We are on a course that calls for us to pursue faith, and we have to pursue it until that faith is perfected in us, meaning until we have the degree and quality and kind of power that God our Father possesses" ("Lord, Increase Our Faith" 6).

The Gradual Nature of Attaining Salvation

The plan of salvation revealed in these latter days includes all that is needed for us to return to our Father in Heaven and live with him once again, but it unfolds gradually to each of us according to our diligence and faith in following the plan. Faith and salvation are linked together. As mortals we are in the process of ultimately gaining salvation. Faith possesses qualities that move us forward toward that ultimate goal. Wendell O. Rich writes:

> *Faith is active. . . .* [It] *"will impel to action." . . . Faith is specific.* . . . [It] is vested in, and has force and power as it relates to particular individuals, teachings, principles, and relationships. *Faith is individual. . . .* As a principle of growth and action it must be won, with the help and power of God, by each within himself. . . . *Faith is spiritual insight.* [It is] "the evidence of things not seen" (Hebrews 11:1) . . . *Faith is assurance.* It is a feeling of inner certainty. . . . From such a feeling of assurance the ancient psalmist exclaimed, "The Lord is my light and my salvation; whom shall I fear? The Lord is the strength of my life; of whom shall I be afraid." (Psalms 27:1) *Faith is creative. . . .* [It] moves men to solve problems, to find solutions, to ask questions believing that there are answers to be found. . . . *Faith is divine companionship.* He who has faith in a Divine Father is never alone. Faith in God carries with it the promise of divine companionship (70-73; emphasis in original).

Fruits of Faith Bring Power to Endure Trials

It is the remarkable reality of the promise of this divine companionship that fills our souls in peaceful and troubled times and assures us we are never alone. We have covenanted with God and he with us. When we went into the waters of baptism and covenanted to keep his commandments, he also covenanted with us that he would never desert us, never leave us, but that we could always have his Spirit to be with us. It is faith in this companionship with the Lord Jesus Christ and obedience to his commandments that allow us to endure all of the vicissitudes of this mortal sojourn so necessary for our spiritual growth.

We see the great power of faith in the lives of our brothers and sisters in various degrees and in various circumstances. This unseen but very real force often appears more evident during times of trial and testing. President Pablo Choc of the Patzicia Branch of the Guatemala, Guatemala City Mission was one whose faith was tried. While attending "a Mormon funeral for a 15-year-old boy, [he] was impressed by the spirit at the meeting. . . . [He] asked the missionaries to stay and teach him" when the service had ended. He was baptized and in time he served as branch president twice (7 years) over a period of sixteen years.

> But . . . his service to his fellowman was never greater than during the 1976 Guatemalan earthquake. At the same time the fearsome earthquake was knocking the supporting beam on top of Elder Randall Ellsworth while the young missionary was sleeping in the Patzicia Branch cultural hall, it was tumbling the walls of Pres. Choc's home, killing his wife, a young son and daughter. After he had seen to the needs of his family, and taken care of the bodies of his wife and two children, Pres. Choc immediately went to the branch chapel to check on the damage there. At the building he assisted in freeing Elder Ellsworth and helped transport the missionary to Guatemala City for medical aid, knowing all the while that his beloved wife and children lay dead back in Patzicia.
>
> [Later, President Choc shared his feelings.] "I am of course saddened by the death of my wife and children, . . . and I will miss her in helping to raise our six remaining children. We were married very young, and in all those years of marriage we never had a real problem. Then in the three weeks after her death I did a lot of praying to the Lord, more than I had ever done before, and I found a lot of strength in my prayers and felt myself getting closer to the Lord. . . . Because of this I don't think my faith ever weakened or wavered for a moment."
>
> During this time the Choc's eldest son, Daniel, had been called on a mission and had been teaching the American missionaries the Mayan dialect so proselyting could be stepped up in the mission district. As a result of the earthquake, the missionaries had been assigned to assist in the cleanup work with the members of the Church in their area. Elder Choc was cleaning up the inside

of a home as an aftershock occurred. His companion and two other missionaries scrambled to safety, but Elder Choc was trapped by a falling wall and killed. As Pres. Choc talked about the deaths in his family, tears began to well in his eyes and slowly slide down his dirt-stained face.

"I was sad, very sad when Daniel was killed, but in a way I am very happy. There are so many of my Mayan people on the other side that Daniel, his mother and the other two children are spending their time teaching them the Gospel message in their native language, and they are spending their time serving the Lord. . . . This is really the Lord's work" (Livingood 5).

It is only with faith in God that we are able to face the events of this life.

We often face the daily basic routine happenings, hardly recognizing the vital moving force that accompanies our comings and goings. However, like the ebb and flow of the waters on the shoreline, there come occasions of high tide when the power of faith is activated in ways that we recognize as miraculous, and they become the very fruits of faith. They bear evidence of the realities of God and our relationship to him. It is then that we can draw deeply from a reservoir of faith gradually accumulated over years of learning and living the gospel and coming to know the Savior. With unwavering faith in God and the righteous desire of our hearts, we can call upon the Lord and actually witness his hand in our own personal lives. I know this to be true.

President Harold B. Lee, speaking to seminary leaders at Brigham Young University, said:

Yes, the Savior, too, is in our midst. His eyes are upon us, but we can't always see him. But the day can come when we could see him. It isn't the Lord who withholds himself from us; it is we who withhold ourselves from him. And if we were living completely worthy, we could see him and have a personal visitation and we would have the assurance, even though we couldn't see him, that he was there, walking, talking, listening, aiding, directing. Make no mistake—this is his work (Goates 319-20).

We would expect to see such faith among the prophets. But we also see it in the lives of all of his children who truly believe.

I recently received a letter from a thirteen-year-old Beehive class president. This young girl, called of God and set apart by the authority of his holy priesthood, wrote the following:

> This past month has been a real trial for me. Dealing with my grandfather's death, then my mother is in the hospital, and then my grandma died. All within a month's time.
>
> I now realize the power and influence that I have with the Beehive girls, and the difference I can make in their lives. I love this gospel, and I will strive to live the commandments of God all my life.
>
> I know that I'm a daughter of a Heavenly Father who loves me, and I love him. I will stand as a witness of God at all times, in all things, and in all places. . . . I will be prepared to make and keep sacred covenants, receive the ordinances of the temple, and enjoy the blessings of exaltation! I hope that I can always be an example to others that they might be touched by my strong testimony of the gospel.
>
> I hope that I can find the lost sheep of the Lord's flock. I *will* stand for truth and righteousness. I *will* hold my torch high for everyone to see that I love the Lord and his gospel.

How plentiful the fruits of faith can be, even in one so young.

Knowledge of God as One of the Fruits of Faith

In the process of gradually growing in faith, we gain a sure knowledge of God. It is in coming to know God in the full and true sense of the word that we gain all things pertaining to life and godliness. And so we each ask the question posed in Lecture 7:18:

> How were they to obtain the knowledge of God? (For there is a great difference between believing in God and knowing him— knowledge implies more than faith. And notice that all things that pertain to life and godliness were given through the knowledge of God.) The answer is that through faith they were to obtain this knowledge; and, having power by faith to obtain the knowledge of God, they could with it obtain all other things which pertain to life and godliness.

This experience of gradually growing in faith should never be viewed as a casual half-hearted endeavor. President Lee gave specific advice. He said: " 'Learning by faith is no task for a lazy man. Someone has said, in effect, that such a process requires the bending of the whole soul [through worthy living]—the calling up from the depths of the human mind and linking them with God. It makes those who follow this course great in the sight of the Lord' " (Goates 539).

It is a great comfort to know firsthand that we can walk by faith on a daily basis. We should never get discouraged by thinking that it requires a mighty leap of faith before God will respond to our earnest supplication. The prophet Alma speaks words of hope and encouragement as he counsels, "But behold, if ye will awake and arouse your faculties, even to an experiment upon my words, and exercise a particle of faith, yea, even if ye can no more than desire to believe, let this desire work in you, even until ye believe in a manner that ye can give place for a portion of my words" (Alma 32:27).

Then comes the glory and absolute promise—

> And because of your diligence and your faith and your patience with the word in nourishing it, that it may take root in you, behold, by and by ye shall pluck the fruit thereof, which is most precious, which is sweet above all that is sweet, and which is white above all that is white, yea, and pure above all that is pure; and ye shall feast upon this fruit even until ye are filled, that ye hunger not, neither shall ye thirst. Then, my brethren, ye shall reap the rewards of your faith, and your diligence, and patience, and long-suffering, waiting for the tree to bring forth fruit unto you (Alma 32:42-43).

Praying and Pondering

The example of Enos provides a guide for each of us as we seek diligently. First, he remembered what he had been taught; then he went before God with a specific desire. The words of his father regarding eternal life sank into his heart. His soul hungered. He cried out in mighty prayer. He was answered by the voice of the Lord and received a remission of his sins. He asked how it was done and was told that it came because of faith in Christ. His faith in the Lord became unshaken. He continued to pray, now in behalf of his brethren. The Lord said, "I will grant unto thee according to thy desires, because of thy faith. . . .

Whatsoever thing ye shall ask in faith, believing that ye shall receive in the name of Christ, ye shall receive it" (Enos 1:12, 15).

Enos followed these steps, and we read his final testimony:

> And I soon go to the place of my rest, which is with my Redeemer; for I know that in him I shall rest. And I rejoice in the day when my mortal shall put on immortality, and shall stand before him; then shall I see his face with pleasure, and he will say unto me: Come unto me, ye blessed, there is a place prepared for you in the mansions of my Father (Enos 1:27).

The fruit then comes as a witness after our diligence, our faith, our patience, and maybe more important, "after the trial of [our] faith" (Ether 12:6).

After praying and pondering, we become attuned to promptings which help us discern truth from error and bring thoughts to our minds. Promptings come as surely as we live from day to day; to this I testify. We can hear the words and thoughts as they are formulated in our minds. We can learn to recognize promptings when they come. They are usually fleeting and faint, never imposed.

President Lee repeated instruction given by President David O. McKay concerning the promptings and impressions of the Spirit. He reported,

> The President made the statement that . . . when we are relaxed in a private room we are more susceptible to those things [spiritual promptings]; and that so far as he was concerned, his best thoughts come after he gets up in the morning and is relaxed and thinking about the duties of the day; that impressions come more clearly, as if it were to hear a voice. Those impressions are right. If we are worried about something and upset in our feelings, the inspiration does not come. If we so live that our minds are free from worry and our conscience is clear and our feelings are right toward one another, the operation of the Spirit of the Lord upon our spirit is as real as when we pick up the telephone; but when they come, we must be brave enough to take the suggested actions (Lee 15-16).

I have always known the power of faith and prayer. But since my call as Young Women General President, I know it more surely than I have known before, perhaps because I have sought more diligently, more earnestly, more fervently. My prayers have been more specific. There are occasions after inquiring of the Lord in prayer concerning important matters that words and thoughts have filled my mind. I take a pencil and pad and attempt to record all the insights and impressions as quickly as I can. Many times those very thoughts and words have been significant to my assignment. As we, our Father's children, have these undeniable experiences, is it any wonder we find ourselves striving, yearning, reaching to feel the operation of the Spirit of the Lord upon our spirit regularly and, if possible, constantly?

How do we develop faith? Faith requires effort and every individual can qualify to receive this gift. The process is simple and clear but requires diligence. It involves study, prayer, and obedience to the commandments.

First, we study. In the 88th section of the Doctrine and Covenants, the Lord instructs: "And as all have not faith, seek ye diligently and teach one another words of wisdom; yea, seek ye out of the best books words of wisdom; seek learning, even by study and also by faith" (v 118).

Second, we pray. The promise of the Lord is that "the Spirit shall be given unto you by the prayer of faith" (D&C 42:14). The Spirit enlightens our minds and teaches gospel truth. It witnesses the truth to us and carries it into our hearts.

Third, we strive to keep the commandments. The Savior gives us this glorious promise and insight in the Doctrine and Covenants: "I give unto you these sayings . . . that you may come unto the Father in my name, and in due time receive of his fulness. For *if you keep my commandments*, you shall receive of his fulness, and be glorified in me as I am in the Father; therefore, I say unto you, you shall receive grace for grace" (93:19-20; emphasis added).

Spiritual Confidence

As we strive to increase our faith in God and gain knowledge through our own experience, often the hardest thing to do is to believe in our own worthiness, our personal righteousness.

Is there a soul alive who has not had an occasion to cry out and plead with God at some time, with a burning desire to increase in personal righteousness, to reach and stretch far enough to connect? We yearn to know not only how to call upon the Lord in faith, but desire to do everything possible to activate the power of faith. Often, after extended periods of fasting and prayer, have we not asked, "But, Father, what more can I do? What should I understand about working by faith?" At those very times when we may feel least worthy and least comfortable in calling upon the Lord in faith, when we have a keener sense of our imperfections, when the flesh is weak and our spirit suffers disappointments knowing the frailties of our lives are shouting at us, in those moments our faith may waiver. It is then that we must trust in the Lord completely to compensate for our weaknesses after we have expended our own best efforts.

Our Savior, in his great understanding and love for each of us, has promised, "I will not leave you comfortless" (John 14:18). Through the process of cleansing our souls, when we have become meek and lowly of heart, then "cometh the visitation of the Holy Ghost, which Comforter filleth with hope" (Moroni 8:26). Christ invited "all to come unto Him and partake of his goodness; and he denieth none that come unto him" (2 Nephi 26:33). With this hope, and being in tune with the Holy Spirit, we can be guided each day of our lives. As our ability increases, our capacity and desire increase, and we grow "grace for grace" (see D&C 93:20).

To increase in righteousness and in confidence before the Lord, Elder Bruce R. McConkie counseled:

> Treasure up the words of light and truth. Hear the gospel taught by legal administrators. Study the revelations and believe what they say. Actually believe the recorded word from God and his prophets, with the result that the hearing of the word is taken into your soul. Then build on that foundation by righteousness and devotion and seeking the Lord, by compliance with his law—and the inevitable result will be to grow in faith ("Lord, Increase Our Faith" 10).

As we face each day and seriously consider those things that are worthy of our attention, we learn to exercise our faith every day. These matters of concern calling for increased faith might include such things as a desire to strengthen our faith, strengthen family relationships, increase understanding and sensitivity to the gift of the Holy Ghost, increase physical health, study the scriptures, magnify Church callings, continue in education, or increase employment skills. Through prayer and the promptings of the Spirit, we can develop our own personalized list according to our individual needs.

In the same talk, Elder McConkie counseled further:

> Don't go out and try to move mountains, but go out and start in a small degree to do the thing you need to do in your life to get what you ought to have temporally and spiritually. . . . Work on the projects ahead, and when you have taken one step in the acquiring of faith, it will give you the assurance in your soul that you can go forward and take the next step, and by degrees your power or influence will increase until eventually, in this world or in the next, you will say to the Mt. Zerin's in your life, "Be thou removed." You will say to whatever encumbers your course of eternal progress, "Depart," and it will be so (11).

Perfection Comes Through Faith

Mental Exertion

Let us consider those things that may not move a mountain right away but will move us forward toward a more complete faith. Again we must ask, "What should I understand about working by faith?" To that searching supplication, we find this answer in Lecture 7:3:

> We understand that when a man works by faith he works by mental exertion instead of physical force. It is by words, instead of by exerting his physical powers, with which every being works when he works by faith. God said, "Let there be light: and there was light" (Gen 1:3). Joshua spake and the great lights which God had created stood still (Joshua 10:12-13). Elijah commanded and the heavens were stayed for the space of three years and six months, so that it did not rain; he again commanded and the heavens gave forth rain (1 Kings 17:1; 18:1, 41-45). All this was done by faith.

And the Savior says: "If ye have faith as a grain of mustard seed, ye shall say to this mountain, Remove . . . and it shall remove (Matt 17:20); or "say unto this sycamine tree, Be thou plucked up . . . and . . . planted in the sea; and it should obey you" (Luke 17:6). Faith, then, works by words; and with these its mightiest works have been and will be performed.

Prayer (thoughts and words) represents mental exertion. We need to learn to access power by pleading our cause in words that are specific to our needs.

Elder Bruce R. McConkie encouraged us to learn how to pray "boldly and efficaciously, not in word only but in spirit and in power, so that we may pull down upon ourselves . . . the very powers of heaven" ("Why the Lord Ordained Prayer" 9).

There are times when we may even feel at a loss to know for what we should pray. On those occasions, we read from the scriptures, "Likewise the Spirit also helpeth our infirmities: for we know not what we should pray for as we ought: but the Spirit itself maketh intercession for us with groanings which cannot be uttered" (Rom 8:26).

Pondering and meditating are additional ways of learning through mental exertion. We first have the desire, then we seek and draw upon our personal experiences. We search for additional enlightenment and edification in an effort to expand our understanding. We study the principles of the gospel and consider how they might be related to the question at hand. Our Father in Heaven has promised that when we seek diligently, ask, and knock, "it shall be opened unto [us]" (D&C 88:63).

Thought allows us to create, to envision, to experience something in our mind. When we see clearly and become specific about what it is we are seeking and feel it is a righteous desire and according to the will of God, we can focus our thinking with a concentration of power so that we can bring our faith, the energy of our mental processes, to bear upon the thing for which we are praying. Through prayer we can then call upon the powers of heaven, the enabling power that allows us to exercise our faith. It is why we are counseled in the Doctrine and Covenants that our "eye be single to [his] glory" and that our "minds become single to God" (D&C 88:67-68). In a very literal sense, we see in our mind as with an "eye of faith" (Ether 12:19).

As we learn to control our mind and our thoughts through mental exertion and set aside all doubts and fears and ask in faith, we can experience personal revelation through direct communication with God.

I am impressed by the words of Orson Pratt. On this subject he writes, "If a person trains his mind to walk in the spirit, and brings his whole mind to bear upon its operations, and upon the principles of faith which are calculated to put him in possession of the power of God, how much greater will be his faculties for obtaining knowledge" (*Journal of Discourses* 7:155-56).

I remember one time as a young girl worrying about the importance of gaining knowledge. In anguish I asked my father, "If the glory of God is intelligence and you are not smart, what will happen to you?" And my very wise and learned father, who never graduated from high school but was self-taught and intelligent through diligent *study* and great *faith*, eased my concern as he explained, "My dear child, if you are diligent in your studies and do your very best and are obedient to God's commandments, one day, when you enter the holy temple, the university of the Lord, you will be prepared in your mind and spirit to learn and know all you need to know to return to your Father in Heaven." It was faith in that promise that seemed to unlock my mind. Study and faith were then put to work together. And I emphasize the relationship of work to both study and faith—plodding toil, whole-souled devotion, mental exertion. Over time, the realization of the Lord's promise came: "Seek me diligently and ye shall find me; ask and ye shall receive; knock, and it shall be opened unto you" (D&C 88:63).

Being One with Christ

Let us anticipate the consequence of this gradual unfolding of faith that takes us over mountain peaks and into valleys, allowing us to be tried and tested in all things. And after the trial of our faith, what can we expect? Salvation is the greatest gift of all the gifts of God, the most glorious of all the fruits of faith. And this is what we can expect. This is a promise if we choose to qualify. In describing saved beings, Lecture 7:9 states:

> They must be persons who can work by faith and who are able, by faith, to be ministering spirits to them who shall be heirs of salvation. They must have faith to enable them to act in the presence of the Lord; otherwise, they cannot be saved. And what constitutes the real difference between a saved person and one not saved is the difference in the degree of their faith. One's faith has become perfect enough to lay hold upon eternal life, and the other's has not.

Paragraph 8 of that lecture states:

> When men begin to live by faith, they begin to draw near to God; and when their faith is perfected, they are like him. And because he is saved they are saved also; for they will be in the same situation he is in, because they have come to him. And "when he shall appear we shall be like him; for we shall see him as he is" (1 John 3:2).

Elder McConkie taught:

> To be saved is to be like Christ, inheriting, receiving, and possessing as he does. To gain salvation is to grow in faith until we have the faith of Christ and thus are like him. Our nearness to him and to salvation is measured by the degree of our faith. To gain faith is to attain the power of Christ, which is God's power. To believe in Christ in the full and true sense is to "have the mind of Christ" (1 Cor 2:16), that is, to believe what he believes, think what he thinks, say what he says, and do what he does. It is to be one with him by the power of the Holy Ghost (*New Witness* 206-07).

Lest we become discouraged, it is important to understand and remember the process by which we grow spiritually. It is not intended that we reach perfection in this life. On one occasion Joseph Smith made the following declaration:

> *When you climb up a ladder, you must begin at the bottom, and ascend step by step, until you arrive at the top; and so it is with the principles of the gospel—you must begin with the first, and go on until you learn all the principles of exaltation. But it will be a great while after you have passed through the veil before you will have learned them. It is not all* to be comprehended in this world; it will be a great work to learn our salvation *and exaltation even beyond*

the grave (*Teachings of the Prophet Joseph Smith* 348; emphasis in original).

So many scriptures make reference to the Savior's statement that he came to fulfil his Father's will. Our purpose is to make our will the same as his will, even as expressed by Mary, "Behold the handmaid of the Lord; be it unto me according to thy word" (Luke 1:38).

As we feast upon the words of Christ through earnest study to know his will, then humble ourselves and learn to bend our will as well as our knees, our faith increases, becoming stronger and stronger. We have an ever-increasing desire to know his will and to carry it out, and we become able and anxious to follow the pattern set by the Nephites as recorded in the book of Helaman: "Nevertheless they did fast and pray oft, and did wax stronger and stronger in their humility, and firmer and firmer in the faith of Christ, unto the filling their souls with joy and consolation, yea, even to the purifying and the sanctification of their hearts, which sanctification cometh because of their yielding their hearts unto God" (3:35).

As we learn to yield our hearts to God in all things, we can experience the glorious promise given by our Savior as he comforted his disciples just prior to his crucifixion: "Peace I leave with you, my peace I give unto you: not as the world giveth, give I unto you. Let not your heart be troubled, neither let it be afraid" (John 14:27).

As we continually strive to make our will the same as that of our Father and his Son, Jesus Christ, we will gradually begin to think as they think, speak as they speak, do as they do. Through faith our hearts will not be troubled, and we will be free of fear.

To the reality of this principle and power of faith leading us to salvation, I bear my personal witness. I watched a man of great faith experience the precious fruits of quiet submission, peace, and spiritual confidence as he faced the final stages of his mortal probation.

Not many years ago, my father, who then lived with us, was diagnosed as having cancer. Following his surgery, he came home from the hospital weak in body but undaunted in spirit.

Over the next many weeks I saw his body steadily weaken. It was as though his spirit was magnified by his increased faith as his body steadily wasted away. Sometimes I would wait outside his bedroom door while he was on his knees for what often seemed a very long time and pondered the two-way communication I knew was taking place. His meals consisted of a spoonful of baby food—all he could manage. But he expressed thanks for it and gratitude for the lessons of each day.

He taught us continually as he prepared himself for what he referred to as his graduation. At his last fast and testimony meeting, he spoke only briefly, quoting Mosiah concerning the need to yield to the enticings of the Holy Spirit and to become "as a child, submissive, meek, humble, patient, full of love, willing to submit to all things which the Lord seeth fit to inflict upon him, even as a child doth submit to his father" (Mosiah 3:19).

A few days later Dad stayed in bed, sleeping off and on during the day.

> I had decided to sit with him. It seemed his eyes were open, yet he wasn't seeing me. I took his hand in mine, a hand that had spanked me and blessed me and caressed me throughout my life. "Dad," I whispered. He didn't respond. "If you know I'm here, please squeeze my hand." I wasn't sure if there was a squeeze, but it didn't seem like it. I bent over and put my cheek next to his very bony cheek, with my hand on the other side of his face. I waited just a second, then straightened up. It was as though his gaze returned from a long way [off]. He looked at me just a moment, and in his eyes I saw complete peace. Joy, trust, confidence, and anticipation all mingled together in that look. A tear escaped from the corner of his eye. I pressed my cheek to his again. There are things we cannot find words or even sounds to express, but in that moment we spoke spirit to spirit, [and I knew he knew God was near].
>
> Shortly after, . . . [my] father's eternal spirit left his mortal body. [We as a] family gathered together. I [had seen] what had taken place, but what I felt was more real than what I saw. Dad was not there in the body, but he was there with us extending his great

strength that had sustained us over the years. We knelt by his bed to give thanks. With tears of gratitude binding us together as a family, we knew that, because of what we had experienced but could not explain, we understood and felt that peace of which he had so often spoke [—that peace that passeth all understanding] (Kapp, *Echoes* 111-12).

Many times after this experience, I returned to my father's room to remember and to try to recapture the tangible warmth of the Spirit that had been there to comfort and reassure us of the reality of the plan and ultimately the promise of salvation, the greatest of all the fruits of faith.

Brothers and sisters, the plan of salvation gives meaning and direction, vision and hope. It is with faith in God that we begin and end this mortal life. God is our Father. We are his children and to become like him is our eternal quest, our destiny. While this striving for perfection will continue on after this life, we can witness evidence of the great saving power of faith and its fruits all along the journey. Of these eternal truths, I bear my personal witness.

BIBLIOGRAPHY

Benson, Ezra Taft. " 'You Are a Marked Generation.' " *Ensign* (Apr 1987) 17:73-74.

Goates, L. Brent. *Harold B. Lee, Prophet and Seer.* Salt Lake City: Bookcraft, 1985.

Journal of Discourses. 26 vols. 1854-86.

Kapp, Ardeth G. *Echoes from My Prairie.* Salt Lake City: Bookcraft, 1979.

———. *Miracles in Pinafores and Bluejeans.* Salt Lake City: Deseret Book, 1979.

Lee, Harold B. "Prayer." Unpublished Address to Seminary and Institute Teachers (6 Jul 1956). Copy in Church Historical Department.

Livingood, Jay. "Quake's Heavy Hand Didn't Crush Testimony." *Church News* (23 Apr 1977) 5.

McConkie, Bruce R. "Lord, Increase our Faith." *Speeches of the Year, 1967-1968*. Provo, UT: Brigham Young Univ, 1968.

———. *A New Witness for the Articles of Faith*. Salt Lake City: Deseret Book, 1985.

———. "Why the Lord Ordained Prayer." *Ensign* (Jan 1976) 6:7-12.

Nibley, Hugh W. *Nibley on the Timely and the Timeless*. Salt Lake City: Publishers Press, 1978.

Rich, Wendell O. *Our Living Gospel*. Salt Lake City: Bookcraft, 1964.

The Rising Generation. Salt Lake City: Deseret Book, 1987.

Teachings of the Prophet Joseph Smith. Comp. Joseph Fielding Smith. Salt Lake City: Deseret Book, 1976.

Ardeth G. Kapp is the Young Women General President of The Church of Jesus Christ of Latter-day Saints.

Appendixes

Appendix A

Preface to the 1952 RLDS Edition
of the Lectures on Faith*

In Volume I of our *Church History* we find reference to "Lectures on theology for publication in the Book of Doctrine and Covenants, which the committee appointed last September now compiling." These lectures were published as part one of the first edition (1835) of the Book of Doctrine and Covenants and had a place in that book and in some of the earlier editions sponsored by the Reorganized Church.

In that first edition (1835) the members of the First Presidency published a "preface" from which we quote:

> The first part of the book will be found to contain a series of Lectures as delivered before a Theological class in this place [Kirtland, Ohio], and in consequence of their embracing the important doctrine of salvation, we have arranged them into the following work.

Through recent years occasional references have been made to these "Lectures on Faith" as they were entitled in the book itself, and we frequently have received inquiries about them.

---

*This preface, published by The Reorganized Church of Jesus Christ of Latter Day Saints, 1952, was written by Israel A. Smith, RLDS President.

To what extent the views expressed in these Lectures are interpretations under inspiration or otherwise of the Prophet Joseph Smith is a matter left to conjecture, because the record is not explicit on that point. What implications may be indulged with respect to the question because those "theological" classes were held as a part of the "school of the prophets" is also left to conjecture.

During the Kirtland occupancy references to the work of the "school of the prophets" were found in the *Messenger and Advocate*, in one of which the Prophet Joseph is quoted as saying:

> During the month of January, I was engaged in the school of the elders, and in preparing the Lectures on theology for publication in the Book of Doctrine and Covenants, which the committee appointed last September [1834] were now compiling.

In view of this statement, and the fact that Joseph Smith was one of the committee on selection and publication that arranged and printed the Lectures as a part of the first Doctrine and Covenants, if we cannot with full assurance hold that the Lectures were his interpretations, we must infer, I believe, that they received his approval or endorsement.

In reprinting these Lectures we do so for their historical value mainly and do not present them with any thought that the church has ever expressly or specifically or by implication endorsed everything in them. Let them be read in the light of the facts as above stated.

Israel A. Smith

Appendix B

Selected Bibliography
for the Lectures on Faith

Books, Theses, Dissertations, Journals,
Pamphlets, and Manuals

Alexander, Thomas G. *Mormonism in Transition.* Chicago: Univ of Illinois, 1986, pp 281-82.

Allen, James B., and Glen M. Leonard. *The Story of the Latter-day Saints.* Salt Lake City: Deseret Book, 1976, pp 69, 96, 167, 481.

Andrus, Hyrum L. *Principles of Perfection.* Vol 2 of *Foundations of the Millennial Kingdom of Christ.* 3 vols. Salt Lake City: Bookcraft, 1968-73, p 20.

Backman, Milton V., Jr. *The Heavens Resound.* Salt Lake City: Deseret Book, 1983, pp 217, 232, 268-70.

Barrett, Ivan J. *Joseph Smith and the Restoration.* Provo, UT: Brigham Young Univ, 1973, pp 218-21.

Bowen, Walter D. "The Versatile W. W. Phelps." Master's thesis. Provo, UT: Brigham Young Univ, 1958, pp 62-66.

Cook, Lyndon W. *The Revelations of the Prophet Joseph Smith.* Provo, UT: Seventy's Mission Bookstore, 1981, pp 182-200.

Cowan, Richard O. *Doctrine and Covenants: Our Modern Scripture.* Provo, UT: Brigham Young Univ, 1978, pp 5, 140-41.

Selected bibliography compiled by Larry E. Dahl.

Doxey, Roy W. *The Latter-day Prophets and the Doctrine and Covenants.* 4 vols. Salt Lake City: Deseret Book, 1963-65, 3:220-21.

Evans, John Henry. *Joseph Smith: An American Prophet.* New York: Macmillan, 1933, pp 95-96.

Fitzgerald, John W. "A Study of the Doctrine and Covenants." Master's thesis. Provo, UT: Brigham Young Univ, 1940, pp 68, 343-46.

Flake, Chad. *A Mormon Bibliography, 1830-1930.* Salt Lake City: Univ of Utah, 1978, pp 574-75.

History of the Church. 7 vols. Salt Lake City: Deseret Book, 1978, 1:349-50, 400-01 (footnote), 417-18; 2:xxiv, 142, 165-66, 169-70, 175-76, 180, 200, 218, 227, 243-46, 250-51.

History of the Reorganized Church of Jesus Christ of Latter Day Saints. 8 vols. Independence, MO: Herald House, 1967-76, 1:282-83, 530, 553, 588, 596, 597; 5:342.

Howard, Richard P. *Restoration Scriptures.* Independence, MO: Herald House, 1969, p 236.

Journal History of the Church. Salt Lake City: Historical Department, The Church of Jesus Christ of Latter-day Saints, 1906- . See 16 Sep 1835.

Journal of Discourses. 26 vols. 1854-86, 12:157-60.

Journal of History. 18 vols. Lamoni, IA/Independence, MO: Board of Publication of the Reorganized Church of Jesus Christ of Latter Day Saints, 1908-25, 15:262-69.

Lambert, Asael Carlyle. *The Published Editions of the Book of Doctrine and Covenants of The Church of Jesus Christ of Latter-day Saints in All Languages 1833 to 1950.* N.p.: A. C. Lambert, 1950.

Ludlow, Daniel. *A Companion to Your Study of the Doctrine and Covenants.* 2 vols. Salt Lake City: Deseret Book, 1978, 1:36.

Lyon, T. Edgar. *Introduction to the Doctrine and Covenants and the Pearl of Great Price.* Salt Lake City: LDS Department of Education, 1948, pp 33-35.

McConkie, Bruce R. *A New Witness for the Articles of Faith.* Salt Lake City: Deseret Book, 1985, pp 71-77.

———. *Mormon Doctrine*. 2nd ed. Salt Lake City: Bookcraft, 1966, p 439.

MacGregor, Daniel. *Changing of the Revelations*. Milwaukee, WI: Harold B. Miner, n.d., pp 15-16.

Partridge, Elinore H. "Characteristics of Joseph Smith's Style and Notes on the Authorship of the Lectures on Faith." Task Papers in LDS History Series. Salt Lake City: The Church of Jesus Christ of Latter-day Saints, 1976 (Dec), no. 14, p 28.

Peterson, Orlen Curtis. "A History of the Schools and Educational Programs of The Church of Jesus Christ of Latter-day Saints in Ohio and Missouri, 1831-1839." Master's thesis. Provo, UT: Brigham Young Univ, 1972, pp 34-42.

Phipps, Alan J. "The Lectures on Faith: An Authorship Study." Master's thesis. Provo, UT: Brigham Young Univ, 1977.

Powell, William M. "Preliminary Study of the Lectures on Faith." Unpublished paper. [Compares the broadside of Lecture 1 with the first publication in 1835.] Transcript in the BYU library.

Ropp, Harry L. *The Mormon Papers*. Downers Grove, IL: InterVarsity Press, 1977, pp 67-68.

Salt Lake School of the Prophets Minute Book, 1883. Ed. Merle H. Graffam. Palm Desert, CA: ULC, 1981, p 44, under the date 11 Oct. [In typescript copy, same publisher, same date, p 66.]

Smith, Hyrum M., and Janne M. Sjodahl. *Doctrine and Covenants Commentary*. Salt Lake City: Deseret Book, 1954, pp xvii, 567-68.

Smith, Joseph Fielding. *Church History and Modern Revelation*. 2nd series. Salt Lake City: Council of the Twelve Apostles, 1947, p 137.

———. *Doctrines of Salvation*. 3 vols. Salt Lake City: Bookcraft, 1956, 2:304; 3:194-95.

———. *Essentials in Church History*. Salt Lake City: Deseret News, 1922, p 186.

———. *Seek Ye Earnestly*. Salt Lake City: Deseret Book, 1970, p 194.

Sperry, Sidney B. *Doctrine and Covenants Compendium*. Salt Lake City: Bookcraft, 1960, p 555.

Widtsoe, John A. *The Message of the Doctrine and Covenants.* Salt Lake City: Bookcraft, 1969, p 2.

Wood, Wilford C. *Joseph Smith Begins His Work.* 2 vols. [Vol 2 is a photographic reprint of the original Book of Commandments, Doctrine and Covenants, Lectures on Faith, and the fourteen Articles of Faith, all published in 1833] Salt Lake City: Wilford C. Wood, 1962.

Woodford, Robert J. "The Historical Development of the Doctrine and Covenants." PhD dissertation. 3 vols. Provo, UT: Brigham Young Univ, 1974, 1:86-87.

Articles and Book Chapters

Alexander, Thomas G. "The Reconstruction of Mormon Doctrine: From Joseph Smith to Progressive Theology." *Sunstone* (Jul-Aug 1980) 5:24-33.

Cowan, Richard O. "The Living Canon." *Hearken, O Ye People.* Sandy, UT: Randall, 1984, pp 17-30.

Crawley, Peter. "A Bibliography of The Church of Jesus Christ of Latter-day Saints in New York, Ohio, and Missouri." *BYU Studies* (Sum 1972) 12:499.

Gentry, Leland H. "What of the Lectures on Faith?" *BYU Studies* (Fall 1978) 19:5-19.

Jessee, Dean. "The Writing of Joseph Smith's History." *BYU Studies* (Sum 1971) 11:443-44.

Larsen, Wayne A., and Alvin C. Rencher. "Who Wrote the Book of Mormon?" *Book of Mormon Authorship.* Ed. Noel B. Reynolds and Charles D. Tate, Jr. Salt Lake City: Bookcraft, 1982, pp 183-84.

Lyon, T. Edgar. "Doctrinal Development of the Church During the Nauvoo Sojourn, 1839-1846." *BYU Studies* (Sum 1975) 15:437-38.

McConkie, Bruce R. "The Lord God of Joseph Smith." *Speeches of the Year, 1971-1972.* Provo, UT: Brigham Young Univ, 1972.

———. "Lord, Increase Our Faith." *Speeches of the Year, 1967-1968.* Provo, UT: Brigham Young Univ, 1968.

Matthews, Robert J. "The Olive Leaf." *The Doctrine and Covenants*. Vol 1 of *Studies in Scripture*. 7 vols. Ed. Robert L. Millet and Kent P. Jackson. Sandy, UT: Randall, 1984, pp 354-55.

Penrose, Charles W. *Conference Report* (3 Apr 1921) pp 9-17.

Richards, Charles C. "The Priesthood as Teachers." *Improvement Era* (Nov 1910) 14:18.

Van Wagoner, Richard S., Steven C. Walker, and Allen D. Roberts. "The 'Lectures on Faith': A Case Study in Decanonization." *Dialogue* (Fall 1987) 20:71-77.

Widtsoe, John A. "Contents and Testimony of the Book." *Modern Revelation: The History and Message of the Doctrine and Covenants*. Young Men's Mutual Improvement Associations Manual #10, 1906-07. Salt Lake City: General Board of YMMIA,1906, pp 31-38.

Woodford, Robert J. "The Doctrine and Covenants: A Historical Overview." *The Doctrine and Covenants*. Vol 1 of *Studies in Scripture*. 7 vols. Ed. Robert L. Millet and Kent P. Jackson. Sandy, UT: Randall, 1984, pp 8, 18.

Periodicals and Newspapers

Evening and Morning Star. [Church newspaper published in Independence, MO, and Kirtland, OH, June 1832 through September 1834. Ed. Oliver Cowdery.] Republished by Eugene Wagner, Basel, Switzerland. Printed in Muhringen,West Germany by F. Wochner K. G., 1969. See (Sep 1834) pp 186-87.

Latter day Saints' Messenger and Advocate. [Church newspaper published in Kirtland, OH, Oct 1834 through Sep 1837. Ed. Oliver Cowdery and John Whitmer] 3 vols. Photographic reproduction. Salt Lake City: Modern Microfilm, 1965. See (May 1835) 1:122-26; (Aug 1835) 1:161-64, 170, 176; (Mar 1836) 1:237.

Latter-day Saints' Millennial Star, The. [Church periodical published in England, May 1840 through Dec 1970 by Parley P. Pratt, Thomas Ward, Rulon S. Wells, and successive eds.] 132 vols. See (Sep 1840) 1:129-33; (Oct 1840) 1:137-50; (Nov 1840) 1:169-74; (Feb 1841) 1:241-45; (Dec 1842) 3:135-38; (Jan 1843) 3:150-52; (Feb 1843) 3:165-69; (Aug 1897) 58:522.

Messenger and Advocate of the Church of Christ. [Published in Pittsburgh and Greencastle, PA, by Sidney Rigdon, Oct 1844 through Sep 1846. Originally entitled *The Latter Day Saint's Messenger and Advocate* until April 1845.] 2 vols. See (Oct 1845) 1:360, 364-66; (Nov 1845) 1:385-89; (Dec 1845) 1:405-07; (Jan 1846) 1:422-24; (Feb 1846) 1:443-45; (Mar 1846) 2:449-52.

Times and Seasons. [Church newspaper published in Commerce and Nauvoo IL, Nov 1839 through Feb 1846.] 6 vols. Photo reprint. Independence, MO: Independence Press, 1986. See (15 Apr 1845) 6:868.

Subject Index

Example, of Christ, 98–101, 192,
230–31, 235, 268
Existentialism, 206

— F —

Faith, and works, 169, 174
daily, 268, 273
effects of, 95–104
eternal perspective through, 263–68
false, 200–201
first principle in science of theology,
35, 96, 241–42, 264
fruits of, 2, 263–83
obtained through sacrifice, 2, 92–94,
243, 244, 247–61
of God, 33, 39, 51–52, 76, 81, 166,
207–8, 264
perfection through, 2, 97–98, 104,
263, 277
principle of action, 31–33, 35–36, 95,
164–75
principle of power, 33–34, 36–37, 95,
96, 166, 169
Fall of Adam, 41–43, 45, 53, 181, 185,
208, 245, 247
False doctrine, 239
False faith, 200–201
False gods, 179, 200–201, 204–6
False prophets, 193
Family relationships, 277
Fanaticism, 204
Fast and testimony meeting, 185, 266,
282
Fasting, 188, 276, 281
Fear, 68, 78, 94, 164, 261, 267, 279, 281
of God, 92
First Presidency, 287
First Vision, 183–84, 224–25, 265–66
Fitzgerald, John W., 15, 18
Flood, 49, 159
Foreknowledge, of God, 257
Foreordination, 83, 88, 216
Forgiveness, 68, 84, 243
Freedom, 173
Funerals, 270
Future, 164–66, 171, 173, 176

— G —

Gedeon, 34, 37
Generations, 184
Genesis, book of, 40
Gift of the Holy Ghost. See Holy Ghost,
gift of

Gifts of the Spirit, 104, 193–94
Glory of God, 100–101, 211, 229
God, anthropomorphic nature of, 203
attributes of, 35, 65, 66, 70, 75–82,
83, 85, 91, 199, 206–19, 222, 242,
250
becoming like, 223, 235–36
character of, 65–73, 75, 81, 83, 91,
199, 200–201, 206–19, 222, 242, 244,
250
commandments of, 171–73
condescension of, 228–29
confidence in, 91–92, 242, 243, 244
conversed with Adam, 40–43, 50–51,
53, 58
crimes committed in name of, 204
existence of, 39–64, 201–2
eye single to glory of, 279
faith of, 33, 39, 51–52, 76, 81, 166,
207–8, 264
fatherhood of, 206
fear of, 92
foreknowledge of, 257
glory of, 100–101, 211, 229
happiness of, 218
integrity of, 211
judgment of, 77–81, 84, 208–9, 230
justice of, 76, 78, 80, 81, 200, 214–17,
230
knowledge concerning, 43, 45–51,
53–54, 58, 64, 65, 179–88, 190–91,
200–201, 219, 266, 267, 272
knowledge of, 76, 77, 80, 81, 103,
104, 196, 208, 221, 247
love of, 68, 71, 73, 79, 208, 217–18,
265, 272
mercy of, 67, 68, 71, 72, 77, 79, 80,
81, 103, 212–14, 215, 230
nature of, 2, 244, 265
no respecter of persons, 68, 69, 71, 73,
215
of order, 186
omniscient, omnipotent, omnipresent,
207, 223
perfections of, 65, 66, 70, 83, 85, 91,
199, 222, 223, 242, 250
personage of spirit, glory, and power,
83, 85–86, 223–28
personal visitation from, 271
physical nature of, 224–28
power of, 76, 77–78, 80, 81, 86, 207,
208, 223, 247, 264–65
relationship to, 250, 271
revelation from, 66, 69–70, 71, 75–76,
96–97, 194–96, 249–51

on love, 218
on perfection, 280–81
on prophets, 188
on revelation, 194–95
on School for the Elders, 12
on suffering of the Saints, 237, 254
on trial of Abraham, 256
on vengeance of God, 215–16
testimony of, 180, 183–84, 266
trials of, 257
understanding of the Godhead, 221–39
Smith, Joseph F., 232
vision of the redemption of the dead,
185
Smith, Joseph Fielding, 18
on Lectures on Faith, 239
Spirit, synonym for glory and power,
225–26
Spirit of prophecy, 188, 189, 194
Spirit of prophecy and revelation,
193–94, 196
Spirit of revelation, 188, 191–92, 194–96,
256
Spiritual gifts, 193–94
Spirituality, 258
Spontaneity, 173–74
Strength, 176
Study, 275–79, 281
Submission, 281
Sufferings, 92, 244, 252, 254

— T —

Tabernacle in the wilderness, 196
Talmage, James E., 18
on Christ, 213
Taylor, John, 10, 16n
on trials, 256
Teaching, 195
Temple, in Jerusalem, 196
in Nauvoo, 197
prayer roll in, 264
Temple ordinances, 185, 272, 279
Temples, 196
Temptations, 80
Ten commandments, 204–5
Terah (father of Abraham), 23, 48–50,
59–63
Testimony, 46, 51, 54, 63–64, 93–94,
103, 180–83, 185, 188–89, 196, 236,
244, 245, 248, 249–50, 252, 264,
267, 272
of Joseph Smith, 180, 183–84, 266
test of, 248
Testimony meeting, 185, 266, 282
Tests, 255–60, 280

Theology, revealed science, 35, 96,
241–42, 246, 264
Third heavens, 102
Thought, 278–79
Time, 164–65
Timothy, 253
Tongues, gift of, 104, 194
Tradition, 236, 237
Treasure hid in a field, parable of, 251
Tree of knowledge of good and evil, 40
Trials, 80, 252, 255, 259, 269, 280
Tribulations, 78–80, 94, 212
Trust, 253
in God, 68, 77–78, 208, 213, 242,
265, 276, 282
Truth, 170, 210
of God, 68, 69, 72–73, 77, 79–81, 92,
179, 211, 230, 244

— U —

Uinta Mountains, 266
Understanding, 80, 277
Unity, 99–101, 186, 210, 211, 245
of Lectures on Faith, 163

— V —

Veil, 41, 202, 280
Virtue, 167–68, 170–73, 175–76, 199
Vision of the redemption of the dead,
185
Visions, 102, 104, 218, 221, 237, 250,
251

— W —

Wealth, test of, 260
Western civilization, 165
Whitney store, 11
Wickedness, 245
Widtsoe, John A., 18
Williams, Frederick G., 3, 8, 30
Wisdom, 32, 80, 104, 169, 264
of God, 211, 217, 247
offered by Lectures on Faith, 163
Woodruff, Wilford, 232
on Joseph Smith, 236–37
Words, faith worked by, 95–96, 277–78
Work, 279
World, overcoming, 94
Worlds, framed by faith, 33, 34, 36, 95,
166
Worry, 274
Worship, 43, 92, 235
Worthiness, 172

Scripture Index

2 Samuel
22:33 — 86
24:24 — 258

1 Kings
17:1 — 96, 277
18:1, 41–45 — 96, 277

1 Chronicles
29:11 — 86

Nehemiah
9:17 — 77

Job
11:7 — 202
11:7–9 — 66, 71
26:7–14 — 86

Psalms
9:7 — 77
9:16 — 77
27:1 — 269
29:3 — 86
31:5 — 77
50:3–5 — 93
79:9 — 86
89:14 — 76, 77
90:2 — 67
103:6–8 — 66
103:17–18 — 67

Proverbs
23:7 — 174

Ecclesiastes
1:2 — 200
12:13 — 173

Isaiah
14:12–15 — 210
14:24, 27 — 76
40:9–17 — 53
45:21 — 76
45:22 — 52
46:9–10 — 76
60:19 — 85

Jeremiah
32:17 — 86
51:15–16 — 53

Zephaniah
3:5 — 76

Zechariah
9:9 — 76

Malachi
3:6 — 67

NEW TESTAMENT

Matthew
3:16–17 — 88
3:45–46 (JST) — 88
5:44 — 217
5:48 — 99
7:15 — 193
13:44, 45–46 — 251
16:4 — 184
17:19–20 — 33, 37
17:20 — 96, 278
19:4 — 191
19:17 — 208
19:24 — 259
24:11 — 193

Mark
9:23 — 102, 265
12:10 — 191
16:16 — 32, 36

Luke
1:35 — 88
1:38 — 281
1:45 — 102
4:16–21 — 191
17:6 — 96, 278
24:27, 44–45 — 191
24:39 — 203

John
4:24 — 203, 227
4:25–26 (JST) — 227
4:26 — 203
5:30 — 88
5:39 — 191
6:38 — 89
10:10 — 230
10:30 — 89
11:35 — 217

BOOK OF MORMON

DOCTRINE AND COVENANTS

130:19–20	215	133:51–52	216
130:22–23	17, 225	133:53	217
132:27	217	138	185

PEARL OF GREAT PRICE

Moses		5:19–23, 32–40	45
1	225	5:58	182
1:3	201	5:58–59	183
1:9	226	6:7	183
1:15	226	6:8–9	227
1:20	226	7:28–40	217
1:39	209	7:31	211
2:26	85		
2:26–29	40		
3:15–17, 19–20	41	Abraham	
4:14–19	41	2:7	207
4:22–25	42	3:6–10	214
4:28	85	3:17	207
5:1, 4–9	43	3:19	211
5:4–9	181	3:22–23	216